THE GREAT AMERICAN MASQUERADE

THE GREAT AMERICAN MASQUERADE

by
Harold Beaver

VISION
and
BARNES & NOBLE

Vision Press Limited
Fulham Wharf
Townmead Road
London SW6 2SB

and

Barnes & Noble Books
81 Adams Drive
Totowa, NJ 07512

ISBN (UK) 0 85478 046 7
ISBN (US) 0 389 20585 0

© 1985 by Harold Beaver
First published in the U.S.A. 1985

Printed and bound in Great Britain by
Unwin Brothers Ltd.,
Old Woking, Surrey.
Phototypeset by Galleon Photosetting,
Ipswich, Suffolk.
MCMLXXXV

Contents

Introduction

All societies are ruled by standards of decorum and indecorum, of correct and incorrect posture. But this very dichotomy hints at the possibility of a third term lurking beyond both: that of imposture, which is the fiction of posture, enacted in masquerade.

Such masks are never simple. They may be carnival masks of joyous regeneration, as M. M. Bakhtin has argued, or secretive masks hiding nothing but vacuum or dread. They may be anarchic or gothic. But inevitably they are connected with the desire for 'change and reincarnation'. No wonder that America, from the very start, seemed a stage set for masquerade, since Americans by their origins placed a peculiar insistence on rites of transition and of metamorphosis. The nation was formed by the violation of racial and historical frontiers. American culture, by definition, lacked a coherent identity. The immigrant, or new-found man, was necessarily initiated into a prolonged and intricate masquerade, whose gestures and postures often seemed grotesque to the more resistant conventions of transatlantic visitors. The carnival tradition of America, to this day, insists on an inexhaustible play of mobility, transformation and fun.

Constance Rourke, in *American Humor* (1931), was the first to link white masquerade with black, not merely blackface nigger minstrels with grinning sambos, but the po-faced Yankee with the cockalorum of backwoodsmen. 'Masquerade was as common to him', she wrote of the Yankee, 'as mullein in his stony pastures.' Or again:

> The mask was a portable heirloom handed down by the pioneer. In a primitive world crowded with pitfalls the unchanging, unaverted countenance had been a safeguard, preventing revelations of surprise, anger, or dismay. The mask had otherwise become habitual among the older Puritans as their more expressive or risible feelings were sunk beneath the surface.

7

Whether the conviviality was secret or brimming over in tall tales, both were masks so blankly worn that (in her words) they 'closed down without a crack or seam to show a glimpse of the human creature underneath'.

Ralph Ellison, himself black, is peculiarly sensitive to masking 'motivated not so much by fear as by a profound rejection of the image created to usurp' identity. That is from an essay, first published in 1958, entitled 'Change the Joke and Slip the Yoke'. The feat, he argues, is not merely black but universally American. It is in the American grain to challenge those who presume, across the psychological distance created by race or sex or manners, to know his identity. Benjamin Franklin allowed the French to mistake him for Rousseau's Natural Man; Hemingway posed as a butch athlete; Faulkner as a farmer; Abe Lincoln as a simple country lawyer. 'Here the "darky" act', Ellison writes, 'makes brothers of us all.'

> America is a land of masking jokers. We wear the mask for purposes of aggression as well as for defense; when we are projecting the future and preserving the past. In short, the motives hidden behind the mask are as numerous as the ambiguities the mask conceals.

The essays that follow explore this theme in various guises: the American as Indian among Indians; or as missionary in the South Seas; or tourist in the Middle East; in blackface, or as youthful entrepreneur, or passionate hero, or urbane cosmopolitan; as mystagogue, charlatan, sham bohemian, or master of hieroglyphs. There are masquerades here not only of sex or of politics or of art but, in their broadest and ubiquitous reduction, of *style*. Tom Wolfe prowls about contemporary America like a star-struck playgoer penetrating backstage. For in this hall of mirrors art too is reduced to masquerade. From Poe and Hawthorne and Mark Twain to Thomas Pynchon and John Barth, Americans have tended to blur the edge between image and experience, between nostalgia and play, between the meaning (of something) and the making (of something else). The extreme, speculative end-games of post-modernism were anticipated long ago by Melville's *The Confidence-Man: His Masquerade* (1857).

8

Introduction

Long before Hollywood, the projection of the New England Yankee or nigger minstrel in stories or on the stage heightened the self-conscious effect in America of masquerade. It was as much a matter of amusement as of concealment or of self-stylization. 'Emotion seldom crept through this assumed disguise', Constance Rourke declared;

> none at all was shown by the Yankee characters or those who belonged to the backwoods, though the backwoodsman could indulge in a characteristic mock melancholy. In minstrelsy emotion was nearer the surface, surging obscurely through the choruses and walkarounds.

Minstrelsy, in fact, with whites masquerading as sambos, was a double masquerade; and minstrelsy was the first American popular form of entertainment to find an enthusiastic export market abroad.

Such is an integral part of the American inheritance, whether deployed for Macchiavellian motives or sheer enjoyment, whether embodied in Brer Rabbit or in President Nixon. These essays range wide from the earliest explorers to the present, from New York to California, from Mississippi to Maine. But a thread that again and again reappears, uniting all their many aspects, is that of the great American masquerade.

Acknowledgements: most of these pieces have appeared previously, themselves in various differing guises, in *Books and Bookmen*, *Book Choice*, the *Journal of American Studies*, the *Listener*, the *Literary Review*, the *Modern Language Review*, the *New England Quarterly*, the *New Statesman*, *Quarto*, the *Yearbook of English Studies* and, above all, the *Times Literary Supplement*.

Extensive parts of Chapter 1 first appeared in the *New England Quarterly*, Vol. 48 (March 1975), 84–103, reprinted here by permission.

Parts of Chapter 4 first appeared in the *Modern Language Review*, Vol. 77 (July 1982), 703–8; the opening section of Chapter 6 first appeared in the *Yearbook of English Studies*, Vol. 8 (1978), 40–53; and the closing section of Chapter 7 first appeared in the *Yearbook of English Studies*, Vol. 12 (1982), 186–93. All are reprinted here by permission of the Editor and Publishers (Modern Humanities Research Association).

I wish to thank all these journals for permission to reprint parts or versions of essays which first appeared in their pages.

1

In Search of Lost Time

The Indian, from the start, was invisible. For he belonged to a timeless land, without history, without origin, perhaps even without a soul. How else is one to read the exuberant, often fanciful-seeming accounts by the early explorers of North America's landscape, Jacques Cartier or Jean Ribaut, for example, or such Elizabethans as Arthur Barlowe, Thomas Hariot and Sir Walter Raleigh? The common approach in recent decades has been double-edged. Such descriptions, it is agreed, represent some kind of exotic mirror image (however inapplicable), revealing more about the closed, conceptual landscapes of the European reporters than of their actual American discoveries. In any case, such reports must be viewed with the utmost caution, usually reserved for estate agents' brochures, as advertisements for the soil, the fauna, the climate, the timber, the harbours, the natural abundance of this land of Cockaigne to promote emigration and trade with the New World. George Alsop's *A Character of the Province of Mary-Land* (1666) provides a prime example of the type:

> So that he, who out of curiosity desires to see the Landskip of the Creation drawn to the life, or to read Natures universal Herbal without book, may with the Opticks of a discreet discerning, view Mary-Land drest in her green and fragrant Mantle of the Spring. Neither do I think there is any place under the Heavenly altitude, or that has footing or room upon the circular Globe of this world, that can parallel this fertile and pleasant piece of ground in its multiplicity, or rather Natures extravagancy of a superabounding plenty.

Both Leo Marx and Howard Mumford Jones pursued this double vision. In mythical terms North America was seen

11

either as a new Arcadia (through classical eyes) or a new
Canaan (through Hebrew eyes). Whether cast in the rôle of
Adam or satanic rapist, the Indian was inscribed from head to
toe with scalp-knots, weird tattoos and cannibal accoutre-
ments. He became a walking emblem, a symbolic mountebank
hawking his mysterious parables to readers of European
broadsheets. The dual image was deliberately deployed to
consolidate colonial settlement against European nostalgia
(eastward across the Atlantic) and terror of the Indian frontier
(westward across the Appalachians). As George Alsop has it:
'The Trees, Plants, Fruits, Flowers, and Roots that grow here
in Mary-Land, are the only Emblems or Hieroglyphicks of our
Adamitical or Primitive situation.' But round that pastoral
retreat, that garden beyond the Garden of the Hesperides,
hyperborean cyclones may strike and rage; the new Eden is
encompassed on all sides by an unbounded wilderness where
'basilisks their rattles shake'.

Such descriptions, however, are not just a matter of
conflicting topics, in a series of New World theses and
antitheses, but of confusing, though accurate, accounts of
confused and bewildering experiences: of initial enthusiasm
turned to disappointment; of gloomy forebodings transported
to wonder and joy. The very reach for magniloquent imagery
is often an attempt to grasp the wholly unexpected. Take Sir
Walter Raleigh's first glimpse, in Guiana in 1596, of a distant
cataract:

> and there appeared some tenne or twelve overfals in sight, every
> one as high over the other as a Church-tower, which fell with
> that fury, that the rebound of water made it seeme, as if it had
> bene all covered over with a great shower of raine: and in some
> places wee tooke it at the first for a smoke that had risen over
> some great towne.

John Josselyn, in 1672, evoking the White Mountains of New
England, is equally precise with a diminutive imagery: 'The
country beyond these hills northward is daunting terrible,
being full of rocky hills, as thick as mole-hills in a meadow,
and cloathed with infinite thick woods.' Not everyone travelled
or wrote, like Thomas Morton, with the mystery of Leda at
their fingertips or Florio's Montaigne in their pocket. Even

descriptions of Indian encounters occasionally suggest a shock of recognition. Cartier recording that the Indians 'did as friendly and merily entertaine and receive us as any father would doe his child' is more than patronizing the Noble Savage.

Gardens too may occur, not to trigger off some time-worn emotion, but to pinpoint a peculiar and wonderful experience. Like George Percy, in 1607, lost in Virginia thickets, suddenly emerging

> into a most pleasant Garden, being a hundred paces square on every side, having many Cotton-trees growing in it with abundance of Cotton-wooll, and many *Guiacum* trees. We saw the goodliest tall trees growing so thicke about the Garden, as though they had beene set by Art, which made us marvell very much to see it.

Even so-called promotional literature may mainly be promoting the truth. Estate agents' brochures, after all, are by no means all lies. That heady scent reported by Arthur Barlowe off the coast of Virginia, for one, is clearly true. The eastern seaboard in 1584 was as perfumed as the coast of Zanzibar today. Giovanni da Verrazzano, from afar in 1524, had smelt the same 'soauissimi odori'; Marc Lescarbot, off Cape Breton twenty-five years later, could almost feel their dense weight: '*Nous tendions noz mains, comme pour les prendre, tant elles estoient palpables.*' Lake Superior was still as magically clear in 1770, for Jonathan Carver gazing down into its depth, as Walden Pond for Thoreau:

> I could sit in my canoe, where the depth was upwards of six fathoms, and plainly see huge piles of stone at the bottom, of different shapes, some of which appeared as if they were hewn. The water at this time as pure and transparent as air; and my canoe seemed as if it hung suspended in that element.

Far from twisting, or consciously adulterating, the truth, most writers seem engrossed in attempting to plumb the mystery of the new experience, as Edward Williams in 1650 pondering the mystery of the Virginia mulberry-tree and vine and silkworm. Such mysteries, under pressure of Calvinist theology, could readily be turned to emblems for mysticism. Most movingly by Jonathan Edwards in *Images or Shadows of*

13

Divine Things, where the passage from New England snow to muddy spring, for example, could be transfigured to a spiritual resurrection:

> The surface of the earth is, as it were, dissolved in the spring; the ground is loosened and broke up and softened with moisture, and its filthiness never so much appears as then, and then is the most windy, turbulent season of all.

It is mainly in poetry, in fact, that European clichés dominate. There the concepts of 'wild' and 'noble' savage, of garden and wilderness, pursued their own relentless, if often self-contradictory, patterns. By the eighteenth century a Horatian poetics flourished, reflecting the Augustan aspirations of the first British Empire and the increasingly republican values of its colonial leaders living in their pastoral villas from Monticello to Mount Vernon to Quincy, Massachusetts. At the very moment when American prose writers were seriously bent on taking up the challenge of their landscape, American poetry retired to an inane Arcadia of Zephyr breezes and Philomel warbling in transatlantic Tempes below a new Parnassus. For American prose holds a number of surprises for those brought up on English chronologies of the sublime or picturesque, anticipating John Dennis as well as Addison on the 'Pleasures of the Imagination'. As Leo Marx long ago observed, Robert Beverley's *History and Present State of Virginia* (1705) was published when James Thomson was five years old. Equally surprising is William Byrd's *History of the Dividing Line* (1729), where the educated, urbane gentleman camps out under the stars—like the bookish Washington Irving and Henry Thoreau after him—surveying his own unexpected limits as much as the disputed Virginia/North Carolina boundary.

But it is William Bartram, son of a famous father, who caps this pre-revolutionary generation. Long before Audubon, he was the botanist inspecting an exotic southland with eyes of wonder:

> The great Rose Hibiscus, The most eligant Crimson Hybiscus, that rises tall above all Plants, spreading into inumerable branches forming a Piramedal Top larger than some Trees, bearing multitudes of Vast Crimson flowers, so resplendant

14

when the Sun shines upon it in the morning the Eye can't behold it without injury to the sight.

An almost Homeric catalogue of birds on the lagoons ends in a prose hymn to 'the Silver plum'd Heron', 'the Sonorrous Stork & Whooping Crains'. Like some New World Odysseus he faces the alligator in the swamps of Florida, 'pierceing the water with his strongplated Tail 5 or 6 feet high, flourishing it in the air, lashing the River into a foam, & roaring like furious waters breaking out of the earth'. A contemporary of Linnaeus, he is at once a naturalist, a spokesman for a classical-minded culture, and an inspiration to a generation of Romantics that included Chateaubriand, Wordsworth, and Coleridge.

Nowhere was there a more rapid disintegration of a spell. Even Old World enchantments were doomed, as if America offered some never-to-be imparted secret whose attainment (in Poe's words) was destruction. Travelling about the country in 1837, Washington Irving recalled Ariosto's account of the moon,

> in which the good paladin Astolpho found everything garnered up that had been lost on earth. So I am apt to imagine that many things lost in the Old World are treasured up in the New; having been handed down from generation to generation, since the early days of the colonies. A European antiquary, therefore, curious in his researches after the ancient and almost obliterated customs and usages of his country, would do well to put himself upon the track of some early band of emigrants, follow them across the Atlantic, and rummage among their descendants on our shores.

He himself was well aware of his own limits. 'I seek only to blow a flute accompaniment in the national concert', he wrote from London in 1819, 'and leave others to play the fiddle and French Horn.' His was a whimsical, fastidious, ironical, sly *obbligato* in the manner of Lamb. The joke is that he was treated much as Caribbean or African writers were to be received a century later. 'It has been a matter of marvel, to my European readers,' he recorded in the preface to *Bracebridge Hall* (1822),

15

that a man from the wilds of America should express himself in tolerable English. I was looked upon as something new and strange in literature; as a kind of demi-savage, with a feather in his hand instead of on his head; and there was a curiosity to hear what such a being had to say about civilized society.

For Irving is a *petit maître* of what he himself called 'filligree work', much of it of German, French and Spanish folk origin. He moved to Madrid at the age of 44 to work on his *Life and Voyages of Christopher Columbus* and *The Conquest of Granada*. On his return to New York in 1832 he had lived away from the States, journeying about Europe from Paris to Prague, for seventeen years. Yet he remained at heart an American. Of the great streams and rivers that flow through American fiction all remember Mark Twain's Mississippi; some linger with Thoreau on the Concord and Merrimack rivers; but few recall the master of Tarrytown whose spirit still haunts the Hudson. Within months of resettling in New York he took off on the western trail, camping throughout the Oklahoma Territory. *A Tour on the Prairies* was published in 1835; and *Astoria*, commissioned by his friend John Jacob Astor, a year later.

But it was his *Sketch Book* (1819) and stories that brought him fame. Like James Fenimore Cooper, that other patrician from New York State, he was a life-long conservative and antiquarian. He tinkered with the romance of the American past, whether of Dutch or Indian or Creole background. Since the New World was an appendage to the Old, even an antiquarian (as Cecil Sharp was to discover several generations later in tracking down English folk songs in the Appalachian mountains) could find material on the Hudson or Mississippi. But however rich the local tales and superstitions, whispers or enchantments of the past, the restless urgency of the American population soon trampled them underfoot. 'Besides, there is no encouragement for ghosts in most of our villages', he laments in *The Legend of Sleepy Hollow*,

> for they have scarcely had time to finish their first nap, and turn themselves in their graves before their surviving friends have travelled away from the neighborhood; so that when they turn out at night to walk their rounds, they have no acquaintance left to call upon. This is perhaps the reason why we so seldom hear of ghosts, except in our long-established Dutch communities.

Irving loved ghost tales. Both *Rip Van Winkle* and *The Legend of Sleepy Hollow*, his two most powerful fables, are essentially ghost tales from such withdrawn, yet long-established, riverside communities. Like Nathaniel Hawthorne and Henry James after him, he was to be a natural expatriate for long periods of his life, but with a far more limited range of folklore and peasant nostalgia to support him. For his most urgent theme, almost literally recorded in *Rip Van Winkle*, is that of time lost—and never regained. Rip escapes the harassment of Dame Van Winkle, his wife, only to rediscover the post-revolutionary harassment of citizens' rights, party politicking, and congressional elections. Sleepy Hollow is soon to be disturbed by 'the great torrent of migration and improvement, which is making such incessant changes in other parts of this restless country'. The evocation of the feudal past is a last desperate effort to stem the radical proletarian present, loud with 'the magic phrases, "town lots", "water privileges", "railroads", and other comprehensive and soul-stirring words from the speculator's vocabulary'. No wonder 'the almighty dollar'— that sardonic phrase which passed rapidly into circulation— was Irving's coinage, first used in 1837. His one theme early exhausted, Irving withdrew to establish himself as America's first national historian, chronicling the life and ventures of Christopher Columbus, John Jacob Astor and George Washington.

The whole prophetic enterprise of art in nineteenth-century America (from Hawthorne to Melville, Whitman to Thoreau) was an attempt to repossess that imaginative vision, to reintegrate that spell. But the boldest, and least fruitful, experiment was Parkman's *Oregon Trail*, deliberately planned as an exercise in time regained. On meeting a waggon-train out west, Parkman records the following exchange:

'Whar are ye from? Californy?'
'No.'
'Santy Fee?'
'No, the Mountains.'
'What yer been doing thar? Tradin'?'
'No.'

'Trappin'?'
'No.'
'Huntin'?'
'No.'
'Emigratin'?'
'No.'
'What *have* ye been doing then, God damn ye?' (Very loud, as we were by this time almost out of hearing.)

For the quest by now was too metaphysical to share with mere traders and trappers and hunters. There were no quick and easy answers. Except as historian. The journey was undertaken, he wrote in the foreword to the first edition, 'on the writer's part with a view of studying the manners and characters of Indians in their primitive state'. Or as he had written in a letter three years earlier:

> I have been occupied for six or eight years in the study of Indian history and character, both by means of the large collections of books in Cambridge and elsewhere, and such limited observations as I could make in several journeys that I have undertaken for the purpose.

Yet reliance on Henry Rowe Schoolcraft—the one pseudo-ethnologist he had sought out in New York—might seem to warp or diminish Parkman's 'observations' to the point of no return. He displayed a good deal less penetration, in fact, than Prince Maximilian of Wied on his Western Tour ten years earlier. 'How shall we account for these extraordinary customs?' he asks, confronted by squaws who may not mention their husbands' names, or sons-in-law who may not speak to their mothers-in-law. Yet, throughout his tour, he clung to romantic fictions such as:

> Indian phlegm and apparent immobility may, in part, arise from temperament, but it is also the result of long training. If the child cries, or becomes angry, the mother says, 'You will never be a warrior'. Under such influences he grows up, accustomed not to suppress the emotion, but to conceal it. The man is encased in this impenetrable exterior—within he may be full of hatred, malice, and suspicion, but none of this appears. He is a statue!

In those pre-Freudian days, suppression (it seems) was civilized and good; concealment, savage, deceptive and bad.

Was not this statuesque Indian of the *Journal*'s opening page
an emblem—or secret sharer, rather—of this Bostonian's own
concealed and tormented inner self?

To resolve all such half-truths and ambivalences must mean
in the end confronting young Parkman himself—not merely as
observer but romantic observer. For 'a young gentleman of
leisure', Henry Nash Smith rightly remarked, 'could afford
better than anyone else to indulge himself in the slightly
decadent cult of wilderness and savagery which the early
nineteenth century took over from Byron.' It means taking
seriously, for a start, Parkman's response to the rituals of the
Sun Dance, the self-inflicted wounds and violence. For the rest
of his long life a Sioux shield, lance, pipe, medicine pouch, bow
and arrows (trophies of his frontier escapade) hung on the
walls of his Boston study; they must have beckoned him to flee
the restrictions of his class and time. As he wrote in 1850 to a
friend in Nicaragua:

> I owe you a grudge, as [your narrative] kindled in me a burning
> desire to get among fevers and volcanoes, niggers, Indians and
> other outcasts of humanity, a restless fit which is apt to seize me
> at intervals and which you have unmercifully aggravated.

But confronting those very 'outcasts', his entire body revolted
in dizziness, blindness, nausea. 'The whole central episode' of
The Oregon Trail (according to Howard Doughty) 'comes to us
heightened by the almost hallucinative perceptions of nerves
in a state of hyperesthesia from illness and exhaustion'. And
on his return, the crack-up. For two years he was in doctors'
hands, shuttled from spa to sanitorium, the immobilized
invalid in tub-baths, sitz-baths, shower-baths and sprays. 'To
the maladies of the prairie', he was to write in a frankly
autobiographical letter,

> succeeded a suite of exhausting disorders, so reducing him that
> circulation at the extremities ceased, the light of the sun became
> insupportable, and a wild whirl possessed his brain, joined to a
> universal turmoil of the nervous system which put his philosophy
> to the sharpest test it had hitherto known. All collapsed, in
> short, but the tenacious strength of muscles hardened by long
> activity. The condition was progressive, and did not reach its
> height, or, to speak more fitly, its depth, until some eighteen

months after his return. . . . The desire was intense to return to
the prairie and try a hair of the dog that bit him, but this
kill-or-cure expedient was debarred by the certainty that a few
days' exposure to the open sunlight would have destroyed his
sight.

The more obvious recurring symptoms were partial
blindness, severe heart pangs, and constant headaches as if he
were going out of his mind: insomnia, depression, crippling
rheumatism, arthritis. 'Seven modern physicians', W. R.
Jacobs writes,

> who have examined his life story, especially the relevant data in
> his letters, agree that his symptoms are indicative of an
> underlying neurosis. Unconsciously he created for himself what
> is called a 'struggle situation'. He forced himself to play the part
> of an exceedingly vigorous and aggressive man of action at the
> cost of tremendous physical and mental tension. Struggle
> became the keynote of his life, and through adherence to it he
> maintained his self-respect.

Again:

> Yet the possibility of a neurotic element in Parkman's anxiety
> about his eyes cannot be overlooked, and it is within the realm
> of probability that there was a neurotic element in his heart
> trouble and in his arthritis.

But what was this 'neurotic element' that turned a devoted
scholar to an aggressive he-man? In what way was this
Byronic cult of the wilderness and savagery 'slightly decadent'?

His Indians have been called 'the only really plausible
Indians in the whole literature of the subject'. But plausible to
whom? To fellow scholars? Fellow New Englanders? Or Sioux
Indians? Plausible as *art* is the inherent reply. *The Oregon Trail*
must be read in the same autobiographical genre of Yankee
romance that includes, in these years, Melville's *Typee* and
Omoo, Dana's *Two Years before the Mast* and Lewis H. Garrard's
Wah-to-Yah and the Taos Trail. Parkman on the Oregon Trail,
that is, must be interpreted in the same creative, rather than
journalistic, light as Dana in California or Melville in Tahiti or
the Marquesas.

Is savagery a world of mindless drift versus the consciousness

and wilfulness of civilization? Or is this merely the terminology
of one, oddly abortive, American romance? It is indicative that
none of Parkman's critics attempts to retrieve Parkman's
Indians from his own, romantic terms. As literary savages,
noble or ignoble, they continue to be thoughtlessly exploited.
But as an exploration of Parkman's own muddled depths and
groping inspiration, the signpost is here. It was precisely this
search, this *recherche du temps perdu*, this deep dive into
anthropological lost time, as he conceived it, that set up the
tensions which were to plague Parkman, like Melville, for the
rest of his long working life. Yet curiously all the critics array
Melville against Parkman, merely because one yielded to, the
other flinched from, savage blandishments. Doughty explicitly
notes: 'the erotic bias toward the masculine that partly colored
Melville's feeling' was 'foreign to Parkman's temperament'.
Yet is it not possible that the similarities between Melville and
Dana and Parkman go further than the mere forms and
itineraries of their separate quests? Kanaka culture, like that
of the Indian, was a world of naked male splendour which
must have aroused an extraordinarily mixed whirl of appre-
hensive guilt and erotic longing in such urban white collegiate
males. Melville perhaps—certainly Whitman—could un-
ashamedly react to this invitation. Parkman, drawn from
adolescence to the naked freedom of forest and Indian, felt
shamefaced and confused. His alone was the agony. His alone
was the crack-up.

He was both drawn to this romance of his deepest self and
resisted. He persisted and yet he resisted with endless pent-up
tensions and ambiguities. In defying James Fenimore Cooper,
in defying his romantic dreams, in defying the deepest
meaning of his own experience, unlike Dana or Melville, lay
the meaning of his literary narrative. He had visited the depth
of the naked self and returned home (all accounts paid and
baggage checked) unscathed. Yet especially the earliest
version—the *Knickerbocker* version—of *The Oregon Trail* revealed
a man 'growing steadily weaker as he moved westward in
space and backward in time'. 'Parkman was sickest when he
was in the Oglala village' his editor perceives. That was the
crux to which his mind would always return; 'both his
notebooks and *The Oregon Trail* itself show that his health

began to mend after he left Fort Laramie for the Pueblo, Bent's Fort, and civilization.'

Both Mason Wade and Doughty set the same passage from the *Journal* against the finished narrative. It is the scene of Old Smoke's village crossing the creek at Laramie. Both deplore the stagey literariness of the book:

> As each horse gained the bank he scrambled up as he could. Stray horses and colts came among the rest, often breaking away at full speed through the crowd, followed by old hags, screaming after their fashion on all occasions of excitement. Buxom young squaws, blooming in all the charms of vermilion, stood here and there on the bank, holding aloft their master's lance, as a signal to collect the scattered portions of his household.

Both praise the precise impressionism of the journal:

> —dogs barking, horses breaking loose, children laughing and shouting—squaws thrusting into the ground the lance and shield of the master of the lodge—naked and splendidly formed men passing and repassing through the swift water.

But what both fail to notice is the disappearance of 'Men and boys, naked and dashing eagerly through the water'—those 'naked and splendidly formed men'—in favour of the 'old hags' (a new touch) and the decorous inclusion of 'buxom' and 'blooming' squaws, whose vitality in the passage is as suspect as the language is specious. For Parkman is visibly re-editing his experience and redirecting his reader's gaze, as he does elsewhere in excising his more sadistic notions. Near the beginning of Chapter 13, 'Hunting Indians', for example, an old medicine man is 'perched aloft like a turkey-buzzard, among the dead branches of an old tree'. The original, serialized version in the *Knickerbocker Magazine* continued:

> He would have made a capital shot. A rifle bullet, skilfully planted, would have brought him tumbling to the ground. Surely, I thought, there could be no harm in shooting such a hideous old villain, to see how ugly he would look when he was dead, than in shooting the detestable vulture which he resembled.

Class and racial snobbism aside, three dominant traits of the age compelled him: a belief in prudery, in property, in industry. But his self-conscious sexual discrimination seems to underlie the other two. For men, as peculiarly sexual creatures, might share—as even Parkman's private correspondence occasionally shows—all kinds of phallic innuendoes and jokes. But womanhood, true Victorian womanhood, is an asexual state repeating annually the divine mystery of the virgin birth. Thus the real antithesis to Parkman's 'naked and splendidly formed' males are his ubiquitous, wrinkled and 'witchlike' hags. Physical attraction is matched by physical revulsion, not man by woman. Thus Parkman's shock, too, at Indian squaws—their frolics, their freedom, their earthy awareness of the male:

The women are full of jokes and raillery. *3 July*

It is astonishing, what abominable indecencies the best of the Inds. will utter in presence of the women, who laugh heartily. *4 July*

. . . listened to the constant joking and trickery of the squaws. *5 July*

As the pipe passed the circle around the fire in the evening, there was plenty of that obscene conversation that seems to make up the sum of Ind. wit, and which very much amuses the squaws. The Inds. are a very licentious set. *29 July*

The gross indecency of many Indian names, even of the most distinguished men. *7 & 8 August*

Such strictures blend with outrage at the males, in their inert and cosseted state, their compliant passivity, their total lack of willpower, of drive to achievement:

The utter laziness of an Ind.'s life. It is scarce tolerable to us, and yet is theirs from year's end to year's end. Bull Bear, a young chief, famous for his intrepidity, ambition, and activity, lies kicking his heels by the fire like the rest. *2 July*

In fact, the greater part of a trapper's or an Ind.'s life is mere vacancy—lying about, as I am now, with nothing to do or think of. *6 July*

Dozed away the afternoon in Raynal's lodge, thinking of things
past and meditating on things to come. Here one feels overcome
with an irresistable laziness—he cannot even muse consecu-
tively. *29 July*

Such laziness spells an 'unsatiable appetite for food and
presents', imposing unpredictable, communal sanctions on
that innermost bourgeois sanctum of private property. Thus
the mixed-up Victorian reaction (part Malory, part counting-
house) to White Shield: 'He was a very splendid and
chivalrous-looking figure; but he is a notorious beggar, like the
rest. *26 July*' For Parkman's only response to communal needs
is a bourgeois version of Pauline charity. 'So much for the
affection and tenderness experienced by the sick in an Indian
lodge', he shrugs, after evoking their lack of sentimentality at
disease and bodily affliction. 'So much for generosity and
public spirit', he scoffs, dismissing the shared obligations and
shared rewards of a buffalo hunt.

'*J'ai l'intelligence néolithique*', asserted Claude Lévi-Strauss.
Such ironic inversions were hardly accessible, of course, to a
Bostonian. But far from identifying, Parkman irresistibly
needed to distance the Yahoo/Savage even further into the
museum laboratory: as 'a good specimen of a Dacotah warrior',
'a female animal of more than two hundred pounds weight',
'living representatives of the "stone age" '. Audubon, too, a few
years earlier, had witnessed the end of a buffalo hunt on the
Dacota Prairie:

> Now one breaks in the skull of the bull, and with bloody fingers
> draws out the hot brains and swallows them with peculiar zest;
> another has now reached the liver, and is gobbling down
> enormous pieces of it; whilst, perhaps, a third, who has come to
> the paunch is feeding luxuriously on some—to me—disgusting-
> looking offal.

But Parkman glories in his own censorious detachment:

> The surrounding group of savages offered no very attractive
> spectacle to a civilized eye. Some were cracking the huge
> thigh-bones and devouring the marrow within; others were
> cutting away pieces of the liver, and other approved morsels,
> and swallowing them on the spot with the appetite of wolves.
> The faces of most of them, besmeared with blood from ear to
> ear, looked grim and horrible enough.

24

The conclusion is not unlike that of the demented Gulliver on his return to England.

> For the most part, a civilized white man can discover very few points of sympathy between his own nature and that of an Indian. With every disposition to do justice to their good qualities, he must be conscious that an impassable gulf lies between him and his red brethren. Nay, so alien to himself do they appear, that, after breathing the air of the prairie for a few months or weeks, he begins to look upon them as a troublesome and dangerous species of wild beast.

No wonder Theodore Parker and Melville were shocked. Again and again in *Typee*, Melville had called the Marquesans 'savages', playing on all the ambiguities of that word. But

> when . . . we are informed that it is difficult for any white man, after a domestication among the Indians, to hold them much better than brutes; when we are told, too, that to such a person, the slaughter of an Indian is indifferent as the slaughter of a buffalo; with all deference, we beg leave to dissent.
>
> It is too often the case, that civilized beings sojourning among savages soon come to regard them with disdain and contempt. But though in many cases this feeling is almost natural, it is not defensible; and it is wholly wrong.

Parkman's mind, however, was beyond such appeal. The case was closed. The whole of his historical opus was to be based precisely on this set piece of the Indians as childishly passionate, yet cunning, treacherous, rapacious, coarsely unmusical, dull, cowardly, lazy, lying, boastful, superstitious and absurd visionaries. Child of nature, the Indian was a natural wolfchild, or *homo lupus*. In the same year as Thoreau's lecture, *Essay on Civil Disobedience*, this Yankee republican castigated the Indians for overindulgence of their children,

> whom they . . . never punished, except in extreme cases, when they would throw a bowl of cold water over them. Their offspring became sufficiently undutiful and disobedient under this system of education, which tends not a little to foster that wild idea of liberty and utter intolerance of restraint which lie at the foundation of the Indian character.

Unwittingly he had stumbled on an acute psychological key, even political key: 'Indians cannot act in large bodies.' However divided and degraded, they were still dangerous and nakedly potent, 'with their dark busts exposed to view as they suffered their robes to fall from their shoulders'.

It is this mingling of force and potency that was so peculiarly thrilling. Like 'The Panther':

> As he suffered his ornamented buffalo-robe to fall in folds about his loins, his stately and graceful figure was fully displayed; and while he sat his horse in an easy attitude, the long feathers of the prairie-cock fluttering from the crown of his head, he seemed the very model of a wild prairie-rider.

These 'graceful', yet vigorously muscled, athlete-warriors were objects of sexual contemplation, but also subjects of romance: The Hail-Storm and The Rabbit sharing 'with one another almost all that they possessed'; Parkman with 'my friend The Panther' riding and hunting together and lying under the trees 'studying the Ogillallah tongue'. For sexual contemplation could always be disguised aesthetically, as Melville had done among the Typee, and Alfred Wallace was soon to do along the Amazon:

> Others again stood carelessly among the throng, with nothing to conceal the matchless symmetry of their forms. There was one in particular, a ferocious fellow, named The Mad Wolf, who, with the bow in his hand and the quiver at his back, might have seemed, but for his face, the Pythian Apollo himself. Such a figure rose before the imagination of West, when, on first seeing the Belvedere in the Vatican, he exclaimed, 'By God, a Mohawk!'

Mrs. Cooper, too, could invoke that vision in defending her husband's work, to argue that

> it was a matter of course that he should dwell on the better traits of the picture rather than on the coarser and more revolting, though more common points. Like West, he could see Apollo in the young Mohawk.

But Parkman can enjoy the aesthetic savagery *and* dwell on 'the coarser and more revolting' traits of the picture. The need was always to distance this psychological tension of love/hate to objects and pictures (seen from without) and somnambules or automata (interpreted from within). At one moment the 'picturesque' scene is 'worthy of a Salvator'—'a noble subject for a painter' or 'the pen of old Scott'. At another, the inner man, devoid of 'speculation and conjecture', is equally stalled: 'his reason moves in its beaten track. His soul is dormant. . . .'

The emotive effect, then, is both figuratively and literally dumb—with pre-Darwinian contempt linking hunters to the hunted (bears, wolves, deer, tortoises) from whom 'they even claim the honor of a lineal descent.' Or again (with a traditionally Protestant alienating effect) the Indian warrior is transformed to a handsome, endearing Satanic child, complementing his hag-ridden world of hobgoblins and witches. The Fox Dance of the 'Strong Hearts' society stamps and whoops, brandishing 'their weapons like so many frantic devils'. Kongra-Tonga's features, as he tells his exploit of the Snake Indian shot, captured, scalped alive and tossed on a blazing fire,

> were remarkably mild and open, without the fierceness of expression common among these Indians; and as he detailed these devilish cruelties, he looked up into my face with the air of earnest simplicity which a little child would wear in relating to its mother some anecdote of its youthful experience.

There is already a touch here of the *fin de siècle*: of evil beauties, especially male evil beauties, with erotic overtones (from *Turn of the Screw* to *Death in Venice*). No wonder Parkman, back at Fort Laramie, pored over his Byron (that 'unmanly character') 'fairly revelling in the creations of that resplendent genius'.

This was the very time, too, of Gustave Flaubert's and Maxime Du Camp's escapades in exotic Syria and Egypt. For sexual rôles on a nineteenth-century Cook's tour—the use of adolescents *'pour se polluer'*, the amused exploitation of native nakedness and *'les moeurs bizarres'*—were but an extension of political rôles: between master and servant, white and native, the leisured and the destitute. From the bazaars of Cairo to the campfires of the prairie, erotic favours were showered on the tourist. But Parkman held aloof. He rejected all such offers. His ultimate and sole narcissistic romance was with his gun: 'I was accompanied by a faithful friend, my rifle, the only friend indeed on whose prompt assistance in time of trouble I could wholly rely.' His hidden summons, rather, were to vengeance,

in a kind of counter assault for self-vindication—self-gratification even. 'A military force and military law are urgently
called for', he insisted. In the mirror of that very pond, by
which he lay with The Panther 'studying the Ogillallah
tongue', he could read the parable of the minnows and the
monster:

> A shoal of little fishes of about a pin's length were playing in it,
> sporting together, as it seemed, very amicably; but on closer
> observation, I saw that they were engaged in cannibal warfare
> among themselves. Now and then one of the smallest would fall
> a victim, and immediately dissapear down the maw of his
> conqueror. Every moment, however, the tyrant of the pool, a
> goggle-eyed monster about three inches long, would slowly
> emerge with quivering fins and tail from under the shelving
> bank. The small fry at this would suspend their hostilities, and
> scatter in a panic at the appearance of overwhelming force.
>
> 'Soft-hearted philanthropists,' thought I, 'may sigh long for
> their peaceful millennium; for, from minnows to men, life is
> incessant war.

In that pastoral interlude even, among the mountains, he
could express this heartfelt, complacent salute to 'overwhelming force'.

Thus the 23-year-old graduate, like any twentieth-century
voyeur/voyageur, had devised his self-protective dark glasses
from behind which to spy the aesthetic savages and plot
revenge. But what his masquerade reveals is merely a desperate
lack of comprehension. His sense of exclusion seemed vindi-
cated, maybe, by all those muddled clichés about the red man
as ferocious, malignant, bloody beast. Feeling alienated, he
needed constantly to alienate his experiences into aesthetic
objects (for contemplation) or satanic perversity (for damnation). Since what he could not understand, the white man had
to control—polemically, politically, economically, and liter-
arily by a restless, observant attention to factual detail. The
aesthetic processing of this 'material' (with asides on Salvator
Rosa and Sir Walter Scott) demanded a tireless, sensual, all-
inclusive accountancy of the Dahcotahs on mountain and
prairie. The *Oregon Trail Journal* aptly concludes with page on
page of scrupulously recorded travelling expenses, from tiny
items like 'tea' and 'Porter', 'Bath' and 'Ale', to fares, purchase

of horses and carts, pistols, powder, and payment of advance wages.

In a final preface, written in 1892, almost half a century later, Parkman still thrills to the paradoxes of male savagery ('hateful', 'terrible', yet somehow charming), while recoiling from the symptoms of modernization ('tame', 'ugly', not to say 'effeminate' caricatures). Within such masochistic dilemmas the bourgeois remained forever locked: repressing his own masculinity, only to despise the resultant effeminacy. Only by such masquerades could time be recycled, Parkman discovered, if not exactly regained. Last of the Yankee Byronists (enthralled by *Childe Harold*) Parkman's achievement was to transform 'a history of the American forest' to romantic tragedy in the encroaching century of the common man; to celebrate an heroic past in the face of a suicidal Civil War; to create a monumental prose *Iliad* at the very moment when the contemporary stage was set for the final destruction of the Plains Indians and their transformation into dime fiction villains for pulp press, Hollywood and TV—that endlessly variegated, commercially promoted pop saga of cowboy-versus-Indian.

2

The Transcendental Savage

De Tocqueville's magisterial summing up, towards the end of the first volume of *Democracy in America* (1835), is based on a racial absolute: *white* (as the blues singer has it) is *right*.

> The first in enlightenment, power, and happiness, is the white man, the European, man par excellence; below him comes the Negro and the Indian. . . . Might one not say that the European is to men of other races what man is to the animals? He makes them serve his convenience, and when he cannot bend them to his will he destroys them.

At once this racial absolute engenders two mutually exclusive variants: subjection or destruction.

For the syntactic play of 'white-plus-red' is very different from that of 'white-plus-black'. Red for Tocqueville seems to signify a kind of gipsy stereotype. As he remarks of one Indian he met: 'There was a sort of barbarous luxury in the Indian woman's dress; metal rings hung from her nostrils and ears; there were little glass beads in the hair that fell freely over her shoulders.' Red, according to Las Casas in the sixteenth century, meant physically weak, but intelligent: the antithesis of the Aristotelean slave. Yet this intelligent, though frail kind of American gipsy, was also a warrior and hunter. From that self-contradiction Tocqueville elaborated a series of verbal manoeuvres, based on the body/mind duality that always has a way of superimposing itself on white colour codes.

His key is this: the Indian and the Negro both live under pressure, in states of extremity. The Indian lives on the extreme edge of freedom. But if his body is brutalized, his pride and will remain intact:

> Far from wishing to adapt his mores to ours, he regards barbarism as the distinctive emblem of his race, and in repulsing civilization he is perhaps less moved by hatred against it than by fear of resembling the Europeans.

Far from cowardly treachery, then, his is a barbaric pride. Thus Tocqueville seeks to mitigate those earlier satanic traits, which the *Encyclopedia Britannica* was still listing as late as 1793 under 'propensity to violence' and 'perfidy combined with cruelty'. But such pride is doomed:

> If they remain savages, they are driven along before the march of progress; if they try to become civilized, contact with more civilized people delivers them over to oppression and misery. If they go on wandering in the wilderness, they perish; if they attempt to settle, they perish just the same.

Thus the logic terminates with inevitable dispossession, subjugation, extermination. To this day European discourse is most readily adapted to structures that move from 'bloodthirsty savage' to 'dead Injun'. If not dead, as good as dead. 'But this is a culture in arrestment', wrote Charles Olson in his *Mayan Letters*: '(Christ, it makes me burn: their inactivity ain't at all beautiful. They are fucking unhappy. What graces they have are traces only, of what was & of what, I'd guess, can be.)'

The Negro, by contrast, suggests an apelike prototype. Tocqueville, like Jefferson before him, conjures with the orang-outang (*simia satyrus*) as missing link: 'His face appears to us hideous, his intelligence limited, and his tastes low; we almost take him for some being intermediate between beast and man.' For black denotes something brutal and tough. Yet to cast him in the rôle of cultivator seems equally self-contradictory. If the Indian lives on the extreme edge of freedom, the Negro has 'reached the ultimate limits of slavery'. If the *body* of the one is brutalized, the *mind* of the other is destroyed. Servile, riddled with self-contempt, he becomes abject, insinuating: 'He adapts himself to his oppressors' tastes, adopting their opinions and hoping by imitation to join their community. . . . His intelligence is degraded to the level of his soul.'

Thus the Indian is victim of the white man's superior force

31

The Great American Masquerade

merely, the Negro of his superior fiction. He assumes the white man's definitions as self-definitions: 'and he has learned nothing but to submit and obey. So he has reached this climax of affliction in which slavery brutalizes him and freedom leads him to destruction.' The logic again terminates with inevitable destruction. But not by armed domination this time, rather by a kind of spiritual extinction. Again European discourse was most readily adapted to structures that moved from the limping slave (with the Jim Crow shuffle) to such blackface zombies as Rastus, Brudder Tambo and Brudder Bones.

Tocqueville, in the 1830s, drew his own conclusion:

> The Negro would like to mingle with the European and cannot. The Indian might to some extent succeed in that, but he scorns to attempt it. The servility of the former delivers him over into slavery; the pride of the latter leads him to death.

He draws that self-fulfilling deduction and rules his double lines in the ledger with the grim satisfaction of an accountant. But then Tocqueville, despite his birth, *was* something of an accountant. He believed both in 'an aristocracy founded on visible and indelible signs' and in the utilitarian age that preferred the cultivator to the hunter and contrasted white progress to red stagnation and degeneration. As he declared in the introduction to his first volume:

> Although the huge territories just described were inhabited by many native tribes, one can fairly say that at the time of discovery they were no more than a wilderness. The Indians occupied but did not possess the land. It is by agriculture that man wins the soil, and the first inhabitants of North America lived by hunting. . . . Providence, when it placed them amid the riches of the New World, seems to have granted them a short lease only; they were there, in some sense, *only waiting*. Those coasts so well suited for trade and industry, those deep rivers, that inexhaustible valley of the Mississippi—in short, the whole continent—seemed the yet empty cradle of a great nation.

Indians, in short, were invisible. Providence had placed them in the New World with this (for us) curiously providential lack of 'foresight'. 'If thou hadst seen this district of country, as I did, when it lay in the sleep of nature', Judge Temple remarks in Cooper's *The Pioneers*. For its dream maidens and dream

32

Indians, like an urge of nature, can only be glimpsed from some Mount Pisgah in the wilderness (as in Cooper), or some crossroads of time (as in Thoreau). The converse of the utilitarian ethos of settlers and surveyors had, from the start, been the lonely epiphany. The sleeping land could only be glimpsed, as it were, in a waking dream:

> Unimproved and wild as this district now seems to your eyes, what was it when I first entered the hills! I left my party, the morning of my arrival, near the farms of the Cherry Valley, and, following a deer path, rode to the summit of the mountain that I have since called Mount Vision; for the sight that there met my eyes seemed to me as the deceptions of a dream. The fire had run over the pinnacle, and, in a great measure, laid open the view. The leaves were fallen, and I mounted a tree, and sat for an hour looking on the silent wilderness. Not an opening was to be seen in the boundless forest, except where the lake lay, like a mirror of glass. The water was covered by myriads of the wild fowl that migrate with the changes in the season; and while in my situation on the branch of the beech, I saw a bear, with her cubs, descend to the shore to drink. I had met many deer, gliding through the woods, in my journey; but not the vestige of a man could I trace during my progress, not from my elevated observatory. No clearing, no hut, none of the winding roads that are now to be seen, were there; nothing but mountains rising behind mountains; and the valley, with its surface of branches. . . . Even the Susquehanna was then hid, by the height and density of the forest.

So Buffalo Bill lies buried on Lookout Mountain, near Golden, Colorado. It is this Augustan vision of the American sublime (mountains rising behind mountains) that will also admit, in the same novel, a lone figure in the landscape: stern, simple, proud, taciturn Chingachgook. But the bifocal vision divorces man from transcendent nature, activity from contemplation, clearings from mirror and mystery, Indians from history.

Even before his retreat to Walden Hawthorne had recognized Thoreau, not as an original merely, but as a kind of aboriginal 'inclined to lead a sort of Indian life among civilized men'. What most vividly struck him was Thoreau's refusal to work, 'the absence of any systematic effort for a livelihood'. He noted

Thoreau's 'strange stories' of his friendship with fish, birds and beasts, as well as herbs and flowers. His weather forecasts were astonishingly accurate. He could handle a boat with only one paddle. Most uncanny of all was his skill in finding arrowheads and relics. It was as if the red men's spirits, Hawthorne recorded, 'willed him to be the inheritor of their simple wealth'.

That was in 1842. Yet the odd fact remains that Thoreau hardly knew a single Indian. Nor did he go out of his way to meet an Indian, let alone make the effort to live among Indians. Francis Parkman, his contemporary, actually travelled as far as Wyoming, in his short-sighted way, to join the Dacota Sioux. Edmund Wilson, that even more improbable Indian, explored not only the literature but the reservations of the Iroquois in upper New York State and Canada a century later. But Thoreau's contact with Indians was limited to his two Penobscot guides in Maine; and they, by the 1850s, turned out to be Protestants and lumbermen in red flannel shirts, living in two-storey clapboard houses with blinds. His three trips, in any case, were brief, lasting no more than two or three weeks; and he never experienced Indian community life.

When finally he did make his great trip west, to Minnesota in 1861, it was already too late. He was in the last stages of tuberculosis and weakened by bronchitis. His excursion to the Sioux agency on the Minnesota river was short and, what was worse, made in the company of officials and sightseers. It is clear that he knew nothing of the tensions that would break into open warfare a year later. But, like Parkman, he brought back trophies from his frontier escapade. The buckskin suit and snowshoes given him by the Sioux are still at Concord.

For Thoreau was a literary Indian, in contact not with living so much as archaeological red men, whom he traced from their field paths and fishing weirs, their pestles and flints. 'I feel no desire to go to California or Pike's Peak,' he wrote in his journal, 'but I often think at night with inexpressible satisfaction and yearning of the *arrowheadiferous* sands of Concord.' Everywhere he discovered hints of Indian red: in the clay of the railroad embankment, the blood-speckled rocks, the dwarf andromeda leaves across a pond, even the robin redbreast. He was the first imaginary Indian—without the statutory plait and headband of a more recent generation—attempting to re-create in his own work that aboriginal hold on the American continent.

But though he was to read Henry Rowe Schoolcraft's translation of Ojibwa tales and Longfellow's *Hiawatha*, he still knew little or nothing of Indian art itself. He praised 'the chant of the Indian muse', but assumed such songs were all of the war dance. He knew nothing of their sun dance lodges or sweat-baths; no more than he recognized their Asiatic origins, only to be established after his death by Lewis Henry Morgan. Gazing with astonishment at a bird-headed pestle, ploughed up near the Concord river, he concluded: 'It brings the maker still nearer to the races which so ornament their umbrella and cane handles.' His twelve Indian notebooks, amounting to some 2,800 pages of source material, from the Jesuit *Relations* to Schoolcraft and Heckewelder, are now in the Pierpont Morgan Library; his collection of arrowheads at Harvard.

So consistent and creative was this relationship with the exterminated tribes that a second paradox has too easily been missed: astonishment at discovering a raw Indian under the sober habits of a New England hermit. For this peace-loving, literate, uncommonly chaste and educated loner was anything but an American Indian of any conceivable tribe or kind. His hippie heirs, turned flower children, were certainly never noted either for chastity or literacy. Gregarious rather, founders of communes, they seem essentially closer (in whatever aberrant way) to authentic Indian life. For Thoreau remained victim to the end of that overwhelming, romantic myth, enshrined by Cooper in *The Last of the Mohicans*, of the doomed and solitary Indian.

Like Cooper's hero, Leatherstocking, Thoreau chose to explore a middle ground between civilized and savage America. Both were attempts to formulate a new rôle, founded on an Indian education. But Thoreau's was by far the most complex: for his was the more educated attempt. Thus his vast compilation of readings in the 'Indian books' was only another aspect of the poet's trail in search of older Indian trails. His very production as a scholar-poet, interweaving close reading and close observation into the permanence of art, was as refined and unmarketable (he claimed in *Walden*) as Indian wickerwork:

35

> I too had woven a kind of basket of a delicate texture, but I had not
> made it worth any one's while to buy them. Yet not the less in my
> case, did I think it worth my while to weave them, and instead of
> studying how to make it worth men's while to buy my baskets, I
> studied rather how to avoid the necessity of selling them.

Thoreau's overriding insight was that the Indian, like the
wilderness, is the essential precondition of American culture.
Since actual Indians, in their archaic vigour, had all but
disappeared, it followed (as he noted as early as 1842) that
'there is only so much of Indian America left as there is of the
American Indian in the character of this generation'.
Fortunately the wilderness itself promoted and preserved that
essential character. There lay the one hope of human—let
alone national—survival.

That is the key to all that is finest, most original and lasting
in his work: the attempt to cross a European with an Indian
education; to construct singlehanded a bridge from Rousseau's
Promenades to the hunters and shamans of North America. So
much can be, and has been, made of the Emersonian or
transcendental cast of his thought that his unique rôle in
reclaiming savagery, as the essential and suppressed element
of our white heritage, has been unduly obscured. Yet it is this
Indian element in all his endeavours that makes him the
harbinger and, in a sense, patron spirit of such vastly
influential movements of the twentieth century as Baden-
Powell's Boy Scouts and Girl Guides, the United States
National Parks (beginning with Yellowstone in 1872),
Britain's more recent Operation Neptune, and the whole new
wave of ecological concern.

'In Wilderness is the preservation of the World.' Not
necessarily on the scale of Yosemite or Snowdonia. For
Thoreau associated swamps with red men. Both were wild
remnants; both restored him.

> I enter a swamp as a sacred place, a *sanctum sanctorum*. There is
> the strength, the marrow, of Nature. The wildwood covers the
> virgin mould, and the same soil is good for men and for trees. A
> man's health requires as many acres of meadow to his prospect
> as his farm does loads of muck. There are the strong meats on
> which he feeds. A town is saved, not more by the righteous men
> in it than by the woods and swamps that surround it.

Such an ecology proved radical:

> Most revolutions in society have not power to interest, still less
> alarm us; but tell me that our rivers are drying up, or the genus
> pine dying out in the country, and I might attend.

He loved the wilderness ferociously. As a young man, he once
wrote: 'I grow savager and savager every day, as if fed on raw
meat, and my tameness is only the repose of untamableness.'
He wanted to be 'nature looking into nature with such easy
sympathy as the blue-eyed grass in the meadow looks in the
face of the sky'. Or, in the words of a memorable passage from
Walden:

> As I came home through the woods with my string of fish,
> trailing my pole, it being now quite dark, I caught a glimpse of
> a woodchuck stealing across my path, and felt a strange thrill of
> savage delight, and was strongly tempted to seize and devour
> him raw; not that I was hungry then, except for that wildness
> which he represented.

That is the opening of the chapter entitled 'Higher Laws'.
For such radicalism had to be redemptive—both for the
wilderness and for the human self. Such transformations of
nature into consciousness, with all their bewildering setbacks
and inadequacies (now on the side of nature, now of consciousness), the self-defeats of a vision searching for paradise
on earth, lie at the heart of the paradoxical patterns of
Thoreau's major works. As the woodchuck passage continues:

> I found in myself, and still find, an instinct toward a higher, or,
> as it is named, spiritual life, as do most men, and another
> toward a primitive rank and savage one, and I reverence them
> both. I love the wild not less than the good.

As flesh seeks to devour flesh, so spirit craves spiritual
fulfilment. Back and forth Thoreau rocked on this see-saw, to
find a point of equilibrium on what he deeply believed to be a
continuum of experience. Just as he tried to find a pastoral
point of equilibrium between the town and the railroad, the
civilized and wild, the forester and the farmer. Rejecting the
blood-lust of the one (in spite of that woodchuck) and the
drudgery of the other (in spite of his beans), he reverted to
some kind of primitive gatherer (of clams and berries). His

most typical mood is one of meditative, alert, timeless silence—
that of a bird-watcher or fisherman—until, like Walden pond
itself, his studious reflections (with a deliberate pun) turn him
into 'a perfect forest mirror'.

As the 'Indian books' make clear, Thoreau knew nothing
of the vision quests, later recounted by Black Elk, for
example, or Lame Deer. Yet his retreat to Walden can be
described as the vision quest of a transcendental savage, who
rejected village society for a more perfect Indian wisdom.
Those very 'Indian books' (started at Walden pond and kept
for some fourteen years) are not a literary reservation, but a
commonplace book feeding all his literary interests, beginning with *A Week on the Concord and Merrimack Rivers*; though it
is possible that by Number 8 (1853) he was searching for
some more specific Indian topic. As he informed the
Association for the Advancement of Science in December, his
interest was 'the Manners & Customs of the Indians of the
Algonquin Group previous to contact with the civilized man'.
But if so, the search was defeated by two further expeditions
to Maine in 1853 and 1857; and there at last he met—as
objects of the closest, prolonged scrutiny—two real-life
Indians: Joe Aitteon (whose mongoloid features were recently
discovered on a tintype at the University of Maine) and Joe
Polis (a much-travelled landowner, eight years older than
Thoreau).

It was Thoreau's triumph to present both men with
absolute candour. Truly Robert F. Sayre remarks: 'As Jim in
Huckleberry Finn is the most realistic black portrait by a white
writer in nineteenth-century American literature, Joe Polis is
the most realistic and attractive native American.' So realistic,
in fact, that Thoreau was too embarrassed to publish the
account in his own lifetime, turning down a bid from James
Russell Lowell for the *Atlantic Monthly*, since Polis was literate
'and takes a newspaper, so that I could not face him again'.
Emerson, in his funeral eulogy, named Polis with John Brown
and Walt Whitman as the three men with the greatest
influence on Thoreau in the last years of his life.

'Wordsworth', he had decided long ago, 'is too tame for the
Chippeway'; and in Joe Polis, gibbering like a muskrat, he had
discovered at last both a practising Christian and aboriginal

wild man. As when Polis, hungry for muskrat, had hushed him with a 'Stop, me call 'em':

> and sitting flat on the bank, he began to make a curious squeaking, wiry sound with his lips, exerting himself considerably. I was greatly surprised,—thought that I had at last got into the wilderness, and that he was a wild man indeed, to be talking to a musquash! I did not know which of the two was the strangest to me. He seemed suddenly to have quite forsaken humanity, and gone over to the musquash side.

From 'Higher Laws' to his ascent of Katahdin, that was the risk Thoreau continued to face. To the end the question haunted him: which of the two was the strangest? He died not with 'Transcendence' or 'Wordsworth' on his lips, but murmuring 'moose' and 'Indians'.

The waking dream was no longer a white man's epiphany, nor a red man's quest; it had become the half-caste's prerogative. Thoreau was a Natty Bumppo from Harvard. He was the first of a whole line of spiritual half-castes who were finally to displace the Indian altogether from the national stage. Sexual contact had been established by the Elizabethans.

John Rolfe was the first British colonist in America to marry an Indian. Nicknamed 'the Playful One', baptized Rebecca, Matsoaks'ats lies buried at Gravesend. But her son, Thomas Rolfe, returned to Virginia; and to this day many prominent Virginia families claim descent from Pocahontas. Within a few years, more than forty settlers had married Indian women and several English women had married Indians.

Yet even John Rolfe had not been ignorant 'of the heavy displeasure which Almighty God conceived against the sons of Levi and Israel for marrying strange wives'. By 1691 the province instituted severe penalties against living with Indians, banishing for ever any English man or woman who married a negro, mulatto, or Indian. After second thoughts, the law was modified to fines and imprisonment. But this was meaningless further west. By the eighteenth and early nineteenth centuries most trappers and *voyageurs* had Indian wives. Toussaint Charbonneau, interpreter for the Lewis and Clark expedition, had his 16-year-old Shoshone wife, Sacajawea. Jim Bridger, who established Fort Bridger on the Oregon Trail, had three Indian wives. Francis Parkman's guide, Henri Chatillon, had married the daughter of old Bull Bear, great chief of the Oglalas. Squaws not only supplied domestic comfort, cured robes and skins, but ensured the trapper's immunity.

'Sometimes they had more than one "wife" ', writes Parkman,

> since a solitary white man's safety among the Indians was partly dependent upon the number of his savage relations who might be expected to avenge his death. When a trapper made a trading visit to a normally hostile or semihostile tribe, he was usually given a squaw for the duration of his visit by the chief, who wanted to trade and to protect the trapper. In such cases the squaw was a business asset, but also a liability because her relatives had to be shown with presents that he loved her. From the squaw's point of view, trappers were extremely desirable husbands, gentler than any Indian and furnishing their wives with store clothes and ornaments, knives and utensils, and other articles that they would never otherwise have seen.

Lewis H. Garrard, on the *Taos Trail*, was even more enthusiastic about squaws who would 'descend from the position of a ministering angel down, down below any scale of degradation conceivable'. In 1933 Hemingway's Nick Adams was to recall with relish their 'plump brown legs, flat belly, hard little breasts' and 'quick searching tongue'.

The celebrated Sequoya was the son of a trader and Cherokee mother. Osceola was reputed to be part white, part possibly Negro. Jesse Chisholm, who opened the trail from Kansas through Oklahoma to Texas, was a Cherokee half-caste. James Fenimore Cooper's fictional concern is all with white squaws; but more commonplace were the squaw men, including runaway Negroes who joined Indian tribes. 'Red Niggers' was the cant term for them. (Ralph Ellison, who grew up in Oklahoma, could remember all kinds of half-bloods, Indians 'as wild as wild Negroes, and others who were as solid and as steady as bankers'.)

Alexis de Tocqueville acclaimed these half-breeds as 'the natural link between civilization and barbarism'. But Crèvecoeur, like Cooper, rejected the resultant 'half-andhalfs'. 'However I respect the simple, the inoffensive society of these people in their villages,' he wrote in his twelfth *Letter from an American Farmer*, 'the strongest prejudices would make me abhor any alliance with them in blood: disagreeable, no doubt, to nature's intentions which have strongly divided us by so many indelible characters.' Indians alone, paradoxically, would be excluded from that western frontier where 'individuals of all nations are melted into a new race' (as he had pronounced in his third letter).

For racial prejudice, before Darwin, was divinely colour-coded, descending on a scale of pigmentation from white to yellow to brown to red to black; from Caucasian, Mongolian, Malaysian, American to Ethiopian. The racialism is explicit in Samuel Morton's *Crania Americana* (1839) and Josiah Clark Nott's *Types of Mankind* (1856). George Bancroft in the third volume of his *History of the United States* (1840) duly adds this Lavater-like, pseudo-scientific touch:

> . . . the nose is broad; the jaws project; the lips are large and thick, giving to the mouth an expression of indolent insensibility; the forehead, as compared with Europeans, is narrow. The facial angle of the European is assumed to be eighty-seven; that of the American, by induction from many admeasurements, is declared to be seventy-five. The mean internal capacity of the skull of the former is eighty-seven cubic inches; of the barbarous tribes of the latter, it is found to be, at least, eighty-two.

The Indians, in their way, confirmed the theme. In Chief Seattle's words at the Port Elliott Treaty in 1855: 'No, we are two separate races, and we must stay separate. There is little in common between us.' Though this did not prevent a little miscegenation when opportunity offered. Captivity narratives, mainly of women, were the stock-in-trade of puritan pamphleteering to display 'the Sovreignty & Goodness of God, Together with Faithfulness of his Promises Displayed' (as Mary Rowlandson put it). Charles Brockden Brown, Cooper, Bancroft, Samuel Drake (in his *Indian Captivities*, 1839), Mark Twain, Theodore Roosevelt, all emphasize the brutal sexuality, the lechery of Indians who will gang-bang their innocent captives. As young women, captured in the 1879 Ute rising, testified at a court of enquiry:

> 'Of course we were insulted a good many times; we expected
> to be.'
> 'What do you mean by insult? And of what did it consist?'
> 'Of outrageous behavior in the night.'

Ebenezer Cook, in *The Sot-Weed Factor* (1708), had spoken
more alluringly of an Indian's sexual charm:

> His manly Shoulders such as please,
> Widows and Wives, were bath'd in Grease
> Of Cub and Bear, whose supple Oil,
> Prepar'd his Limbs 'gainst Heat or Toil.

Even Shakespeare, after all, or collaborators on *King Henry the
Eighth*, had taken in the myth of his genital power. 'Is this
Moorfields to muster in?' cries the porter of palace yard; 'or
have we some strange Indian with the great tool come to
court, the women so besiege us? Bless me, what a fry of
fornication is at the door!' By the nineteenth century numerous
mixed marriages took place not only on the frontier but with
Indian lads in missionary colleges or in the big city. Black Elk,
on tour with Buffalo Bill, was a great favourite with Wasichu
girls, as he calls them, in Paris.

Yet none were as much despised as half-castes, or half-
breeds, or half-bloods, or *bois brulés* as the French named their
mixed bloods. (All terms are equally compromising with their
suggestion of adulteration, of the dilution and pollution of
'pure' blood.) Cooper rejected them as 'altogether more
barbarous than the real savage', condemning them to the
worst of both worlds: 'the depravity of civilization without the
virtues of the savage'. Mark Twain rubbed it in. His Injun Joe
is the 'half-breed devil' and 'bloody-minded outcast' of *The
Adventures of Tom Sawyer*. He is a grave-robber and murderer
and secret avenger haunting St. Petersburg, planning to slit
the Widow Douglas's nostrils and 'notch her ears like a sow'.
But at last the score is settled. The fate of Injun Joe is not
simply extinction; it is extinction by squeezing out, starving
out, crunching raw bats and candle ends, until he lies

> stretched upon the ground, dead, with his face close to the crack
> of the door, as if his longing eyes had been fixed, to the last
> moment, upon the light and the cheer of the free world
> outside.... To this day the tourist stares longest at that

pathetic stone and that slow-dropping water when he comes to
see the wonders of McDougal's cave. Injun Joe's cup stands
first in the list of the cavern's marvels.

Twain, of course, was right. The fate of the Indian was first
to be expropriated, then segregated, and then turned into a
tourist attraction, a memento for white trippers. But half-
breeds—at least for fellow southerners—could play quite
another rôle. Apart from Injun Joe, I can think of four literary
half-breeds in major American fiction: Poe's Dirk Peters (of
The Narrative of Arthur Gordon Pym), Hemingway's Dick Boulton
(of *In Our Time*), and Faulkner's Boon Hogganbeck and Sam
Fathers (of *Go Down, Moses*). All are pariahs in some sense—
quick-witted, tough, valiant even—who are revealed as the
ambiguous saviours of white men. Or white youths, rather.
For their charges are all adolescents, closely identified with
their authors, as they launch out on their ritual quest after
experience. In each case it is a half-breed who acts as guardian
spirit—for Arthur Gordon Pym, for Nick Adams, for Ike
McCaslin—to shelter or guide them on their initiations.

Dirk Peters is a half-breed Crow from the Black Hills. With
his bearskin wig and demonic laugh, his very appearance is
hybrid: part white, part red, with an immense head indented
like a Negro's. It is this anthropoid ape—half lover, half
fiend—who rescues Pym from drowning and his suicidal dive
off a cliff-face. Dick Boulton coolly turns the tables: for it is this
Ojibwa half-breed who accuses the doctor (alias Hemingway
Senior) of stealing, of grabbing (frontier-style) what is not
legally his. Standing up to the doctor, he abets Nick Adams in
his own youthful rebellion. Boon Hogganbeck is the whiskey-
sodden quarter-Indian who finally knifes the Bear. But Sam
Fathers, son of a Negro slave and Chickasaw Chief, is ritual
priest of the hunt and of the land. It is he who dedicates Isaac
McCaslin to the mystery of the wilderness. For a half-breed—
like his counterpart the mulatto, it appears—might embody
the worst of white and red. But he might also mirror the
southern hero's incorrigibly split identity (as in Poe), or his
divided stand between civilization and wilderness (as in
Faulkner), or merely his mid-western sense of grievances, his
mixed-up loyalty and morality (as in Hemingway).

For the half-blood may originally have been considered a French-Canadian legacy and so, both psychologically and politically, unAmerican. Yet he was also the natural shuttle, as scout and negotiator and trader, between the tribal Indians and the advancing Anglo-American frontier; and so naturally suspected as a double agent by both sides. It was Indians, far more readily than white men, who integrated half-bloods into their tribes. Mary Jemison, a captive who later married a Seneca, explained that she never returned to white society because it would not accept her half-blood children. Choctaws, Cherokees, Creeks at various times had half-blood chiefs. Later, missionaries were quick to utilize them for a foothold in the reservations.

Nineteenth-century travellers and agents were likely to view half-bloods as 'designing', 'fickle', 'credulous'—in a word, as mischievous bastards. For a sophisticated New Yorker like Washington Irving, the half-blood met in his *Tour on the Prairies* (1835) became symptomatic of America itself: part eastern, part western; part order, part anarchy; part rational, part savage. Pierre Beatte was the first dubious victim of that double exposure. What, then, was to be the rôle of miscegenation in fiction? Was it the inability to fuse a divided heritage? Or the integration that eventually resolves it? Or the sign of a universal conflict between reason and instinct? A pre-Freudian metaphor for ego and id?

Tocqueville's view was something of an exception. Few thought that half-castes formed 'the natural link between civilization and barbarism'. Most southerners, to the contrary, held that half-castes were unnatural, both physically and morally grotesque. (It is a line followed even by Walt Whitman in an early story, 'The Half-Breed'.) Northerners were more likely to welcome mixed blood, as long as it meant the redemption of red by the dominant white in a new and invincible amalgam. The more literary the performance, as that of Poe, or of Hawthorne (in the unfinished *Septimius Felton*), or of Melville (in *The Encantadas*), the less the emphasis was likely to fall on a peculiarly American conflict or American destiny, but on the half-blood as symbol of a universal heritage—of our common crucifixion by the antagonistic forces of the unconscious and the conscious mind.

Yet there was one symbolic integration which was wholly American: Natty Bumppo, of Cooper's *Leatherstocking Tales*. By compounding all that is heroic in the white man and noble in the savage, he displaced the half-blood, self-consciously flinching from any hint of cross-breeding, insisting again and again on the purity of his blood. He is the man 'without a cross', who 'knew no cross of blood'. In Cooper's mythology this new American was to be a hybrid as *spiritual* cross-breed. So physically he had to remain pure. That was all-important. The synthetic American was to replace the genetic half-breed. His legendary ancestor was Daniel Boone.

The creation of this synthetic or symbolic American— mediating between society and savagery, wilderness and civilization—constituted a controlling myth of the American nineteenth century. It shaped the politics of the frontier. It was surely this that distinguishes the fate of the half-blood from that of the mulatto. For the ideal of a white-black hybridization was not a nineteenth- but a twentieth-century product. Only with the rise of jazz and Harlem and *négritude*, was this second spiritual synthesis—this second white takeover on a racial frontier—attempted. Not until Norman Mailer's essay on 'The White Negro' (1957) was it to find its committed champion. By now that particular compound in whiteface has triumphantly overtaken Natty Bumppo and Davy Crockett. The mulatto is the incarnation of youth. He is top of the pops.

3

Dramas of Disorientation

Two missionaries arrived at the Marquesas Islands in 1791. They were brought by the same ship, the *Duff*, that had established the highly successful mission on Tahiti. But while one missionary stayed on to face a long and ultimately frustrating task, the other made off again. Why did Mr. Crook stay on? Why did Mr. Harris sail? The ship's captain, in *A Missionary Voyage to the Southern Pacific Ocean* (1799), tried to explain.

Crook felt encouraged from the start; he enjoyed the ceremonial greeting. But Harris was clearly shaken. He at first declined to go ashore, under the pretext that he needed more time for packing; and even after six days on land returned aboard full of misgivings. Still, he agreed to have another go and again went ashore. Four days later they found him hiding in the hills, having been robbed of his belongings, 'in a most pitiable plight, and like one out of his senses'. As far as the captain could make out, both men had been invited by the coastal chief to make a journey inland. But Harris had refused. So Crook had gone alone with the chief, who left his wife with Harris 'to be treated as if she were his own'. That was meant, the captain realized, as an unmistakable gesture of hospitality. But when Harris again refused, the chief's wife 'became doubtful of his sex' and in the company of some other women entered his hut at night where they 'satisfied themselves concerning that point, but not in such a peaceable way but that they awoke him'. Harris thereupon dashed out of the hut with his trunk and went down to the beach, where he was further scared by a band of males; so he rushed off into the hills, leaving them to plunder his goods.

46

The captain's judgement was stern:

> Discovering so many strangers, he was greatly terrified; and,
> perceiving what they had been doing, was determined to leave a
> place where the people were so abandoned and given up to
> wickedness: a cause which should have excited a contrary
> resolution.

But from the start, Harris had felt inadequate, disorientated,
undermined. When he awoke to find the women examining his
penis, all his repressive psycho-sexual mechanism collapsed.
He was flooded with impulses and emotions that he could not
control. The event was literally unspeakable. It lay on the very
edge of insanity. It could only be expressed in the vehement
condemnation of the Marquesans as 'savage'.

In fact, it seems most unlikely that the women were
'doubtful' of Harris's sex. Marquesans were simply more
fascinated than we are with male genital characteristics.
Melville, in *Typee*, suggests that he and his companion were
subjected to a similar investigation. But for the missionary
Harris, it was a confrontation with horror, the ultimate dread,
the annihilating Boojum. The language of faith alone could
not sustain him; nor could that of 'civility'. The concept of
'civilization' as corroborating power did not yet exist: Dr.
Johnson had refused to admit the word to his dictionary.

Such is the theme of *Marquesan Encounters*.* It is a peculiarly
American theme, since to play the loner on a racial boundary
was to adopt a peculiarly American stance. The original rôle of
the frontier—whether in New England, or Jefferson's Virginia,
or Cooper's New York—was to sustain a Janus face. For if
from one point of view Indian savagery seemed degrading, by
reversing the perspective the frontiersman could catch a view
of civilization which was just as demeaning. Racial boundaries
were defined by an ideology of exclusion: 'Whether the savage
domain is seen as a mess to be straightened out, or as a
fructifying mystery to plunge into, it remains a place of the
mind.' It was a place for testing communal values and
confirming or repudiating such values. Far more than a
geographical zone, it structured American identity.

---

* T. Walter Herbert, Jr., *Marquesan Encounters: Melville and the Meaning of Civilization*
(Harvard University Press, 1980).

The Marquesas Islands, in this sense, typify the American frontier. Though claimed for the United States, the annexation was never ratified. They remained an ideal frontier, defined by three major encounters separated by some fifteen years. First a naval commander: Commodore David Porter sailed into the Pacific during the war of 1812 to destroy the British whaling fleet in Polynesia, taking possession of the Marquesas in 1813. Next the missionaries: the Rev. Charles Stewart arrived in 1829 as chaplain aboard the U.S.S. *Vincennes* and his enthusiastic account prompted a mission, led by William Alexander, to land in 1833. Last a romantic refugee: in 1842 Herman Melville deserted the whaler *Acushnet*, taking refuge in the interior. Each brought to this insular outpost his own model, or paradigm, or interpretative scheme, however inarticulate, of civilization. These systems might (in shorthand) be classed as the Enlightenment, Calvinism and Romanticism. But neither Porter's *Journal of a Cruise Made to the Pacific Ocean* (1815), nor Stewart's *A Visit to the South Seas* (1831), nor Melville's *Typee* (1846) exemplifies any such system. Rather, each records a moment of intense disorientation, and the peculiar rhetoric and dramatic structure, the adaptations and evasions and selective suppressions of each account reveal the writer's instinctive sense of identity. At the moment of crisis it is not social forms merely but identity itself that seems both threatened and confirmed, far beyond habit or prejudice. For if identity founders, reality itself gives way, as it did for poor Harris on Nukuheva. It is the interstices, then, that must compel attention: not merely the said, but the unsaid; not the message only, but its code of metaphors.

For we know next to nothing of the context from outside those sources. So these texts need to be read not only for what they tell us about the Marquesans, but about themselves. They need to be explored for their own hidden premises and devious articulacy. They need to be interpreted not so much as messages about others (savages) as for their own persuasive and civilizing coherence. It is as if William Carlos Williams's famous dictum were to be reversed. Instead of 'No ideas but in things', the modern structuralist, in the wake of Saussure, exclaims: 'No things but in ideas'. It is with a juxtaposition of discourses that such reading is engaged, not a colonial history.

The mission that landed in 1833 was an offshoot of the successful American mission to Hawaii. It consisted of three couples (the Alexanders, the Armstrongs and the Parkers) with their four children. They quickly built a compound on rectilinear lines, with internal partitions for individual privacy and separate areas for each family. Nothing could have been more calculated to shock Marquesan sensibilities, nor to blinker the missionaries' view of their new environment. For a start, they could not grasp a social structure without a visible hierarchy of rank or seniority. They profoundly disapproved of Marquesan sexual exposure and open licentiousness. They were contemptuous of the non-stop clan warfare and Mafia-like feuds. They were horrified by the ritual use of corpses, that ultimate humiliation of enemies by triumphant absorption.

To the Marquesans, however, such cannibalism was heroic, since it made the whole tribe a repository of its bested enemies. Much of their culture, even by Homeric standards, was heroic, with its suspension of fighting during festivals, its prolonged ritual exchanges of taunts but minimal infliction of injuries. An early eye-witness recounts a three-day battle in which a total of four men were killed. The last day of the battle, he reports,

> is more for mirth than war, every one making the best appearance he can. Their Allys meet them on the mountains, makeing a grand appearance of about 4000, evry party bringing their drums and conch shells. A very grand dance ensues: some is fighting, others danceing. At times those that was fighting would set down and talk with each other with as much composure as though they was friends and then rise again and renew the fight.

Between Americans and Marquesans, as the Taipis were to discover, there was a confusion of metaphors. To the Americans war meant power: politics, in the classic phrase, carried out by other means. To the Marquesans war was more like a dance, participation in which was seen as a performance. Their battles, in fact, enacted rather than settled differences. They were a form of communication, as were the heated exchanges between the missionaries and their prospective converts on the subject of food. The Americans claimed that their deified fowls were mere food; the cannibals replied that if the missionaries ate the fowls, which were their gods, they 'also will eat Jehovah'. From which Alexander warily foresaw the possibility of martyrdom.

But it was not their hosts, the Teiis, who were really threatening; it was the Taipis (or Typees) who saw the missionaries as allies of their rivals. This was most disconcerting. It was one thing to be martyred, quite another to be killed as friends of the cannibalistic Teiis. The mission was thwarted. God, they knew, had a plan for the human race. It was a benevolent plan revealed, step by step, as the prophets of light came into conflict with the imps of darkness. They might be worsted in a skirmish, but the war had to be won. It was bound to be won, for it was a war of liberation whose ultimate victory was as predetermined as any Marxist revolution. A war of liberation not from the chains of economic slavery, but from the bondage to sin, with plenty of Calvinist torment and inner wrestling along the way.

It slowly dawned on them that there would be no repeat performance of Hiram Bingham's miraculous conversion of the Hawaiians; that Stewart's vision of the Marquesans as *animae naturaliter Christianae*, instinctively drawn to civilizing picnics, was a fiction; that Dr. Johnson's 'happy valley' was not to be found in Nukuheva; that the Marquesans lacked even the rudimentary language to express concepts of 'law' and 'government'. Yet their satanic idolatry remained an obstinate challenge to a crusade. Even as his mission crumbled around him, Alexander mused that abandoning the Marquesans would be to 'give infidels occasion to say the Gospel is not equal to the work of taming the rude savage of Nukuheva & Satan will exult when he finds he is left unmolested in his old dominions'.

But what did 'taming' mean? It was a euphemism for revolutionary destruction: a total abolition of the old religion; a total reconstruction of character; a total renovation of the culture. The missionaries' vocabulary assigned all Marquesan practices to a code of filth and death and darkness. Their rôle, as they saw it, was to be

> made the instrument of razing to the dust such altars of abomination and blood, and of erecting on the ruins humble chapels of adoration and prayer, where the only offering required is the sacrifice of 'a broken and a contrite heart'.

But this revolution, paradoxically, was to be achieved not by arms, but by force of words. The missionary was the instrument of God. So God's vernacular had to be translated into Marquesan; or rather, the missionary had first to learn the cannibals' tongue. 'I long to have my tongue unloosed', Alexander wrote, 'that I may tell them plainly the glad tidings which angels rejoiced to publish.' For history, too, was ultimately on the mission's side. Only it was not called history in those pre-Marxist days so much as 'providence'; and providence needs a longer run—plus a warship or two. In the short run the Marquesans noticed that Jehovah's so-called power was a fraud, that

> the missionaries did not kill thieves, that they did not use physical force and were also unable to lay hold of the spiritual weapons that were available to the Marquesan holy man. A Marquesan *taua* was competent to lay on curses that would soon have destroyed a thief who made off with his belongings; but the white *taua* (as the Marquesans termed the missionaries) were altogether defenseless.

Commodore David Porter, on the other hand, relied not on spiritual reconstruction, but on education. He wanted to *elevate* the Marquesans, or *advance* them, by technical and commercial processes based on a common understanding and cooperation. This was not a matter of grace so much as knowledge; not of spiritual revolution so much as practical evolution or development. Unlike the missionaries, he was impressed by the Marquesans. He was impressed by their many achievements: their architecture, for instance; their astonishing neolithic techniques, hewing and fitting together stones 'with as much skill and exactness as could be done by our most expert masons'; their skill in navigation; their spontaneous cooperation without legal or political restraints. Like Jefferson lauding the Indian, he concludes:

> They have been stigmatized by the name of savages; it is a term wrongly applied; they rank high in the scale of human beings, whether we consider them morally or physically. We find them brave, generous, honest, and benevolent, acute, ingenious, intelligent, and their beauty and regular proportions of their bodies, correspond with the perfections of their minds.

51

High words which he soon had to circumscribe and redress. These nature's children also turned out to be lazy-minded, superstitious, gullible, muddled:

> They are not fond of trouble, and least of all, the trouble of thinking. They are very credulous, and will as readily believe in one religion as another. I have explained to them the nature of the Christian religion, in a manner to suit their ideas; they listened with much attention, appearing pleased with the novelty of it, and agreed that our God must be greater than theirs.

Religion for them was merely a toy; their shrines were 'baby-houses'; their gods, 'their dolls'. Their nakedness, though, he finds he can defend: it is not dress but manners that maketh woman. But cannibalism proved more intransigent; it was impossible to reconcile that with 'generosity and benevolence'; it seemed incompatible with their cleanliness and personal fastidiousness. 'How then can it be possible,' he asks,

> 'that a people so delicate, living in a country abounding with hogs, fruit, and a considerable variety of vegetables, should prefer a loathsome putrid human carcass to the numerous delicacies that their valleys afford? It cannot be,' he concludes; 'there must have been some misconception.'

There could be no 'fee fi fo fum' here: that would be altogether too irrational, too unnatural.

Culturally, then, the Marquesans were instinctive children, well endowed in body and mind, needing only 'art' to perfect their crude democracy. But events were to put that premise to the test. Commodore Porter had originally landed to refit his ship. Trapped between rival raiding parties, he tried to make peace with both sides, only to be taunted by both sides. Having exchanged names, one Teii chief argued, Porter should share his hatred of the Happahs because they had cursed the bones of his mother who was now Porter's mother. The American knew he was entangled in 'sophistry', but when a Happah attack was mounted, launched a counter-attack. Things immediately went wrong. By Marquesan standards he indulged in overkill; his muskets caused five fatalities. This was unprecedented. Suddenly he had been transformed, in Marquesan eyes, from a coward to a 'demon of destruction'.

The American presented himself as a super-tribal protector who could back his benevolence by an exemplary code of punishment. But to the Marquesans his guns simply exemplified transcendent *power*. Despite a prolonged drought, Porter was now showered with bananas, coconuts, breadfruit, sugar-cane, but above all, with hogs. In exchange he offered pieces of iron. But the Marquesans were trying to restore the ritual equilibrium by their gift of pigs (which, to this day, constitute the symbolic means of exchange on New Guinea). Furthermore they unilaterally declared him a *haka-iki*, or tribal chief, and built him a tribal village. All this is complacently reported: how on the fourth day after the battle,

> upwards of four thousand natives, from the different tribes, assembled at the camp with materials for building, and before night they had completed a dwelling house for myself and another for the officers, a sail loft, a cooper's shop, and a place for our sick, a bake house, a guard house, and a shed for the centinel to walk under.

Taking possession that same evening, Porter remarks that this village 'had been built as if by enchantment'. He named it 'Madison Ville' and, after a salute of seventeen guns, took possession of the island. A fort was built at the entrance to the harbour.

What was viewed by the Americans as a rational balance of convenience was seen by the Marquesans as deference to savage and unpredictable force. When the Americans eventually abandoned Madison Ville, it was razed to the ground (except for a wall built by British prisoners-of-war). With power dispersed, the emblematic attributes of power too had to be eradicated. But first the power balance was to be yet further upset. The Taipis were deeply disturbed by the American-Teii alliance and suspected Porter's offer of peace. Porter reminded them of his victory over the Happahs, but the Taipis defiantly called them cowards and the Americans 'white lizards, mere dirt'. To the Taipis they had become 'the posteriors and the privates of the Teiis', for the white man offered a wholly foreign paradox: an iron hand in a velvet glove. Instead of childlike reason, Porter was confronted by adolescent obscenity.

So he invaded the valley of the Taipis and, after an initial repulse, enacted his final paradox: a trail of terror. The bringer of peace, to his own amazement, destroyed a flourishing culture. The promise of civilization, as so often since, began with devastation: 'Never in my life did I witness a more delightful scene, or experience more repugnancy than I now felt for the necessity which compelled me to punish a happy and heroic people.'

> We had been compelled to fight every inch of ground, as we advanced, and here they made considerable opposition; the place was, however, soon carried, and I very reluctantly set fire to it. The beauty and regularity of this place was such, as to strike every spectator with astonishment, and their grand site, or public square, was far superior to any other we had met with; numbers of their gods were here destroyed.

Melville in *Typee* added an ironic postscript, observing that a 'long line of smoking ruins defaced the once-smiling bosom of the valley, and proclaimed to its pagan inhabitants the spirit that reigned in the breasts of Christian soldiers'.

With that accomplished, Porter set sail, leaving a small holding party. Immediately the political alliance collapsed. The Marquesans started 'stealing' back their pigs; worse still, several Americans deserted to settle among the Marquesans. 'It could scarcely be credited at first', poor Porter recorded,

> that men, even of the lowest order in society, surrounded by savages, and without the possibility of reaching a civilized part of the world, in an open boat, could seriously think of deserting. But on a nearer investigation of the matter, such was found to be actually the case.

Yet the self-evidently superior rationality of American culture had been undermined from the start, for Porter, it turns out, had an interpreter called Wilson. Wilson was British; he had apparently settled in Nukuheva ten years earlier, was tattooed from top to toe, and spoke Marquesan fluently. It was Wilson who had been the constant intermediary between the Americans and the Marquesans. It was Wilson who acted as double agent, now abetting (it seems) the attack on the Taipis, now undermining the fort, co-ordinating the islanders and growing band of deserters in an attack, finally attempting to gun down the last of the absconding fleet.

Civilized conflict, too, for Porter, was imbued with ritual that consolidated values and confirmed difference. It was a rite every bit as testing as a skirmish between Happahs and Taipis. However various their versions of protestant civilization, both Madison Ville and the mission were sustained by a superior power, a secret weapon of incalculable destructive force: the bullet and the Bible. Invincible self-confidence was conferred by these B-bombs. With such an arsenal up one's sleeve, the game of 'Who's Who' on the savage frontier was always worth playing. It contained all the fun of self-identification, with a minimum of risk (*pace* Harris) of self-confusion and self-immolation.

So a challenge was posed by the deserter, the beachcomber, or *omoo* (Marquesan for 'tramp' or 'rover') afloat on the savage/civilized boundary: such as the renegade Wilson; such as Morrison who acted as interpreter for the Rev. Charles Stewart and later advised the Teiis to murder Alexander's missionaries for the sake of their belongings; such as Herman Melville who bolted into the hills of Nukuheva as deserter from the *Acushnet*. Rear-Admiral Dupetit-Thouars was anchored in Taiohae Bay at the time, annexing the Marquesas for France. The young American needed to escape this new fangled French jurisdiction and so blundered into the valley of the Taipis. They soon found he was useless at mending muskets, but handy enough as an informer on the strength of the French squadron. The American, for his part, was humbly grateful for the chief's protection.

Young Herman must have long dreamed of such an adventure. He was a nephew of Captain John DeWolf II, the close friend of G. H. von Langsdorff, the Russian naturalist who had visited the Marquesas in 1804. He was a cousin of Thomas Melville who had served aboard the U.S.S. *Vincennes* in 1829, accompanying Stewart on his excursion into the Taipi Valley. This was no ordinary South Seas salt or layabout, but a learned and genteel cultivator of the picturesque. So he proved something of a conundrum, this gentlemanly deserter, this aloof and superior young fellow in flight from Christian civilization to benign savagery.

For the correlative of a gentlemanly tramp is the noble savage: both victims of a ruthless, materialist culture; both alienated, in a commercial age, from their past; both poignant survivors. As a beachcomber on this literary frontier, Melville was able to straddle both Taipis and missionaries, both native cannibals and French imperialists. He struck a Byronic pose, as if torn between horror and admiration (for the savages), hatred and nostalgia (for civilized life); preoccupied by his own instabilities, his own inner turmoil; fascinated by the clash of strange encounters; ready to borrow, refabricate, lie for the ultimate truth of fiction.

That was the crux. It needed fiction to explore the ambiguous meaning of savagery and challenge of cannibalism. For Porter the Marquesans simply could not be cannibals. For the missionaries the Marquesans inevitably were cannibals. For Melville they were mirrors in which we can study our own anxious selves (a paradox since Montaigne) in Swiftian guise:

> The fiend-like skill we display in the invention of all manner of death-dealing engines, the vindictiveness with which we carry on our wars, and the misery and desolation that follow in their train, are enough of themselves to distinguish the white civilized man as the most ferocious animal on the face of the earth.

For it was discontinuities that intrigued Melville, not cultural closure. His was to be a fiction of shifting perspectives and foiled responses: beginning in pain and depression (focused on a lame leg); succeeded by apathetic resignation (the limp disappears); crowned by delight at this 'Happy Valley' secure from arbitrary codes and civilized cares. Taipi society, the narrator decides, is founded on 'the grand principles of virtue and honor'; he is bowled over by this Garden of Eden that extends before his open eyes. But then he is stalled once more, perplexed. What were those taboos and tattoos but closed systems, after all? They both excluded him and, even more frighteningly, offered to enrol him. So he swung round on a cycle from uncertain misgivings to ambivalent horror, with occasional glimpses of a new radicalism. Might not 'savagery' itself be a concept generated by Western ideology? Might not 'civilization', as the means for transforming Polynesians, merely pave the way for their inevitable degradation? Was not 'progress' perhaps a synonym for white imperialism? His was not a practical project (like Porter's), nor a spiritual project (like the missionaries'), but an aesthetic project. *Typee*, that is, does not impose a meaning; rather it generates a critical diversity of meanings.

Yet in this too Melville was a missionary, though his mission was not to the Marquesans but to his fellow Americans. 'The term "Savage" ', he had written,

> is, I conceive, often misapplied, and indeed when I consider the vices, cruelties, and enormities of every kind that spring up in the tainted atmosphere of a feverish civilization, I am inclined to think that so far as the relative wickedness of the parties is concerned, four or five Marquesan Islanders sent to the United States as Missionaries might be quite as useful as an equal number of Americans despatched to the Islands in a similar capacity.

It was in order to become such a missionary, as it were by proxy, that he had volunteered. Though, of course, he was misunderstood. When he caricatured a fat and prissy missionary's wife being drawn to church in a little go-cart by two islanders, the *Christian Parlor Magazine* refused to see the point. 'Better to earn a subsistence by industry as porters', it intoned, 'than to slaughter and devour each other.' Or perhaps it understood all too well, when it charged him with trying to convert Americans to 'Typeeism'.

As Malinowski recorded in *A Diary in the Strict Sense of the Term*: 'History is observation of facts in keeping with a certain theory; an application of this theory to the facts as time gives birth to them.' These three interrelated narratives staged, within one generation, on a single island make a fascinating laboratory to test the 200-year-old compact between Prospero and Caliban. For the anthropologist had most to learn from Melville. That unstable, mobile, literary identity has become Prospero's professional identity.

But what of Caliban? Must he remain merely a subject for Western discourse? Must he remain for ever an enigma? May he never reverse Roman Jakobson's model of communication and send us a message back? We have no vernacular account of Porter's arrival, nor of the missionaries, of course. No comprehensive name for the islanders even, other than 'the men' (*te tau 'enana*). But there is evidence none the less. As Armstrong recorded:

> The behavior of the natives was a severe trial to my feelings, as it commonly is whenever we attempt to preach to them. Some lie & sleep: some laugh and talk: some quarrel with what is said: and others mock, and mimic the preacher & endeavor to excite laughter in others. Here one sits smoking a pipe, there one sits twisting a rope, and often there is such confusion that the speaker can scarcely hear himself speak. When we request them to sit still and hearken to our words, they reply, 'Yes, let us all sit still, and listen'. One says to another 'sit you still there', and makes a motion as though he would strike him or throw a stone at him; the other must retaliate: and this excites laughter. Thus the whole congregation is a scene of noise & confusion. Not infrequently the half of all present will arise and go off, laughing and mocking. This behavior is no small trial to our patience & faith: I am sometimes tempted to give way to doubt, and ask can such persons ever become civilized & christianized?

They were openly contemptuous of the Christian deity, calling Jehovah *tutai* (dung). They even seemed to have reached out for some form of cultural relativism. A chief's wife, according to Porter, rebuked a missionary for ridiculing their gods, when they did not ridicule his. If his God wished them to be convinced that they should worship only him, she argued, then he should also send his Son to instruct them. They would not kill him, as did the tribe of which the missionary had informed her. They would thank him for his good intentions and give him, as they had given the missionaries, shelter and food while he remained among them. Their gods supplied breadfruit and coconuts. It was the white men who had come to get the produce of their island. 'Why would you visit us, if your own gods and your own island could supply all your wants?' she asked. 'The gods of the white men are intended for them alone. The gods of Nukuheva were intended solely for us.'

That missionary was none other than Mr. Crook, who persisted alone in Nukuheva when Mr. Harris sailed on the *Duff*.

4

Voids and Needs

When Gustave Flaubert entered Jerusalem on horseback in 1850, he let out a fart. *'Nous entrons par la porte de Jaffa'*, he records in his *Notes de Voyages*, *'et je lâche dessus un pet en franchissant le seuil, très involontairement; j'ai même au fond été fâché de ce voltairianisme de mon anus.'* Neither J. Ross Browne nor Herman Melville nor Mark Twain gives off quite this distinctive smell. But then they were North Americans, not the immediate heirs of Voltaire. Nor did they feel the same pressure to cut through the gush of their more flamboyant predecessors—from Chateaubriand and Lamartine to Gérard de Nerval. They may have read Lamartine but their obvious mentors were English. It was the contemporary travel-books of Lady Hester Stanhope, of Alexander Kinglake and Sir Richard Burton, that provided the spice of adventure for their more pedestrian, guided tours.

Tourists, then, rather than adventurers, and roving correspondents rather than pilgrims, all three stuck to well-established trails: Cairo and the pyramids; from Beirut across the Lebanon to Baalbek and Damascus; on, either overland via Mount Hermon to the Sea of Galilee and Nazareth, or disembarking again at Jaffa, inland to Jerusalem for the round trip to Jericho, the Jordan, and the Dead Sea. In 1859 William M. Thomson, of the American Mission in Beirut, produced his bestseller *The Land and the Book*. A few years later Henry H. Jessup, after fifty-three years of missionary work in Syria, helped to found the American University of Beirut.

In the half-century between John Lloyd Stephens's *Incidents of Travel in Egypt, Arabia Petraea, and the Holy Land* (1837) and

Charles Doughty's *Travels in Arabia Deserta* (1888)—the one American, the other English—conditions of travel in the Ottoman Empire had begun to improve rapidly. Egypt and the Holy Land were being opened up for the mass market. By mid-century, paddle-wheel steamships served several Lebanon and Palestine ports. Murray's *Guide to Syria and Palestine* was published in 1858; the first Baedeker followed in 1875. Mark Twain, on the *Quaker City*, covered the first transatlantic cruise in 1867; and Cook's Tours began to operate soon after. By the time the Eastman Company developed the Kodak in 1880 and the American Express Company first issued travellers' cheques in 1891, the foundations for the whole modern travel industry—with its camel rides to the pyramids and tours round the churches of the Nativity or Holy Sepulchre—had been laid.

J. Ross Browne, Herman Melville and Mark Twain well exemplify this shift from would-be adventurer (Browne in 1851) to sceptical pilgrim (Melville in 1857) to confused and irreverent tourist (Twain in 1867). Each wrote up his travel notes with various degrees of creative licence. Most celebrated, no doubt, was *The Innocents Abroad* (1869) which sealed Twain's reputation. Of increasing fame today is Melville's *Clarel*, a long narrative poem in four parts and 150 cantos, published some twenty years after his return in 1876. Least remembered is Browne's *Yusef; or, The Journey of the Frangi* (1853), a light-hearted travelogue featuring his roguish dragoman. Since Melville's journal survives as well as Twain's original articles for the *Alta California*, we can weave in and out from the hurly-burly schedule of the journey to its literary transformation in tranquillity. But equally interesting are their biographical contacts and parallels. Both Browne and Twain were old hands from California and Nevada imposing the same West Coast idiom and frontier ways on the Palestinian scene. Both Browne and Twain, too, were newspaper correspondents, hoping to bring off a coup. Only Melville set out privately as an artist, seeking to gather further material for his art. Yet Melville and Browne too shared contacts: both had served their apprenticeship on a whaling ship. In fact, Browne's *Etchings of a Whaling Cruise* had provided copy for Melville's first published review.

For Browne was an amiable rover and philistine, a booster
for go-ahead America of railroads and democratic conventions, tilting at such autocratic stumbling-blocks as the
pyramids, the Colosseum and St. Sophia. There is a salty
humour in his transformation of Lake Galilee to Lake Tahoe
and the valley of the Lebanon to California's Salinas Valley.
Local fleas are inflated to bumble-bees; Jericho diminished to
a 'ruinous old Khan, eight or ten wigwams built of mud and
bushes'. But there is also the ultimate horror in the crypt at
Bethlehem—a glimpse of the Christ child:

> a strange, disgusting thing, with staring eyes of glass, tawny
> skin, and wrinkled neck; its cheeks puffed out, and its mouth
> slightly open as if it had been suffocated with thick incenses.

This image might conceivably have appealed to the author
of *Moby-Dick*. But Melville came east, more in a Jamesian
spirit, as a 'passionate pilgrim'. He had long been a student of
the Higher Criticism of Niebuhr and Strauss; he had long
shown interest in the archaeological finds at Babylon and
Nineveh; he had long pondered the lore of the pyramids and
the myths of Isis and Osiris. *Moby-Dick* had been a com-
pendium of earlier mythologies presented as a transcendent
American myth. As H. Bruce Franklin argued in *The Wake of
the Gods* (1963):

> Melville saw Egyptian mythology as the direct source of the
> Hebrew mythology and therefore of the myth of the Christ.
> Confronted with the solecisms of the Old Testament's
> prophecies of the Saviour and the New Testament's biography
> of the Saviour, he turned to what he considered their Egyptian
> source. There he found a picture of the saviour which seemed to
> describe more accurately what he could see.

No wonder that Captain Ahab, haunting Stubb's dreams,
'seemed a pyramid'. For as Melville was to confirm in Cairo:

> I shudder at idea of ancient Egyptians. It was in these pyramids
> that was conceived the idea of Jehovah. Terrible mixture of the
> cunning and awful. Moses learned in all the lore of the
> Egyptians. The idea of Jehovah born here.

At last he had traced his hard-won scepticism to its creative
source.

So he rejoiced in the paradox of Muslim shepherds, at prayer in the fields below Bethlehem, facing Mecca; or of the muezzin's call from the mosque of Omar built on the foundations of Solomon's temple close by the church of the Holy Sepulchre. Comparative religion and comparative mythology had long been the central concern of his own mythopoeic imagination; just as his old distaste for the Christian missionaries in Tahiti and Hawaii revived in Smyrna and Jerusalem. It was 'against the will of God', he considered, 'that the East should be Christianized'. Off the coast of Patmos, the author of 'The *Jeroboam*'s Story' confronted a holy man:

> almost naked—ludicrous chased away gravity—solemn idiocy—lunatic—opium eater—dreamer—yet treated with profoundest respect and reverence. . . . Wretched imbecile! base and beggarly Santon, miserable stumbling-block in the way of the prophecies.

For Melville his tour of the Holy Land was the fulfilment of a complex vision, not a revelation.

After Melville's achievement, Mark Twain may seem merely a second, more accomplished J. Ross Browne. In a way he was, not only in his humour but in his mounting hysteria and bleak despair. 'No Second Advent', he jotted in his diary. 'Christ been here once, will never come again.' His foray into the Syrian desert turned into a wild extension of Indian-hating in Nevada. It was fun maybe to call Palestinian Dan Dutch Flat, or Ain Jelud an oriental Jacksonville. But the Hebrew patriarchs, on that analogy, were no better than the Digger Indians of California: 'treacherous, filthy and repulsive'.

> They sat in silence, and with tireless patience watched our every motion with that vile, uncomplaining impoliteness which is so truly Indian, and which makes a white man so nervous and uncomfortable and savage that he wants to exterminate the whole tribe.

Or again:

> As we trotted across the Plain of Jezreel, we met half a dozen Digger Indians (Bedouins) with very long spears in their hands, cavorting around on old crowbait horses, and spearing imaginary enemies; whooping, and fluttering their rags in the

wind, and carrying on in every respect like a pack of hopeless lunatics.

What Mark Twain confronted in the desert was total alienation. A Tom Sawyer in the Holy Land, he found the landscape barren, the Arabs disease-ridden, the language foreign, the Muslim infidel, the relics sham, the guide-books blather, the fellow pilgrims possessive New Englanders filching mementoes. The jester was dog-tired, facetious, finally cornered in despair, with no romantic loop-holes by which to escape into euphoria except the warrior myth (of the Crusades), the pious myth (of the New Testament) and an infantile myth (of Superman's revenge):

> Here was a grand Oriental picture which I had worshipped a thousand times in soft, rich steel engravings! But in the engravings there was no desolation; no dirt; no rags; no fleas; no ugly features; no sore eyes; no feasting flies; no besotted ignorance in the countenances; no raw places on the donkeys' backs; no disagreeable jabbering in unknown tongues; no stench of camels; no suggestion that a couple of tons of powder placed under the party and touched off would heighten the effect and give to the scene a genuine interest and a charm which it would always be pleasant to recall, even though a man lived a thousand years.

If this is jest, it is of the same frantic order as the genocidal climax to *A Connecticut Yankee at King Arthur's Court*.

Back in America there were even more desperate, more chilling voices, questioning the pious myth of the New Testament and its salvation:

> After great pain, a formal feeling comes—
> The Nerves sit ceremonious, like Tombs—
> The stiff Heart questions was it He, that bore,
> And Yesterday, or Centuries before?
>
> The Feet, mechanical, go round—
> Of Ground, or Air, or Ought—
> A Wooden way
> Regardless grown,
> A Quartz contentment, like a stone—

This is the Hour of Lead—
Remembered, if outlived,
As Freezing persons, recollect the Snow—
First—Chill—then Stupor—then the letting go—

The voice, the form, the pace, the whole performance is unmistakable. No one else—neither George Herbert, nor Isaac Watts, nor Emily Brontë, nor Emerson, nor Elizabeth Barrett—has written quite like this. A formal feeling comes; yet the iambic pulse, the metrical count, the rhyme scheme, the grammar, the punctuation, even the linear lay-out of the quatrains, is open to shift and variety. Only once does an exact metrical repetition occur:

A Wooden way
Regardless grown,

and there Emily Dickinson doubles the single line so that we can both *see* how mechanical it sounds and *hear* the emphatic 'Regardless' at the opening of the intercalated eighth line. For her own feet never tramp. Her whole regard, by means of line endings and linear dashes, is to scalpel or hew out—however miniature the seeming scale—a felt form. Made of words, it must become a breathing form, even though her subject so often, as here, is the loss of breath, the loss of life.

The living nerves and heart of the first quatrain are transformed to the mechanical thud of the second; that thud, to the dead weight and crystal transparencies of the third. The patterning is swift. The 'Tombs', the 'Feet', the 'Quartz', the 'Hour of Lead' are never expounded. Or if expanded, it is only to emphasize a numb redundancy: 'A Quartz contentment, like a stone—' As ceremony leads to tombs, so tombs apparently to Calvary—an ageless Calvary, noisy as an American boardwalk.
Or again:

I heard a Fly buzz—when I died—
The Stillness in the Room
Was like the Stillness in the Air—
Between the Heaves of Storm—

The Eyes around—had wrung the dry—
And Breaths were gathering firm
For that last Onset—when the King
Be witnessed—in the Room—

I willed my Keepsakes—Signed away
What portion of me be
Assignable—and then it was
There interposed a Fly—

With Blue—uncertain stumbling Buzz—
Between the light—and me—
And then the Windows failed—and then
I could not see to see—

The effect, at first sight, is like something by Emerson in its
sensuous merging of detail (in the foreground) with ultimate
evanescence (in eternity) by the suppression of the middle
distance (where social life is played). But the attempt at exact
focus and exemplary definition is foiled. The humour (with its
diabolic hint of Beelzebub, Lord of the Flies) turns out to be
that all such attempts must ultimately fail. Dickinson
deliberately subverted Watts (e.g. 'A Prospect of Heaven
Makes Death Easy'), as her English contemporary, Lewis
Carroll, parodied his 'sluggard' and 'busie bee'. In this both
are heirs, in widely differing ways, of Blake's *Songs of Innocence
and of Experience*. Even T. W. Higginson, her first editor,
suggested that she was most like Blake. Though William Dean
Howells, in his review in 1891, corrected this to: 'it is a Blake
who had read Emerson who had read Blake.'

For Emerson was her maestro. He too was a figurative
thinker. It was primarily figures that structured his texts. 'The
eye is the first circle', runs a typical launching phrase (of
'Circles', 1841). In other words, the 'I', or personal vision—in
a kind of permanently extended pun, or rebus—has primacy.
As the eye leads to the horizon, so the horizon to the world,
and the world to God. In its most memorable formulation:

> Standing on the bare ground,—my head bathed by the blithe
> air, and uplifted into infinite space,—all mean egotism vanishes.
> I become a transparent eye-ball. I am nothing. I see all.

But further paradoxes abound. Everything the eye sees within
the circling horizon is gathered in further circles, ciphers,
mysteries. The ideal for each individual visionary is to figure
out the horizon, fill in the ciphers, give imaginative meaning to
the world.

Even by his contemporaries' standards, Emerson stood apart. Even then he seemed singularly devoid of social, or political, or psychological structures for his idealist ambitions. He was not a creative artist, but a liberal theologian turned philosopher. The task of filling those empty horizons became too much for him. No wonder he early lost faith in the real world and in real men. The Emersonian ego was lonely. It refused to be contained or engaged. Its urge for eternal expansion was destructive of normal social relations. As Henry James, Sr. tartly commented: 'He was never the man anyone took him for, for the simple reason that no one could possibly take him for the elusive, irreducible, merely gustatory spirit for which he took himself.'

In one respect at least he was like Shakespeare and Plato: in being almost devoid of biography. His was a settled, rural existence, marked not by physical so much as mental strife. Just as his realm was confined not by Canada or Mexico so much as spiritual or eschatological needs. From youngest manhood he was thought of, in transparent terms, as an 'angel'. Though Henry James, like his father, remained a sceptic. As he mockingly claimed in *Hawthorne*, the Emersonian 'doctrine of the supremacy of the individual to himself' found the ready response it did in the New England of the time because there was so little to feed on, culturally, *outside* of the self. Such a doctrine, James insisted with cosmopolitan élan, 'must have had a great charm for people living in a society in which introspection, thanks to the want of other entertainment, played almost the part of a social resource'. The final effect of the great Transcendentalist on James was of something slim, pallid, bare, almost blank: almost a kind of absence (in his 'unconsciousness of evil') rather than presence, more wraith-like than angelic to haunt and bewilder the American mind. 'We get the impression', he concludes, 'of a conscience gasping in the void, panting for sensations, with something of the movement of the gills of a landed fish.'

Such voids threatened Emerson from the first. 'I dedicate my book to the Spirit of America', the 19-year-old inscribed his 'Wideworld' journal in 1822. The gesture smacked of youthful megalomania. For the dedication was really to himself. From the start he assimilated his personal to the national identity. His was to be an oracular law for the licentious west. Not a Delphic but a new American law. His command to contemporaries and to later disciples was clear: no longer 'Know thyself', but the far more unsettling and intoxicating 'Trust thyself'. Thus, and only thus, could 'the reformation of the world . . . be expected from America'.

A nation of Puritan settlers looked to a redeemer. He was to be the new dissenter, the new Luther whose defiance at the Diet of Worms ('I can do no other!') Emerson consciously echoed on stepping down from the pulpit of the Second Church of Boston in 1832. Like Luther, Emerson could no longer serve the eucharist in good conscience. Like Luther, he cast himself adrift at the age of 30 to serve a personal vision—or indulge a personal need, rather—of unmediated access to the divine. The hero was 'he who is immovably centred', Emerson declared. For it was his own depressions and self-doubts that had to be shored and buttressed by the great essay on 'Self-Reliance'. George Washington was his hero; but, above all, Luther whom he called the George Washington of German history, the very paradigm of the democratic spirit.

It was Luther who taught Emerson, as he taught Carlyle and Melville, to growl his 'mighty No', to become a nay-sayer. But only in preparation for his own eventual 'Yes'. Like Luther, he attracted 'protesters', self-conscious disciples of an independent master. Emerson, Whitman, Thoreau—all three were pioneers in search of a fit ideal for America. But Emerson claimed to be the original explorer 'who invades the coast of an unknown continent and first breaks the silence which hath reigned there since the creation', who

> ceases to be an ordinary adventurer, providing for himself and his son, or his friend,—but becomes the representative of human nature, the father of the Country, and, in a great measure, the Arbiter of its future destinies.

But yea-sayers of the ego—in other words, egotists—never make easy bedfellows. Thoreau physically flinched on meeting Whitman. Whitman commercially made use of Emerson. Emerson felt emotionally confused and sometimes resentful of Thoreau. While Thoreau publicly poked fun at the master in *A Week on the Concord and Merrimack Rivers*. After initial enthusiasm, Emerson tended to back away in his inimitable manner. As described by James: 'he retreats, smiling and flattering, on tiptoe, as if he were advancing.' For Emerson was both attracted to prophetic youngsters and coyly defensive of his own all-American title. He dithered between an excessive self-confidence and a nagging lack of self-trust. Was this the reason that not a single American was eventually included among *Representative Men*?

Not Hawthorne, certainly. Nor Poe. Not for them to be marooned in such intellectual circles. Like Emily Dickinson, rather, they desired to climb out upon circumference. Their gasping conscience was lured by mesmerism, phrenology, phrenomagnetism, homeopathy and spiritualism that flourished in mid-nineteenth century America; and part of the fascination of their work lies precisely in the question it poses on the relation of science to art. Hawthorne himself had seen mesmerism heal the sick. He had married into a family of homeopathic practitioners. He knew how to read character in a face. He had lived at Brook Farm and invested in it. He had edited a popular magazine and was well aware of the public mania for ghosts and spirit-rapping. Hawthorne notoriously slips and slithers and refuses to be pinned down. Yet in that long line of doctors, alchemists, botanists, hypnotists, physicists and inventors inhabiting his romances, something of Hawthorne's attitude to his age does emerge.

What attracted Hawthorne to vicious or crazy scientists like Heidegger, Aylmer, Rappaccini, Chillingworth, Maule, Westervelt, Grimshawe and Dolliver? Why did they grip him so? By interpenetrating experimental science with ethics, Hawthorne defined the new mode of science fiction; it was his key to psychology. That is how he revolutionized Faustian or Gothic fiction. Constantly he toyed with concepts of an *elixir vitae* and of moral diseases. 'A physician for the cure of moral diseases' runs a journal entry. Or another: 'A moral philosopher to buy a slave, or otherwise get possession of a human being, and to use him for the sake of experiment, by trying the operation of a certain vice on him.' Or again: 'A person to be in possession of something as perfect as mortal man has a right to expect; he tries to make it better, and ruins it entirely.' That must be the origin of 'The Birthmark', in which the mad,

Faustian urge of a scientist—play-acting with the stereoscope, daguerreotype and diorama—was to overreach itself by the wizardry of sheer intellectual control. But science is not a religion. An aesthetic flaw should not be equated with a technological flaw, certainly not with a moral flaw. Imperfection is life. The removal of Georgiana's one physical blemish (a birthmark) makes her perfect—but dead.

From the religion of science Hawthorne turned to science as art. In 'The Artist of the Beautiful' Owen Warland tries to 'spiritualize machinery' by creating 'Nature's ideal butterfly', only to have it crushed by a flesh-and-blood baby. The play of creativity may imaginatively transcend organic life but it remains a toy, a trifle, a fiction ultimately, and so unnatural. In 'Rappaccini's Daughter' such miniature casualties of the lab are transformed to the universal death-trap of a lethal radiation. Venomous intellectuals now actively distil their venom. The poisoner's creative art is no fantasy merely. His very daughter is poisonous. This is a revolutionary science of an inverted Eden, where 'as poison had been life, so the powerful antidote was death.'

All three stories, then, tell of experimental self-delusion, of scientific perversion inevitably leading to destruction. Such techniques spy out and probe nature's most intimate secrets, as Chillingworth pries into the dim recesses of Dimmesdale's soul. This is what Hawthorne called the 'Unpardonable Sin':

> The Unpardonable Sin might consist in a want of love and reverence for the Human Soul; in consequence of which, the investigator pried into its dark depths, not with a hope or purpose of making it better, but from a cold philosophical curiosity,—content that it should be wicked in whatever kind of degree, and only desiring to study it out.

Hawthorne's hypnotists—unlike their successors, Caligari and Thomas Mann's Cipolla—never debauch their victims out of political lust for self-gratification. They merely invade the 'virgin reserve', the sanctity of their somnambulists' souls. The hold of Matthew Maule on Alice Pyncheon, or Holgrave on Phoebe, or Westervelt on Priscilla, is not that of sadistic mastery but of cold-hearted voyeurism.

This is what drew Hawthorne so ambiguously to his mad

scientists. As fellow artist, he shared in all their guilt-laden tensions. He too was a technician of fictions. His too was a science probing social and phrenological mysteries in order to immobilize and trap men in his fictional webs. Dr. Heidegger's experiment was his. He too was a spell-binding mesmerist, investigating the dark depths of his own soul. Mesmerism in a sense became for Hawthorne a metaphor of the writer's art, though he never resolved his own dilemma. On his return from Italy, his novels grew more and more fragmented. His artist-mesmerist disintegrated into a confusion of tentative rôles from which he could no longer co-ordinate a plot.

But a master of masquerade, he was Melville's master. For Melville insisted on an opposition of line and circle, of the linear quest and the labyrinthine mandalas of whale tubs and whale-lines and the great whale itself, whose very name means 'roundness or rolling'. Melville's work is all puzzles. The puzzle of *Typee* is: are they or are they not cannibals? The puzzle of *Moby-Dick* is: what and where is the White Whale? The puzzle of *The Confidence-Man* is: is he one or is he many? There may well be an interpreter, either as narrator or protagonist, attempting to unpuzzle the strange case of the lethargic slave-ship ('Benito Cereno'), say, or of the anorexic scrivener ('Bartleby'). Invariably it is a matter of scrutiny and interpretation of signs. But not all such enigmas, by their very nature, are capable of resolution. They present a crux. They demand some kind of insistent, searching penetration. Which is what Ishmael offers. His is a fluid, wayward, spiralling discourse, repeatedly ravelling and unravelling its enquiry, as if spooled on some never-ending shuttle. But there are also obsessional cryptographers, like Ahab, who follow their one fixed code, with an unflinching if baffled will, as if

> some certain significance lurks in all things, else all things are little worth, and the round world itself but an empty cipher, except to sell by the cartload, as they do hills about Boston, to fill up some morass in the Milky Way.

Merely to ask *Why?*, for Hebrew and Greek alike, was commonplace and childish; to ask *What does that mean?* was the mark of the philosopher and prophet. 'The fact must be transformed at all costs into idea,' declared Roland Barthes, 'into description, into interpretation; in short, there must be found for it *a name other than its own.*' This mania for interpretation—this quest for meaning—was still the governing trait of western civilization in the nineteenth century, even in America, in an age that witnessed the triumph of technology and science. Especially in America, perhaps, where it reached some of its most idiosyncratic forms of expression.

Was not America regarded as 'Nature's Nation'? And nature, vice versa, as 'the American Temple'? That temple (as Perry Miller and Sacvan Bercovitch after him have argued) was still a temple of God. America, then, needed to be read as a book of *Revelation*, God's 'other book', a Holy Writ of living hieroglyphs. Such emblems were a peculiarly American preoccupation. Without ruins and monuments, after all, they had nothing but nature to decipher. Nature became their substitute for history. Instead of human traces, they had divine (or natural) traces; instead of social norms and forms, they had the hieroglyphs on the banks of the Missouri and the Mississippi.

It was Champollion's decipherment of the Rosetta stone in 1822 that inaugurated this passion for Egyptian hieroglyphs. The pseudo-Egyptian *Hieroglyphica* had been deeply revered by Renaissance scholars and artists. Their hermetic picture language, devised by Thoth-Hermes, was considered the language of the primitive world, more profound than any discursive description. By the eighteenth century it was revived as the token of spiritual freedom. Revolutionary Egyptianism, Frances Yates has called it. The cult of a Supreme Being, using Egyptian symbols, was the religion of the Revolution. Egypt became a symbol of freedom, to this day reflected in the Egyptian symbols on American dollar bills. Fascination with Champollion's hieroglyphs was profoundly affected by their earlier identification with independence and liberty.

What Champollion introduced was a craze for analytic reading or interpretation. He discovered that hieroglyphics were a composite mode of writing: part pictographic, part symbolic, part phonetic. It had been realized that Greek names, like Ptolemy, must have been written phonetically in Egyptian. But it was Champollion who announced that even the names of Egyptian pharaohs like Rameses and Thothmes at Abu Simbel were composed of phonetic signs. A rebus, that is, functioning on the homonymic principle of a pun, could be turned into an arbitrary, repeated sign to represent any phoneme. As if the picture of an eye, in English, standing for the pronoun 'I' were arbitrarily extended to designate the initial phoneme of names like 'Iris' or 'Ivor'. It all depended on unravelling an inner (hidden) meaning from an outer (visible) shape by means of a logical (if obscure) convention that involved a system of correspondences.

But far from insisting, with modern linguists, on the convention of phonetic signs, Americans remained doggedly metaphysical. For them, as for Paracelsus, nature herself presented an emblematic script, or cipher, from whose signature might be construed the moral intention of the creator. If not read exactly, it could be interpreted by leaps of metaphorical insight. Or it could be analysed, by metonymic selection, to uncover the radical forms—the Saussurian *langue* or Chomskian 'deep structure', so to speak—underlying phenomenal variety. As Thoreau wrote of a thawing sandbank in spring:

> I feel as if I were nearer to the vitals of the globe, for this sandy overflow is something such a foliaceous mass as the vitals of the animal body. You find thus in the very sands an anticipation of the vegetable leaf. No wonder that the earth expresses itself outwardly in leaves, it so labors with the idea inwardly.

For the earth was meaningful; and every cipher demands a key. Such as Swedenborg had supplied in his *Hieroglyphical Key to Natural and Spiritual Mysteries by Way of Representations or Correspondences* (1784). Reversing the code, hieroglyphical bibles had translated spiritual facts back to emblems. Nature preceded the language of men: it was Adam who had called things by their right or original name. Proper names, that is, are the proper Hebrew names whose signifiers embody the signified. Emerson called them 'transparent' in their self-evident mimesis. Only in a fallen world did the pictograph become a conventional sign. After Babel began the never-ending multiplication and dispersal of signs, until usage had distorted, without wholly disguising, their origin. Emerson gives examples in *Nature*:

> Every word which is used to express a moral or intellectual fact, if traced to its root, is found to be borrowed from some material appearance. *Right* means *straight*; *wrong* means *twisted*. *Spirit* primarily means *wind*; transgression, the crossing of a *line*; *supercilious*, the *raising of the eyebrow*.

But the 'language of nature', or 'natural sign', is in itself an absurd confusion or contradiction in terms. Signs are rarely 'transparent', words seldom onomatopoeic. The poet, for Emerson, was the man to whom nature offered all her creatures 'as a picture-language'.

For Emerson's disciple, Thoreau, the simplest aspect of nature was, by definition, hidden from the majority who were too petty, too preoccupied, too degraded. The microcosm of a Walden pond was a mystery demanding the priestly ministrations of its resident interpreter. Those 'leaves' or 'lobes' of the thawing sandbank were the signature of Genesis itself and language incorporated their signs by the fluid interpenetration of *lobe* and *globe*, *leaves/labor/lapsus/lapse/lap/ flap*: 'The radicals of lobe are *lb*, the soft mass of the *b* (single lobed, or *B*, double lobed,) with the liquid *l* behind it pressing forward.' Thus Socrates, in Plato's *Cratylus*, had reduced words to their composite letters and the (phonetic and visual) shape of the letters to *poésie concrète*. That liquid *l* pressing forward on the soft mas of the *b* is much more than a semantic equivalent. It is the semantic manifestation of the sandbank in flux: as 'there pushes forward from the thawing mass a stream of softened sand with a drop-like point'. For what is a *b* but an *l* with a drop-like point? 'If the basic creative process in terms of natural forms is the accretion of fluid matter into globes or lobes, then the word "lobe" is an emblem of that process and of the form that it creates.' If the creator patented such lobed and leafy vegetation, it was Thoreau, not Champollion, who first deciphered their hieroglyphic.

Whitman went further. He presented himself not merely as priest, or prophet, or scholarly cryptographer, but as mystic bard, as 'chanter of Adamic songs'. He was the new Adam of a new Eden, issuing his endless roll-call of words fit for the American experience, attempting to restore language to its original and emblematic signs. As the Bible had influenced his prosody, so *Leaves of Grass* itself became a kind of hieroglyphic Bible. In *Leaves of Grass* Whitman evokes mankind's ability to return to its Edenic childhood:

> There was a child went forth every day,
> And the first object he looked upon and received with wonder
>   or pity or love or dread, that object he became. . . .

In that sense we are all potentially children of Adam:

> Human bodies are words, myriads of words,
> (In the best poems re-appears the body, man's or woman's,
>   well-shaped, natural, gay,
> Every part able, active, receptive, without shame or the
>   need of shame.)

For our bodies are emblematic windows, or hieroglyphs, of the soul; and song alone makes the perfect pictographic fusion possible. When inspiration becomes expiration, how can we know the body from the soul? The contents from the form? The singer from the song?

Poe's whole career was explicitly concerned with upstaging Champollion as intuitive artist and scientist. Or rather artist-as-scientist, or scientist-as-artist: what he called 'a double Dupin—the creative and the resolvent'. As Freud himself was to write: 'the interpretation of dreams is completely analogous to the decipherment of an ancient pictographic script.' Poe was to be the master cryptographer and code-breaker in the decipherment not only of criminal mystery, and cosmic mystery, and metaphysical mystery (within the crypt), but also of dreams.

But Hawthorne and Melville, not Poe, are the most sophisticated hieroglyphical writers: neither bards exactly, nor priestly interpreters, nor enigmatic maestros of cryptanalysis, but mediators between the mystery of art and the mystery of the world. 'The Scarlet Letter' is a hieroglyphic conundrum, indicating its narrative contents and its form, both Adultery and Art, in defiance of ultimate explication. Text and context constitute a kind of hieroglyphic doubling; or rather, the opaque letter, in its duplicity, reflects the relationship between script itself and the pervasive duality of splintered consciousness. As Hawthorne says in 'The Custom-House' section that introduces *The Scarlet Letter*:

> as if the printed book, thrown at large on the wide world, were certain to find out the divided segment of the writer's own nature, and complete his circle of existence by bringing him into communion with it.

If *Walden* could be said to search out and embody the hieroglyphs of nature, *The Scarlet Letter* could be defined as the hieroglyph of the divided self. For as hieroglyphs, by definition, are only partly visible, requiring an imaginative reader for their completion, so the divided circle of the writer's nature is completed by the chance encounters of his text. Only in the expectation of such union can the writer hope to realize himself. Even then it remains a veiled appropriation, a hieroglyphic exposure, in a cipher addressed to those 'few who will understand'.

For Hawthorne and Melville alike the glyph was 'undecipherable', 'a riddle to unfold', a mystery destined to 'be unsolved to the last'. As indeterminate as the colour white which Melville challenges Champollion himself to read:

> Champollion deciphered the wrinkled granite hieroglyphics. But there is no Champollion to decipher the Egypt of every man's and every being's face. Physiognomy, like every other human science, is but a passing fable. If then, Sir William Jones, who read in thirty languages, could not read the simplest peasant's face in its profounder and more subtle meanings, how may unlettered Ishmael hope to read the awful Chaldee of the Sperm Whale's brow? I but put that brow before you. Read it if you can.

So Hawthorne's Pearl is 'a living hieroglyphic'. So Melville's Queequeg, though illiterate, is wholly tattooed or inscribed with 'hieroglyphic marks'. So the great Sperm Whale, with his 'pyramidical white hump', and Ahab, with his 'Egyptian chest', are both 'hieroglyphical'. Perhaps there is not even mystery, after all. Like Ahab, we can strip layer from a little lower layer, but the world (to echo *Pierre*) is found to consist of nothing but surface stratified on surface. To its axis, the world being nothing but superinduced superficies. By vast pains we mine into the pyramid; by horrible gropings we come to the central room; with joy we espy the sarcophagus; but we lift the lid—and no body is there!— appallingly vacant as vast is the soul of a man!

This sense of the self's inherent instability, of its ability to adopt any role or mask, to become anything, precisely because in itself it is nothing, comes more and more to dominate Melville's thought. From *Mardi* to *The Confidence-Man* there is an increasing emphasis on the illusory nature of under-standing; on the possibility of reversing the privileged axes of good and evil; on the subjection of the self to the ceaseless circulation of meanings. A hieroglyphic indeterminancy principle—what might be called the Heisenberg factor in all networks of symbolic relationships—is finally translated from Melvillean terms to those of Derrida's *Grammatology*.

The self, in its god-like independence, may be the ultimate illusion. For Melville's reading had long ranged far beyond Wordsworth or Emerson, Hawthorne, Irving or Poe. He had delved, even if sometimes no further than the encyclopedias, into comparative religion, philosophy, geology, physics, anthropology, zoology. He had moved altogether beyond Transcendental theory. It is the phallic thrust of the chimney that the husband of *I and My Chimney* so deviously defends against female depredations. It is a cock-crow ecstasy that pulses through *Cock-A-Doodle-Doo!*, as it had reverberated through Queequeg. For the cock is charged with an ambiv-alence of sexual energy; and it is sexuality, not philosophy here, that allows the narrator to see life steadily and see it whole. What he has witnessed is a transfiguration and a collapse; yet he continues to exalt such exultation.

How to convert that transfiguration into style is the con-man's secret. It is also Ishmael's lesson of the laughing 'Hyena' (a 'sort of genial, desperado philosophy') and at least one school of whales (the Huzza Porpoises). It is also the lesson of *The Whale*. For the reader must first be lulled, then gulled. As one of the earliest reviewers put it:

As the gull (no inapt emblem, the matter-of-fact philosopher will say, of him who allows another man's imagination so to influence his own)—folds up her wings . . . and is wildly rocked through the hills and hollows of the waves—so does the mind of the sympathetic reader yield an unconscious allegiance to the resistless sway of this powerful writer.
(London *Morning Post*, 14 November 1851)

That same reviewer turned the tables on Melville by parodying the parodist with this variation on 'The Hyena':

There are occasions when the reader is disposed to believe that the whole book is one vast practical joke. We are half inclined to believe that the author is humbugging us, and with that suspicion comes its invariable accompaniment, a sense of offended dignity; but the spell of genius is upon us, and we are powerless to resist.

Other cycles were to follow the *Pequod*'s fatal descent into 'the axis of that slowly wheeling circle'. Bartleby shirked cyclic involvement, preferring the motionless centre—at the still turning point—to his colleagues' rising and setting suns. But Ishmael's ultimate successor as humbugging narrator was the Confidence-Man, constantly recasting himself and the identities of his audience. So *techniques* of irony turn, at a profounder level, to matters of 'confidence'—confidence in the narrator, confidence in ourselves as readers—in a shifty mirror image that itself reflects Melville's shifting theme, which is the crisis of self-confidence. Three times stories are presented at second or third hand—those of Goneril, Colonel Moredock and China Aster—to confuse or negate the narrative form. The aim is to restore reality to the multiplicity of appearance by an art of fiction that can reveal (in Melville's words) 'more reality than real life can show'.

In moral terms it is not a foolish confidence (or trust) which is the prerequisite for acts of charity (or love); an all-embracing love, rather, is the prerequisite for trust. That is what this Mississippi ship of fools, setting out on April Fool's Day, cannot comprehend. That is why the Trickster's own commitment to confidence (whose ultimate source is St. Paul) serves as a mere tool, a highly developed game whose rules are a matter of complete indifference to him. So, too, Melville felt, as he wrote to Hawthorne, on completing *Moby-Dick*. A peculiar contentment was his, a sensation of 'irresponsibility; but without licentious inclination'.

Samuel Clemens's relationship with his audience, by contrast, seems an altogether simpler affair. Masquerading as 'Mark Twain', he wooed listeners and readers alike to place their trust not in his history but his humours. It was the Trickster's archetypal displacement of substance with virtuoso style. It was the making of his first great comic character, Colonel Sellers. All that was asked of an audience was joyous laughter: joy at this madcap Till Eulenspiegel on his national tightrope; joy at his lithe and rapidly improvised shifts of posture; joy at his chameleon-like changes from sensible observer to credulous clown and ironic commentator. Like his own jumping frog of Calaveras County, the aim was to leap across an exhausted culture (whose guide was Baedeker) into a living Jerusalem, the Holy Land of the imagination.

This 'Eastern' became the essential 'Western'. Turning from Judea to the Rockies in *Roughing It*, he substituted insouciance for back-breaking labour, style for fact, the ritual of the tall tale for the codes of an established hierarchy. Huck, from the western frontier, became his final confused incarnation. *Huckleberry Finn* is *all* performance, a total exercise in rhetoric whose meaning can only be understood in terms of 'confidence', 'trickery' and 'style'. 'Style', in fact, proves the very key to the text—its prayers, its superstitious rituals, its juvenile games, its nigger magic. 'Style' is a concept as dear to Miss Watson as to Tom Sawyer and Huck. Huck's hero-worship of Tom suggests a love of 'style' for its own sake. But even more it points to his marginal role, his search for social hierarchy, his need to escape a desperate lonesomeness. His very prayers become a means of self-persuasion to the social will. As Huck says of the King: 'he warmed up and went warbling right a long till he was actually beginning to believe what he was saying *himself*. . . .' What links the man of prayer to the habitual liar and the effective con man, in Warwick Wadlington's words, 'is his ability to give consent not so much to what he is saying as to *his saying* it'. But one thing distinguishes Huck from the Duke and the King, the Granger-fords and the whole cast of loafing con men on the banks of the

Mississippi. He is never an entertainer. Unlike the quacks and the gunmen and the lynch parties, he is never remotely in it for kicks. He is in it for survival, even though (it must be added) this by no means always includes Jim.

Melville's God had been morally 'indifferent'. Mark Twain's, in the end, became actively 'malicious'. But from the masquerades of Nathanael West God has altogether vanished. The sky 'looked as if it had been rubbed with a soiled eraser'. Miss Lonelyhearts, that hysterical high-priest of twentieth-century America, does his best with the sacerdotal rôle; he tries to play the Holy Fool. But he is sceptical of his title; sceptical of the illusions on which it is built. No angels for Miss Lonelyhearts, no flaming crosses, no doves, no 'wheels within wheels'. It is on a Hollywood film lot—in Los Angeles, City of the Angels—that Nathanael West (né Nathan Weinstein) located his final scenario of voids and needs.

5

South from Baltimore

Even in 1849, as Poe lay dying in the gutter of Baltimore, his star was already rising across the Atlantic. His is possibly the strangest case of critical resurrection in all literary history. The poet and story-teller who died as Edgar Allan Poe was reborn in France as Edgar Poe. *Poe—Poë—Poète*: his very name rang provocatively in French ears. His fame was to become identified with the meaning and aspirations of poetry itself.

It is good to know that Poe had an inkling of his French metamorphosis. For Paris had long been his city of imaginary romance. His language was larded with gallicisms, like *outré, recherché, bizarre*. He had read Balzac and Hugo's *Notre-Dame de Paris*. Monsieur Ernest Valdemar (of the ghastly mesmeric experiment), Monsieur Maillard's private *maison de santé* (or experimental asylum) in Provence, and the Duc de l'Omelette, are all somehow French. But most celebrated is his detective amateur—and *raisonneur*—C. Auguste Dupin of *The Murders in the Rue Morgue* and *The Mystery of Marie Rogêt*. For France, above all, was for him the Cartesian land of ratiocination and mathematical analysis—of Condorcet's theory of probability, of the Marquis de Laplace and Cournot's calculus of economic forecasting. How thrilled he must have been in December 1846 to be able to inform his New York Editor 'that some of the Parisian papers had been speaking about my "Murders in the Rue Morgue" '.

By then *The Purloined Letter* and *The Gold Bug* had both been translated into French; and that very winter Baudelaire was reading his first Poe story, *The Black Cat*, in a fever of spiritual turmoil. It was a moment akin to Saul's vision on the road to Damascus. For Baudelaire recognized in Poe a soul brother and mirror image: '*mon semblable,—mon frère!*' He undertook a complete translation of his works. 'Do you know why I so patiently translated Poe?' he asked, when accused of plagiarism.

> Because he resembled me. The first time I opened one of his books I saw, to my amazement and delight, not simply certain subjects which I had dreamed of, but *sentences* which I had thought out, written by him twenty years before.

Or again: 'I found poems and stories which I had thought about, but in a confused, vague, and disordered way, and which Poe had been able to organize and treat perfectly.'

In the words of Champfleury, his friend: 'Baudelaire incarnated Poe.' He wrote to London for copies of all Poe's works; he collected a complete file of the *Southern Literary Messenger* and looked up Americans to borrow other magazines Poe had edited. According to Charles Asselineau, Baudelaire sought out all manner of English speakers, from waiters and stable-boys to sailors and tourists. On one occasion he insisted on questioning an American writer in shirtsleeves who was trying to buy a pair of shoes. But the man seemed to him so prejudiced, so ignorant, that Baudelaire finally stormed out shouting: 'He's nothing but a damned Yankee.'

What particularly enraged him was the American's strictures on the incoherence of Poe—that 'his talk was not at all consecutive.' And that, oddly enough, remains an American line to the present. Baudelaire's first published translation, *Révélation magnétique*, appeared a year before Poe's death in 1848; and he continued his work of translation for sixteen years. Two volumes, published before *Les Fleurs du Mal*, first established Baudelaire's own reputation. Of the twelve volumes of the definitive edition of his works, five contain translations from Poe. The backhanded compliment of his American critics has been precisely that 'a slipshod and a shoddy English prose' (in Malcolm Cowley's words) has been turned 'into admirable French'. Or, as Allen Tate put it, that the thematic coherence is clearer in Baudelaire since the French disguises the characteristic blemishes of Poe's style.

The battle for Poe's reputation, on either side of the

Atlantic, continues. Defamed in the nineteenth century as a debauched, incestuous, drug-addicted drunk, he seemed the only begetter of an unAmerican progeny of nightmare and death—startlingly re-created in the cinema of the 1960s by Roger Corman's films starring Vincent Price. Henry James called 'an enthusiasm for Poe . . . the mark of a decidedly primitive stage of reflection'. Yvor Winters, in his *In Defense of Reason*, was still violently attacking Poe thirty years ago. But in France—through Baudelaire's advocacy—he became the very prototype of the *poète maudit*: of the artist as outcast and rebel against bourgeois society. His *poésie pure* became an inspiration and model for Mallarmé; his pariah rôle, for Rimbaud and Verlaine; his *art poétique*, for a long line of poets from the Parnassians to Valéry. It was T. S. Eliot who first bridged, however ambiguously, these American and French versions of Poe. For Eliot was the first to be equally torn between his American and later symbolist allegiances—between school-boy memories of a 'puerile' Poe and an excited discovery of Baudelaire and Laforgue.

Baudelaire propagated a triple vision of Poe. There was Poe the prankster with his scorn for democracy and progress and the whole utilitarian ethos, sweeping aside its 'rectangular obscenities' and technological obsessions. There was Poe the arch-romantic, deliberately cultivating drugs and drink as a means of releasing the 'artificial paradise' of the imagination. And there was Poe—the virtuoso analyst of 'The Philosophy of Composition', 'The Poetic Principle' and 'The Rationale of Verse'—who believed, 'true Poet that he was' (wrote Baudelaire) 'that the goal of poetry is of the same nature as its principle, and that it should have nothing in view but itself'. It was with Poe's impoverished and isolated life that Baudelaire himself identified: his self-revelation in *Mon coeur mis à nu* was suggested by a phrase in Poe's *Marginalia*, 'my heart laid bare'. The peculiarly exotic, morbid or perverse strain in Poe he developed in his own *Paradis Artificiels* and *Fleurs du Mal*.

The reason that the impact of Poe on Baudelaire and his successors was so profound was partly because it brought the full force of the romantic revolution to bear at last on the Cartesian enlightenment of France. What had seemed merely a sum of theatrical and historical gestures in Dumas and

Victor Hugo was felt suddenly to teeter on the brink of intuition and dream. The French sense of intellect and form was at last undermined by the counter-logic of unspoken desire, of unformulated dread, of half-conscious dreamscapes pervaded by *le démon de la perversité* (Poe's 'imp of the perverse') with his gratuitous acts, his criminal leaning, his longing to let go, to fall, to sink dizzily into the maelstrom, the spinning whirlpool, the abyss.

'There is no passion in nature so demoniacally impatient', Poe had written,

> as that of him, who shuddering upon the edge of a precipice, thus meditates a plunge. To indulge for a moment in any attempt at *thought*, is to be inevitably lost; for reflection but urges us to forbear, and *therefore* it is, I say, that we *cannot*. If there be no friendly arm to check us, or if we fail in a sudden effort to prostrate ourselves backward from the abyss, we plunge, and are destroyed.

The imaginative impulse in Poe, it is clear, has become horribly autonomous and detached. Always the hidden movement is towards a crossroad, at that critical junction of time and space (pinpointed in *The Pit and the Pendulum*) where a personal bid for self-annihilation seems simultaneously to invite a cosmic vision: 'some never-to-be-imparted secret, whose attainment is destruction'. In the closing words of Baudelaire's *Le Voyage*:

> *Nous voulons, tant ce feu nous brûle le cerveau,*
> *Plonger au fond du gouffre, Enfer ou Ciel, qu'importe?*
> *Au fond de l'Inconnu pour trouver du* nouveau!

> This fire so scorches our brain, that we wish
> To plunge into the depths of the gulf, Heaven or Hell, who cares?
> To find something *new* in the depths of the Unknown!

Baudelaire had translated only four of Poe's poems. But Mallarmé—who at the age of 20 had learned English and visited London, he said, 'the better to read Poe'—translated a selection of the poems into prose. His edition of *Le Corbeau* ('The Raven') was illustrated by his friend, Edouard Manet; his volume of the poetry appeared in 1889. The common link between Debussy's *L'Après-Midi d'un Faune* and his interest in Poe is not hard to trace. Gauguin, too, painted a picture entitled 'Nevermore'; Odilon Redon (like James Ensor and Paul Klee after him) drew a series of lithographs based on Poe. For by the late nineteenth century, a further reason for the pervasive influence of Poe was quite simply his availability. What other American author, apart from Fenimore Cooper, stood in such multi-volume ranks on French library shelves? It is with a start of amazement, then, that an English-speaking reader, unriddling Mallarmé's tribute in *Le Tombeau d'Edgar Poe*, recited over Poe's grave in 1875, discovers that his peculiar triumph had been to: '*donner un sens plus pur aux mots de la tribu*; or, as Eliot put it in *Little Gidding*: 'to purify the dialect of the tribe'. The power of verbal ablution through art was yet another twist in Poe's transforming rôle within the French tradition.

'Poetry does not have truth as object, it has only itself', wrote Baudelaire in his *Notes Nouvelles sur Edgar Poe*. But it was Paul Valéry who first took Poe's final cosmological prose-poem, *Eureka*, wholly to heart, with its paean to God as the supreme aesthete: whose Truth (in its 'perfect consistency') is Beauty; whose Beauty, Truth. It was Valéry who defined that high-strung tension between vitality and the void as *vertige* (or vertigo) given *synthèse* (form or design) by art. 'A delirium of lucidity', he called it in a letter to André Gide. For Valéry, building on the perceptions of Baudelaire and Mallarmé, Poe became not only the prophet of symbolism but of a self-conscious formalism (which in America became the original source of the New Criticism).

Such is the grand line of descent, but it by no means completes the circuit of Poe's French influence. It was the French who first saluted Poe as *le créateur du roman merveilleux-scientifique*, or the founder of science fiction. Jules Verne himself acknowledged his debt by completing (so he claimed) the unfinished *Narrative of Arthur Gordon Pym* in *Le Sphinx des Glaces*. It was Freud's French disciple, Marie Bonaparte, following the lead of Émile Lauvrière, who pioneered the psycho-biography of Poe, analysing his fictions as the re-creation of his neuroses. But it was also the French who resisted that psychological thesis (which identified the breakdown, in fiction, of 'the House of

84

Usher' as Poe's own disintegration) by emphasizing the cerebral, impersonal logic of his art, his 'lucid intelligence of the order of Pascal's'.

The intuitive range of that logic has also been a special preoccupation of the French: in Gaston Bachelard's important work on water and dreams, *L'Eau et les Rêves*, and Georges Poulet's *Studies in Human Time*, centring on Poe's eternal present—the enveloping dream of closed time in the image of the whirlpool. Even today, the influence of Poe on French criticism is by no means dead. The structuralist critic, Jean Ricardou, associated with *Tel Quel*, included an essay on the waters of Pym's Tsalal in *Problèmes du nouveau roman*, while Jacques Lacan and Jacques Derrida more recently have engaged in a lengthy polemic concerning a seminar on *The Purloined Letter*. For what else is structuralism but a semantic outgrowth of the Parnassians' 'Art for Art's sake' and Valéry's aestheticism, awarding primacy to the verbal system (*langue*) in which a statement (*parole*) is made? No wonder contemporary French critics continue to find Poe's works appropriate as texts for the consideration of basic critical or theoretical problems.

For all writing, by structuralist formulas, is inevitably concerned with its own inscription. Thus *The Narrative of Arthur Gordon Pym* is no longer to be read as a voyage *au bout de la nuit* but to the bottom of the page, exploring the possibility of its own textual existence at the same time that it prefigures its own erasure. Like Mallarmé's celebrated swan, or Arthur Gordon Pym lost in the dazzling glare of the Antarctic, Poe's fiction, too, in this final French metamorphosis, becomes a 'blank paper defended by whiteness'.

In such ways Poe has continued to exert the full force of the creative charge of poetic play on the French tradition from Baudelaire to Derrida: as a story-teller who for ever seems on the very point of engagingly baring his psyche, while he disengages as narrator; who for ever holds out the promise of hidden truth, while contriving to offer forgeries, imitations, hoaxes. Those final hieroglyphs on Tsalal may form a kind of signature, the first extended clue in Poe's work to his obsession with cipher. So much for Poe as creator and resolver of conundra. On either side of the Atlantic the debate is likely to continue. For he was both detached observer—scientist, explorer, detective—and imaginative artist; both master and mystagogue. What is a hoax at one end can easily become (to use his own word) the art of 'mystification'. But it is the French who have pitched the debate to its extremest terms. Was Poe's fiction a monumental bungle—that is their question—or the achievement of a transcendent genius?

Similar questions are asked today of other maverick Southerners: Mark Twain, William Faulkner, Carson McCullers, Flannery O'Connor, John Barth. But what is a Southerner? That is the question. What is Southern literature? What is the South?

By the mid-nineteenth century there was a fair consensus. A Southerner was a kind of swaggering, military braggadocio. Parodies were rife, such as Mark Twain's Colonel Grangerford or Poe's Brevet Brigadier General A. B. C. Smith: 'He was, perhaps, six feet in height, and of a presence singularly commanding. There was an *air distingué* pervading the whole man, which spoke of high breeding, and hinted at high birth.' But what lay behind that facade of glossy hair, unimaginable whiskers and brilliant teeth? Nothing, was the answer. 'They are mere bladders of conceit', wrote Emerson in his journal:

> The young Southerner ... has conversed so much with rifles, horses and dogs, that he has become himself a rifle, a horse and a dog, and in civil, educated company, where anything human is going forward, he is dumb and unhappy, like an Indian in a church. ... His pugnacity is all they prize in man, dog, or turkey.

The older Mark Twain, long resident in Connecticut, was wrily to admit as much:

> Ignorance, intolerance, egotism, self-assertion, opaque perception, dense and pitiful chuckleheadedness—and an almost pathetic unconsciousness of it all, that is what I was at nineteen and twenty, and that is what the average Southerner is at sixty today.

This ironic stereotype found its classic embodiment in Henry Adams's portrait of Roony Lee, son of Robert E. Lee, at Harvard in the years just preceding the Civil War:

Tall, largely built, handsome, genial, with liberal Virginian openness towards all he liked, he had also the Virginian habit of command. . . . For a year, at least, Lee was the most popular and prominent young man in his class, but then seemed slowly to drop into the background. The habit of command was not enough, and the Virginian had little else. He was simple beyond analysis; so simple that even the simple New England student could not realize him. No one knew enough to know how ignorant he was; how childlike; how helpless before the relative complexity of a school. As an animal, the Southerner seemed to have every advantage, but even as an animal he steadily lost ground. . . . Strictly, the Southerner had no mind; he had temperament. He was not a scholar; he had no intellectual training; he could not analyse an idea, and he could not even conceive of admitting two.

Without scholarship or intellectual training there was not much chance of an official Southern literature either. Poe (himself born in Boston) was the first to fight a running battle against the hegemony of the Boston Brahmins. Southern literature was forced to respond, point counter point, to the New England, puritan axis of an Emerson or Hawthorne. It was a game of antitheses, of finding a William Gilmore Simms to match the Northern James Fenimore Cooper in a series where the South was regularly running out of partners. By the 1930s, when the South first seems brimming over with literary talent, a new question arose. Which South? The South of Thomas Wolfe, of Erskine Caldwell, of Richard Wright, or of William Faulkner?

There are two main lines of approach. The first is on a geographical axis. The south-east woodlands of North America, extending beyond the Mississippi to the edge of the great plains between the Missouri and Red rivers, contain three older cultural areas: the Chesapeake Bay, or Tidewater, society (of Virginia and Maryland); the Charleston society (from South Carolina to Georgia); and the Piedmont of North Carolina, including the whole back country of the Appalachians. To this colonial core was added the south-west cotton country of Mississippi and Alabama (Faulkner's Deep South) and the Creole delta country of Louisiana. One answer, then, to particularize Southern literature, is a sense of location and enduring devotion to place—as George Washington Cable was devoted to New Orleans, William Faulkner to northern Mississippi, Ellen Glasgow to Richmond, Virginia, or Flannery O'Connor to rural Georgia. Outsiders too, of course, like Kate Chopin or Lafcadio Hearn, could become fascinated with Creole and Cajun lore. But one key point to note is that twentieth-century imagery (in Wolfe, Carson McCullers, O'Connor, even Faulkner) derives almost wholly from the Piedmont, not Tidewater, aspect of the South.

This may well smack of regionalism in the narrowest sense, like that of some literary coteries in Yorkshire or Wales. But the South, if not so scholarly, was never so provincial either. Its publicized aim was the deliberate and self-conscious creation of a new model of slave capitalism. A second answer, then, to particularize Southern literature, is a sense of participation in the social and political experience of the South. It was, and remains, a mainly rural society, pervaded by blacks, whose past is mirrored in three magically transforming myths—that of an idyllic Golden Age (of John Pendleton Kennedy's *Swallow Barn* or Thomas Nelson Page's *In Ole Virginia*) with its cavalier romanticism abetted by servile, grinning blacks; that of a Gothic terror, stalked by predatory blacks; and a frontier comedy of tall tales.

All are pastoral myths; and a dominant ghost haunting the debate is Allen Tate. As Tate wrote from Paris in 1929: 'We must be the last Europeans—there being no Europeans in Europe at present.' By which he meant that the South must be European in some ideal sense aimed at twentieth-century modernism: a traditional agricultural community, imbued with personal, dramatic and sensual values. As he was to write in 'Remarks on the Southern Religion':

> the Southern mind was simple, not top-heavy with learning it had no need of, unintellectual, and composed; it was personal and dramatic, rather than abstract and metaphysical; and it was sensuous because it lived close to a natural scene of great variety and interest.

Here at last was an answer to New England's smug superiority, now dismissed as 'self-conscious and colonial'. Here was a vision, much like Yeats's vision of Ireland with two important provisos. The South was Protestant, not Catholic. Nor was it a feudal society exactly, but, in Tate's phrase, 'a semi-feudal society'. In fact, black chattel slavery is not feudal at all. Slave society is unorganic, closer in spirit to the Greek and Roman world—that other historical image to which appeal was invariably made. Lewis P. Simpson sums up the Southern impasse:

> Since they did not have any possibility of living by what Tate calls 'the higher myth of religion', they tried to live by what he calls 'the lower myth of history'. They endeavored to imitate historical forms of feeling and emotion. But in adapting the life of European traditionalism to their situation, the southerners succeeded only in being ornamental and meretricious.

The 'Confederate dream', as Henry James remarked, was that the rest of the world would somehow conform to the South. To this end was bent the whole rhetoric of politics and law that dominated the South. A renegade talent like Mark Twain's could draw on the oral tradition of south-western humour and a particular brand of Southern Calvinism to puncture that dream. He could denounce the sham medievalism and chivalric traditions of what he once called 'The United States of Lyncherdom'. He could even publish the memoirs of General Grant. But the most scathing commentaries are by such black contemporaries as Frederick Douglass and William Wells Brown, Charles W. Chesnutt and W. E. B. DuBois.

Take William Elliott's *Carolina Sports by Land and Water* (1846). The literary parallels that can be drawn with Melville and Faulkner seem perfunctory enough. A vivid description of 'devil-fishing' evokes a comparison of the dying manta-ray with the whale. Or again, a deer-chase, with blood smeared like Indian warpaint, evokes the symbolic blooding of Isaac McCaslin by Sam Fathers in Faulkner's *The Bear*. But the question confronted is why the literature of the old South remained so obstinately dilettante, so mediocre. One answer is precisely that serious writing remained too European, too art-inspired. But, what is more, life in the South was *too* personal, too closely meshed in its personal relations for anything other than such light, autobiographical sketches. Aesthetically William Elliott, on the outmost edge of a self-assured cultural empire, made obeisance to its centre; morally he lived in a police state. It was a police state even though the thought-control was self-imposed. As even Thomas Nelson Page was to recognize years later:

> The standard of literary work was not a purely literary standard, but one based on public opinion, which in its turn was founded on the general consensus that the existing institution was not to be impugned, directly or indirectly, on any ground or by any means whatsoever.

The literary superego could not let the slaveholder be stripped of his privileges nor release women or slaves to subvert his narrative. It needed a pariah like Poe to translate such public forms to private nightmare. It would have required the genius of Tolstoyan dimensions to dynamite such a beleaguered consensus.

Mark Twain, of course, began his career after the Civil War; and that career, disengaged not only from the Tidewater South or his own border South, moved on to the Mississippi, and so west, and then back east, embodying a whole process of dislodgement. Not simply the values of the society being left behind, but the tensions of the disengagement itself, are part of the southern experience. Was not his own family history a western migration from Virginia to Kentucky, to Tennessee, to frontier Missouri? Were not Orion and Sam Clemens put in a printshop just because of the overscrupulous and ineffective aristocratic pose of John Marshall Clemens, their father, a small-scale slave-owner who had complacently sold off his slaves (and family furniture) down river to pay his debts? Think of Twain's glee on receiving his honorary doctorate at Oxford. How he longed to wear that glorious scarlet robe all day! Dressed in white, like his own Colonel Grangerford, he used to stroll up and down Fifth Avenue just to be stared at.

Was he ever really sure of his own status? Status for this ex-Southerner—whether of a Colonel Sellers in Washington, or of a Tom Sawyer with his gang, or of a pilot on the Mississippi, or of the Connecticut Yankee at the court of King Arthur, or for that matter of the vagrant Huck partnered by a Duke and Dauphin—reigned supreme. But mixed up with his feeling for impractical, sentimental, credulous gentry were the standards of a natural tough aristocrat who continually sought out the meaning of real honour and an honest conscience. Truly Sam Clemens proved himself to be the frustrated son of the American border with his love-hate both for the Virginia bluebloods and that new-fangled Northern capitalist technology to be blown sky-high in the *Connecticut Yankee*. 'In the Old South', wrote Walter Sullivan, 'the honor and the pride were there, not as individual virtues in isolated men, but as a part of the public consciousness, the moral basis on which the culture was constructed.'

So Willie Morris, in *North Toward Home*, was drawn back passionately to his Southern small-town beginning: with its Negroes, its baseball heroes, its hillside graveyard, its local radio station, its Methodist youth groups, bootleggers, country clubs, football weekends, hunting and fishing in the delta. He wrote of his instinctive alliance in New York with Ralph Ellison, the liberated Mississippi white with the Oklahoma Negro:

> We shared the same easygoing conversation; the casual talk and the telling of stories, in the Southern verbal jam-session way; the sense of family and the past and people out of the past; the congenial social manner and the mischievous laughter; the fondness of especial *detail* and the suspicion of the more grandiose generalizations about human existence; the love of the American language in its accuracy and vividness and simplicity; the obsession with the sensual experience of America in all its extravagance and diversity; the love of animals and sports, of the outdoors and sour mash; the distrust in the face of provocation of certain manifestations of Eastern intellectualism, particularly in its more academic and sociological forms. And in both of us, I felt, as in so many other Southerners in the East, there was a pointed tension just below the surface of things, a strong and touchy sensitivity—usually controlled but always there.

There lay the seeds of tragedy, or at least of heroic moral drama with 'its tangled loyalties', as Robert Penn Warren said of Faulkner, 'its pains and tensions of transition, its pieties and violences'. For the Southern writer, in Louis D. Rubin's words, 'has habitually seen man as by nature a creature of society and has seen his alienation from society as tragic, and he has also depicted the base of human action as essentially moral'. When this vision was linked with the presence of the black man as outsider in a society itself in the process of transition, the results could well be called tragic. The agrarian *I'll Take My Stand* (1930) was itself emblematic of this Janus-faced focus. The Fugitives 'were able to recognize that incipient disruption because they saw it within themselves: because they were already sufficiently distanced from the community to be made conscious of what that community had been and was not . . .'. The great period of Southern literature was inaugurated by the break-up and collapse of the integrated community.

For in 1920 the boll weevil was completing its devastation of America's Cotton Belt. It was the year of the Prohibitionist victory of the Volstead Act. It was also the year that H. L. Mencken first became a byword and bogy throughout the American South. Since General Sherman no one has been so universally reviled as this outsider from Baltimore, this German Herr Menken or Menneken, this journalistic carpet-bagger who dared call the very heartland of American civilization 'almost as sterile, artistically, intellectually, culturally, as the Sahara Desert'. The essay that caused this upheaval of revulsion was 'The Sahara of the Bozart'. First published in 1917, it was the extended version of 1920 that drew down on Mencken the combined wrath of the American South. For what was this mock-hillbilly version of Beaux Arts but an urban parody of the whole cluster of rural and feudal values revered by the Confederate South?

> In all that gargantuan paradise of the fourth-rate there is not a single picture gallery worth going into, or a single orchestra capable of playing the nine symphonies of Beethoven, or a single opera-house, or a single theater devoted to decent plays . . . Nor an historian. Nor a sociologist. Nor a philosopher. Nor a theologian. Nor a scientist. In all these fields the south is an awe-inspiring blank.

The postbellum civilization of the South, according to Mencken, was both puerile and bankrupt: Huck Finn's syndrome without his graces—his saving flight from the horror (of the southern male) and the complacency (of the female of the species). It was not culture at all, in a word, but 'Kultur', a compound of ignorance, prejudice and superstition. Its landmarks were racial segregation, legal prohibition, and a religious fundamentalism that would turn the clock back on evolutionary Darwinism itself.

Yet Mencken was not a revolutionary, or a modernist even, so much as an aesthetic anarchist. His was an aristocratic rearguard action for the Old South. His was an elegy for a lost race 'of delicate fancy, urbane instinct and aristocratic manner—in brief, superior men'. He loved the *ancien régime* 'of manifold excellences ... undoubtedly the best that These States have ever seen'. 'In place of duelling they lynch', he lamented. As a German-American, torn between his roots and adopted ideals, he imposed a Nietzschean solution on American history. For had the Confederacy won,

> no such vermin would be in the saddle, nor would there be any sign below the Potomac of their chief contribution to American *Kultur*—Ku Kluxery, political ecclesiasticism, nigger-baiting, and the more homicidal variety of Prohibition. . . . The old aristocracy . . . would have at least retained sufficient decency to see to that.

Allen Tate called him a 'nostalgic clown'.

But Mencken's nostalgia was veiled by his virulent hatred for the new South of poor whites, evangelists and political demagogues. What he labelled the Bible Belt—or on occasion the Chastity Belt—was a region infested with grotesques and frauds: Methodist and Baptist barbarians, 'ecclesiastical mountebanks', barnyard theologians. A 'sort of Holy Land for imbeciles', he called it. From 1920 to 1935, in a pseudo-Jeffersonian spirit of detached analysis, he produced his 'New Notes on the State of the South' (as it were) in a series of critical assaults on the South's whole sentimental, antiquarian code. Occasionally he even descended from Baltimore into this netherworld of benighted yokels and hillbillies. It was Dayton, Tennessee, in July 1925, that supplied the perfect stage-setting for this connoisseur of farce, where a young high school biology teacher, John Thomas Scopes, was arraigned for teaching evolution in violation of a law passed by the Tennessee state legislature. 'The Monkey Trial' proved Mencken's finest hour.

His firm friendship with James Branch Cabell ('a member of one of the oldest and most distinguished *Junker* families of Virginia', as Mencken insisted for a German audience) underscores his position. What he clearly admired in the author of *Jurgen* was the wholly non-ideological, comic stance of the aesthetic nihilist. His key disciple, however, was to be W. J. Cash, whose *The Mind of the South* (1941), for all its differences of emphasis and interpretation, derives wholly from Menckenite premises.

Of course, Mencken was not to have it all his own way. A counter-attack was eventually launched. Yet when it came, paradoxically, it came from a group with equally backward yearnings, though with a more elaborately developed aesthetic. These were the Agrarians or Fugitives of Nashville—Donald Davidson, Allen Tate and John Crowe Ransom among others. Theirs was an apologia for a defeated rural South of yeoman farmers, somewhere midway between 'white trash' and the planters. 'THE FUGITIVE' warned the Nashville poets in their foreword to the first issue of the *Fugitive*, 'flees from nothing faster than from the high-caste Brahmins of the Old South.' But it was not until the 1930 symposium that their whole anti-Menckenite manifesto was presented, glorifying an organic Southern tradition that was at once agrarian and conservative and religious.

By then it had become clear that a Southern renaissance could never be fostered on the scientific or sociological model of the Midwestern school. One year earlier, in 1929, two novels had appeared (neither reviewed by Mencken) bitingly critical of inbred Southern provincialism and idiocy: Thomas Wolfe's *Look Homeward, Angel* and William Faulkner's *The Sound and the Fury*. Yet both were written with a rhetorical appeal, rooted in Southern myth and tradition, far transcending Mencken's bigoted, rationalist, anti-religious stance. Especially Faulkner—with his substitution of Yoknapatawpha for Poictesme—might have seemed Cabell's heir. But Mencken was still searching for 'a Southern Edgar Lee Masters, or Dreiser, or Sherwood Anderson' to oust the magnolia-and-moonlight school of Thomas Nelson Page and the ladies of Richmond. In the summer of 1930 this scourge of the South actually married a girl from Montgomery, Alabama. Torn between his aristocratic version of an imaginary Old South and his aesthetic obtuseness to the real achievement of William Faulkner, Allen Tate, Robert Penn Warren and John Crowe Ransom, Mencken became increasingly irrelevant. After a final blast at the Agrarians in 1935, he permanently swivelled his sights to the encroaching menace of Franklin Delano Roosevelt.

So the French fascination with the South was echoed by a Southern fascination with Germany. There is a famous exchange of letters between Scott Fitzgerald and Thomas Wolfe. Fitzgerald, that master of invisible scaffolding, had gently proferred Flaubert as a model; Wolfe, in a brusque rebuff, hurled *Don Quixote* and *Pickwick* and *The Brothers Karamazov* and *Tristram Shandy* back across the net—novels that *boil* and *pour*, great for 'the *unselected* quality' of their selection. Scaffolding to Wolfe meant nothing. His ideal was grandiose Russian, but the rhetoric was pure Teutonic; the *Schwärmerei*, Teutonic; the *Weltschmerz* and all-corrosive film of emotion, Teutonic. Wolfe loved Germany and as late as 1935 revelled in Nazi Berlin. His last visit was during the Olympics, in August 1936.

This impassioned American, curiously, paid six separate visits to Europe before plunging west to Colorado and the Pacific coast only three years before he died. Germany was his mystic and adopted homeland. A vision, to haunt him all his days, was of the *Hofbräuhaus* in Munich. 'In this vast smoky room', he wrote to his Jewish mistress,

> there were seated around tables 1,200 or 1,500 people of the lower middle classes. The place was a mighty dynamo of sound. The floors and tables were wet with beer slop; the waitresses were peasant women with smooth, hard kindly old faces—the beer slopped from their foaming mugs as they rushed through this maelstrom. A choir of drunken voices sang beyond the doors—women and men—ugly and hearty, swaying towards each other in a thousand natural powerful mug-lifted postures, as they do in Teniers. The place was one enormous sea-slop of beer, power, Teutonic masculine energy and vitality. It was like watching some tremendous yeast unfolding from its own

bowels—it was the core, heart, entrails of their strength—the
thing unfolding and unpremeditated that cannot be stopped or
stoppered.

After 1936 he felt cut off from his roots. He loved German
'Physical Clean-ness', their health, their 'Concentration of
Natural Energy', though increasingly distrusting their
repression of free speech and 'Cult of Insular Superiority'. 'I
don't like the Jews', he recorded in his notebook, 'and if most
of the people that I know would tell the truth about their
feelings, I wonder how many of them would be able to say that
they liked Jews.' The *Berliner Tageblatt* repaid the compliment,
calling him a typical South German peasant, comparing his
head to certain drawings by Dürer.

His anti-semitism, like his condescension to Negroes, was of
a Southern small-town variety; he inherited it from his fond
little stiff-laced mother (absorbed in real estate deals) as much
as from the whole parochial world of Asheville, North
Carolina. Some have tried to apologize for it or, like his editor,
Maxwell Perkins, brush the matter under the carpet. But
Aline Bernstein—his 'dear Jew', his 'grey-haired Jew'—was
dogmatic: 'He hated us like poison—it was a twist in him that
made me loathe him at times.' The very thought that he might
be taken for a Jew, as once reported by Mrs. Sherwood
Anderson, sent him into paroxysms of abuse. In 1936 he was
actually on a train when a Jew was arrested near the border at
Aachen; and safe in Paris he wrote a memorable account. But
that was an anonymous Jew, 'some nameless cipher out of life'.
It was anonymous people he really liked—the idea of people *en
masse*: in saloons, in restaurants, on the docks, in markets, on
the subway, in latrines. He loved to prowl about cities at night.
By the 1930s he naturally identified with the workers and
playacted the Communist. 'Life is too short', he remarked, 'to
be mixed up in nasty complications with other people.'

For Wolfe was wholly self-centred. He was incapable of
forming adult relationships. Instead he formed two celebrated
liaisons: with Aline Bernstein (his 'grey-haired, wide-hipped,
timeless mother') and Maxwell Perkins. The mother-substitute
was discarded for a father-substitute, himself ruthlessly to be
discarded in his turn. Wolfe's hungry mechanism needed

material. His egoism fed on slights and rejection. Betrayed, he could revenge himself on the turncoats. While Aline sends desperate cables, he records: 'She wrecked me, maddened me and *betrayed* my love constantly, but she will not leave me alone now.' On his deathbed, he could remark of the devout Perkins: 'it's almost as if *unconsciously*, by some kind of *wishful* desire, he wants me to come to grief. . . .' Such was the paranoia that harried him through his short life. He died, aged 37, of miliary tuberculosis of the brain.

'I have felt that sometime as you grew older, you would, with your powers, learn how to go up and on without treading down others', wrote a boyhood friend, his first *femme fatale*. But he never grew up. He was the perpetual adolescent, supported first by his ambitious mother (who saw him through college), later by Aline Bernstein. Women nursed Tom Wolfe; Tom Wolfe nursed his genius. Far from the gangling North Carolina hillbilly he liked to pose, he was an exceptionally well-educated and privileged young American who rode roughshod over his home, his family, all literary acquaintances and friends. Like his father, a funeral mason, he was drunk on words. And what of the grace of wit? What of reverence for language? Time 'with this strange excuse' pardons Kipling, but not Wolfe. He viewed life as from a speeding train. His love affair with language, as his love affair with the Widener Library at Harvard, was undifferentiated, *total*. His Southern froth engulfed every subject. It drowned his books. 'You are covering youself with a mass of words that are a fungus growth', warned Aline. But to Perkins he wrote:

> I have at last discovered my own America, I believe I have found my language, I think I know my way. And I shall wreak out my vision of this life, this way, this world and this America, to the top of my bent, to the height of my ability, but with an unswerving devotion, integrity, and purity of purpose that shall not be menaced, altered, or weakened by anyone.

Those relentless, proliferating triads are like an awful image of the disease that eventually killed him.

Thomas Wolfe appropriated the whole world. Tennessee Williams merely appropriated the name of a state. But Peter Taylor, born and bred in Tennessee, is its witness and chronicler. Much as Faulkner's name evokes Mississippi and Flannery O'Connor's Georgia, Peter Taylor's should evoke the distinctly Southern pattern of family life in and around Memphis and Nashville. Yet while the reputation of John Crowe Ransom and other Fugitives of an earlier generation seems secure, Peter Taylor is still in need of an introduction. His first collection, *A Long Fourth, and Other Stories*, appeared more than thirty years ago; yet he remains something of a dark horse, his growing critical acclaim not matched by an equal fame. Nor is it difficult to see why. His measured, almost neutral narrative voice is wholly at odds with received opinion on Southern style. These well-made tales conceal whole worlds of tension and subterfuge that resist the rhetorical swell of Southern prose, that studiously undercut even dialect tonalities, that largely ignore the religious manias and sexual vagaries and racial throes once inescapably associated with the South. Only the historical traumas remain, hidden in a web of small-town lives, where latter-day heirs of Tom Sawyer still date their girls, settle in comfortable avenues, maybe fight a new thoroughfare, or entertain the governor, or get drunk, or divorce, or escort their widowed mothers to the country club.

Laid bare at last are personal traumas: misery, misunderstandings, misfits groping hopelessly towards each other behind the blank veil of commonplace provincial middle-class stability. Typically the scenes are set in the gentle world of middle Tennessee—particularly the little region around Nashville

> which was known fifty years ago as the Nashville Basin and which in still earlier times, to the first settlers—our ancestors— was known somewhat romantically perhaps, and ironically, and incorrectly even, as the Miro District.

'In the Miro District' itself is the story of a grandfather and his grandson in the 1920s. Grandfather could only confide his feelings to other men. He could only confide them when he had a little whisky in him:

> And what is important, too, is that he only drank alone or in the company of other men. He abhorred what my father and mother had come to speak of in the 1920s as social drinking. Drinking liquor was an evil and was a sign of weakness, he

98

would have said, and just because one indulged in it oneself was no reason to pretend to the world that there was virtue in it. *That* to him was hypocrisy. Drinking behind closed doors or in a secluded hunting lodge, though one denounced it in public as an evil practice, signified respect for the public thing, which was more important than one's private character. It signified genuine humility.

But to the new generation with their frolicsome and independent girls all such secrecies were themselves a sign of hypocrisy. And if a weakness for liquor was to be kept private, what about women?

In our part of the world we were all brought up on tales of the mysterious ways of Thomas Jefferson, whose mother and wife are scarcely mentioned in his writings, and Andrew Jackson and Sam Houston, whose reticence on the subject of women is beyond the comprehension of most men nowadays. Did they have too much respect for women? Were they perhaps, for all their courage in other domains, afraid of women or afraid of their own compelling feelings about women?

That question is never answered. But the new generation outfaces the old. It is the older generation that is ousted, the younger which conquers. It is grandfather's seemingly stern shadow that is forced to withdraw at last into the inscrutable stereotype of Confederate Reunions. It is the young first-person narrator who is left to confront his bleak and pyrrhic victory. So he was different from his grandfather; he had made him grasp that. But how was he different? What if, merely as a result of being born when he was and where he was, at the very tail of something, he was like nothing else at all, only incomparably without a character of his own? Such is the *rite de passage* not only of one adolescent but of a whole bewildered society.

It is a rite that, in *A Confederacy of Dunces*, John Kennedy Toole brilliantly turned to farce. Ignatius J. Reilly is an infant inflated to grotesque dimensions. Like Ignatius, his author too had apparently been still living with his mother at the age of 30. It was Thelma D. Toole who relentlessly hawked her son's typescript, which had been unanimously rejected in the 1960s, until she elicited an enthusiastic commendation from Walker Percy. When she publishes her own memoir, it may become possible to disentangle fact from fiction. For what at one point sounds like hilarious satire of American junk culture, at another sounds like self-satire. The loathing shifts remorselessly to self-loathing. John Kennedy Toole committed suicide in 1969, at the age of 32, depressed at his failure to get the novel published.

Who else is the mock-hero of this fiction? Who else this grotesque pasha, this Southern Oblomov, wallowing in his flannel nightshirt in a back bedroom in New Orleans? This lumbering, bloated, belching, hypochondriac slob who is literally a weight round his mother's neck? Mercilessly Ignatius J. Reilly tyrannizes over his mother. Relentlessly he manipulates everyone by his monumental sloth and size. A true Southerner of the old school, he rants against the modern world. A royalist and medievalist at heart, he yearns for the luminous age of Abelard and Thomas à Becket. Boethius's *De Consolatione*, Hroswitha and Batman are his guides as he swings up and down—mostly down—the cycles of Fortuna.

This inert blob of domesticated tissue is compulsively drawn (like the hero of Walker Percy's *The Moviegoer*) to movies, greedily studying the credits for performers, assistant producers, even hair designers that had previously roused his loathing, nauseating himself on close-ups, inspecting smiles for cavities and fillings. A purulent mess, he seeks out his mirror image in the world. His gloating lust is all expended on the movies and TV (that hang-up was all too true of the 1950s and early '60s), while he lashes out at heterosexuals, homosexuals, Protestants, 'newspaper reporters, stripteasers, birds, photography, juvenile delinquents, Nazi pornographers'. He dreams of terrorizing the white proletariat.

This man-mountain of heaving fat—all lethargy and rancour—is a wholly novel compound: both Rabelaisian, with his gargantuan farts, and melancholy as melancholy Jaques, and coyly virginal as Oliver Hardy. Inflated with gastric gas, when his pyloric valve snaps shut, he bumbles and floats into disaster-prone, knockabout regions of pure farce, like another Pyecraft. But Ignatius is not the only memorable character. There is also a supporting cast of zany patrolmen, bag-ladies, night-club proprietors, hustlers, strippers, queers, Jewish industrialists, black vagrants, hot-dog vendors and female militants crisscrossing the wide sweep of the Crescent City from Canal Street to the suburbs, from the French Quarter to the wharves along the Mississippi. Bourbon, Royal, Chartres, St. Peter, Dumaine: all the lovely names of the Quarter resound. All the accents resound: of the black spivs, the flitty queens, the German and Irish Third Ward. Mark Twain himself might have saluted such an achievement. A spirit of revelry, of Mardi Gras, hovers over all as Ignatius (now a hot-dog vendor), an Italian patrolman, a Negro doorman, and a variety of homosexuals wander about the Quarter in festive drag.

It must be remembered that something like a twenty-year gap divides this text from the 1980s. Like *Sister Carrie*, *A Confederacy of Dunces* has reached us after a long and painful detour. John Kennedy Toole himself died in 1969, a year of revolt and rejuvenation. His novel is still rooted in an earlier decade of snug, sly, cynical seclusion—of verbal sabotage from the dark wombs of cinemas, family bedrooms, bars, bus terminals, rest-rooms, pool-halls and the back rows of seminars. Twice Ignatius sallies out (bugged by his mother to find work) to be incongruously transformed: first into a rabble-rousing leader of sweat-shop labour; next, into a sexual campaigner. But this Satyricon of disguises and depravities and chance encounters necessarily moves to a comic resolution. The mother remarries; the Jewish proprietor returns to his factory; his psycho-babbling wife is worsted; the stripper hits the big time; the vagrant lands a job; the bag-lady is retired; and Ignatius is rescued by his activist college girl-friend. The havoc littering his trail turns out to be wholly beneficial. This costive buffoon on the prowl—this obese onanist—turns out to be the trickster hero of the Carnival City. The anarchy that surrounds him is restorative and mysteriously creative.

For art is masquerade and there is salvation in art. That is the lesson passed on to Southern writers by Edgar Allan Poe. Ultimately that is his incommunicable secret 'whose attainment is destruction'. But for Southern blacks there never had been a choice. Survival for them entailed all the tricks of masquerade. Art for them, from the start, had been a matter of life and death.

6

This Double Consciousness

Some time in the 1780s, a Frenchman was invited to dine with a Carolina planter. That Frenchman was J. Hector St. John de Crèvecoeur on a nightmare stroll into the American forest of the subconscious. 'In order to avoid the heat of the sun,' he wrote in his ninth *Letter from an American Farmer*,

> I resolved to go on foot, sheltered in a small path, leading through a pleasant wood. I was leisurely travelling along, attentively examining some peculiar plants which I had collected, when all at once I felt the air strongly agitated, though the day was perfectly calm and sultry. I immediately cast my eyes toward the cleared ground, from which I was but a small distance, in order to see whether it was not occasioned by a sudden shower; when at that instant a sound resembling a deep rough voice, uttered, as I thought, a few inarticulate monosyllables. Alarmed and surprised, I precipitately looked all around, when I perceived at about six rods distance something resembling a cage, suspended to the limbs of a tree; all the branches of which appeared covered with large birds of prey, fluttering about, and anxiously endeavouring to perch on the cage. Actuated by an involuntary motion of my hands, more than by any design of my mind, I fired at them; they all flew to a short distance, with a most hideous noise: when, horrid to think and painful to repeat, I perceived a negro, suspended in the cage, and left there to expire! I shudder when I recollect that the birds had already picked out his eyes, his cheek bones were bare; his arms had been attacked in several places, and his body seemed covered with a multitude of wounds. From the edges of the hollow sockets and from the lacerations with which

he was disfigured, the blood slowly dropped, and tinged the ground beneath. No sooner were the birds flown, than swarms of insects covered the whole body of this unfortunate wretch, eager to feed on his mangled flesh and to drink his blood. I found myself suddenly arrested by the power of affright and terror; my nerves were convulsed; I trembled, I stood motionless, involuntarily contemplating the fate of this negro, in all its dismal latitude. The living spectre, though deprived of his eyes, could still distinctly hear, and in his uncouth dialect begged me to give him some water to allay his thirst. Humanity herself would have recoiled back with horror; she would have balanced whether to lessen such reliefless distress, or mercifully with one blow to end this dreadful scene of agonising torture! Had I had a ball in my gun, I certainly should have despatched him; but finding myself unable to perform so kind an office, I sought, though trembling, to relieve him as well as I could. A shell ready fixed to a pole, which had been used by some negroes, presented itself to me; filled it with water, and with trembling hands I guided it to the quivering lips of the wretched sufferer. Urged by the irresistible power of thirst, he endeavoured to meet it, as he instinctively guessed its approach by the noise it made in passing through the bars of the cage. 'Tankè, you whitè man, tankè you, putè somè poison and givè me.' 'How long have you been hanging there?' I asked him. 'Two days, and me no die; the birds, the birds; aaah me!' Oppressed with the reflections which this shocking spectacle afforded me, I mustered strength enough to walk away, and soon reached the house at which I intended to dine. There I heard that the reason for this slave being thus punished, was on account of his having killed the overseer of the plantation. They told me that the laws of self-preservation rendered such executions necessary; and supported the doctrine of slavery with the arguments generally made use of to justify the practice; with the repetition of which I shall not trouble you at present.—Adieu.

That cage, that skull, those birds evoke a whole macabre world of southern gothic, familiar from Edgar Allan Poe to Alfred Hitchcock. Not that Crèvecoeur had necessarily visited the South. Like Chateaubriand after him, he was content to explore much of the American South by proxy; those frenchified accents alone suggest the fictional contrivance. For this is a deliberate Gothic fiction whose overt Christian symbolism serves only to underline the un-Christian horror of a slave society. The ironies, at the close, point to the implicit text: 'And there was one named Barabbas, which lay bound with them that had made insurrection with him, who had committed murder in the insurrection' (Mark 15. 7).

This murderer is more than a black Barabbas, however; he is another Christ that the scripture might be fulfilled 'which saith, And he was numbered with the transgressors' (Mark 15. 28). That cage is transformed to another Golgotha, or 'place of a skull'. His mangled flesh and blood become a hideous last supper for greedy insects and birds. Hanging from a tree, as from a cross, for two days this Christ-Barabbas longs for the ultimate release on the third. Yet the irony is directed as much at the visitor as the resident planter. For despite his horror and sudden surge of pity, he passes ineffectively on the other side. His momentary help proves a mere mockery, like that of the bystander at the crucifixion, who 'ran and filled a spunge full of vinegar, and put it on a reed, and gave him to drink, saying, Let alone; let us see whether Elias will come to take him down' (Mark 15. 36).

The messianic cult of the negro was an essentially nineteenth-century perversion, lingering from Twain to Faulkner, from that peculiar institution into that peculiarly haunted gothic South. The whole of *Uncle Tom's Cabin*, in some sense, is a religious parable. It can be read as a kind of last judgement whose moral geography shifts south, ever south, along the great continental riverways, across the Ohio, down the Mississippi, into the Red River, from Shelby's Kentucky to St. Clare's Louisiana and Legree's Arkansas: whose *Paradiso* lies in Canada, across Lake Erie, whose *Purgatorio* in Ohio, whose *Inferno* lost in the swamps and marshland of the Gulf of Mexico. This moral geography is exactly paralleled by the shifting literary modes, opening with the Family Tableau (of Shelby's plantation), moving on to the Sentimental Child Idyll (of the New Orleans French Quarter), closing in the Gothic Diabolism (of Legree's plantation). But, more precisely, *Uncle Tom's Cabin: or, Life Among the Lowly* should be read as a kind of Methodist allegory.

Harriet Beecher Stowe was the daughter, the wife and the sister of Methodist ministers. Her principal source for Tom was a fugitive slave from Maryland who became a Methodist minister. Every form of spiritual devotion was to be embodied in her novel: textual dogmatism that rationalizes scripture (in the doctrinaire clergyman aboard the Ohio steamboat); cold, uncharitable religion of intellectual awareness (in the New England spinster, Ophelia); the intuitive spirit of sanctity which is the grace of the Holy Ghost (in little Eva). But Uncle Tom, as suffering servant, quoting the teachings and hymns of Wesley, is the pervasive moral touchstone at its centre. 'The first part of the book ever committed to writing was the death of Uncle Tom', she later recorded. 'This scene presented itself almost as a tangible vision to her mind while sitting at the communion-table at the little church in Brunswick. She was perfectly overcome by it.'

On that vision ultimately rested the whole topsy-turvy structure, where the black South merely reflects the white South, as the white reflects the black, in an irresponsible mirror imagery of apathy, hypocrisy, and brutality. Two Georges (one black, one white) attempt to slay the dragons on the colour-line: George Harris, by a political solution, following in the tracks of Martin Delany to colonize Africa; George Shelby, by economic reconstruction at home, turning a slave plantation to a Victorian landed estate. But Uncle Tom claims the centre; for Stowe's Methodist-style Christianity was aimed neither at the managerial society nor its acquisitive economy. (The pity was that blacks as ingenious and enterprising as George Harris could not *use* their entrepreneurial skills!) It was aimed at the conversion of individuals. George Harris may be our hero; for his is the rôle of self-redemption. But Tom is clearly *hers*; for his is the real heroic rôle, that of the messianic redemption of others, including his black tormentors, Sambo and Quimbo. Such heroism calls for an heroic Christian response, which is beyond colour.

The trouble with this compassionate feeling, however, is the whole racial stereotype on which it is built. For open intellectual pride remains a white prerogative. George Harris must be a mulatto, inheriting his 'set of fine European features' and 'high, indomitable spirit' from 'one of the proudest families in Kentucky'. The unadulterated African, by contrast, is 'home-loving and affectionate', 'sensitive and impressible', 'sympathetic and assimilative'. The imagery seems essentially feminine or child-like. 'Tom, who had the soft, impressible nature of his kindly race, ever yearning toward the simple and childlike', is himself the calculated stereotype of the eternal child, the eternally exotic child, to be linked first with George Shelby, then with little Eva. A generation later Uncle Tom was to be replaced by Nigger Jim, a consumptive Evangelina by the robust Huckleberry, on another redemptive journey south down the Mississippi. For the eternally exotic child is also the religious child, calling martyr Africa as witness to both plantation slavery and industrial slavery:

> It is the statement of missionaries, that, of all races of the earth, none have received the Gospel with such eager docility as the African. The principle of reliance and unquestioning faith, which is its foundation, is more a native element in this race than any other; and it has often been found among them, that a stray seed of truth, borne on some breeze of accident into hearts the most ignorant, has sprung up into fruit, whose abundance has shamed that of higher and more skilful culture.

Tom, as a 'grave, good-natured' Bishop of Carthage in this allegory is linked to the unsaintly Augustine St. Clare. Tom is the true Pope of this suffering world, its *servus servorum* and tormented black Christ carrying his cross, whose white evangelist was little Evangelina. 'Mas'r,' he pleads with Simon Legree,

> if you was sick, or in trouble, or dying, and I could save ye, I'd *give* ye my heart's blood; and, if taking every drop of blood in this poor old body would save your precious soul, I'd give 'em freely, as the Lord gave his for me. O, Mas'r! don't bring this great sin on your soul!

Jean-Jacques Rousseau long ago, in *The Social Contract*, had summed up such paradoxes:

> Christianity preaches only servitude and dependence. Its spirit is so highly favourable to tyranny that it always profits by such a régime. True Christians are made to be slaves, and they know it and do not mind: this short life counts for too little in their eyes. We are told that a people of true Christians would form the most perfect society imaginable. I see in this supposition only one great difficulty: that a society of true Christians would not be a society of men.

106

Yes, Stowe agrees whole-heartedly; the dependent slave alone is made a true Christian! She accepts Rousseau's position, stripped of all sarcasm. In accepting that servile paradox, she turns the horror of Crèvecoeur's black Golgotha in the South Carolina woods to the sublime uplift of her avuncular black martyrdom in Arkansas. Crèvecoeur's sacrificial murderer (rebel? agitator? zealot?) becomes her grave and child-like Messiah.

Black reaction was ruthless. Expatriates in Canada were particularly damning. 'Uncle Tom must be killed, George Harris exiled!', exclaimed the *Provincial Freeman*. 'Heaven for dead Negroes! Liberia for living mulattoes! Neither can live on the American continent. Death or banishment is our doom, say the Slaveocrats, the Colonizationists and . . . Mrs. Stowe!' But W. E. B. DuBois, writing after the fiasco years of Reconstruction that followed the Civil War, moves beyond mere indignation to expose the whole psychological misconception on which Stowe's Uncle Tom was based. 'The long system of repression and degradation of the Negro', he comments in *The Souls of Black Folk*,

> tended to emphasize the elements of his character which made him a valuable chattel: courtesy became humility, moral strength degenerated into submission, and the exquisite native appreciation of the beautiful became an infinite capacity for dumb suffering.

Moby Dick was the almost exact contemporary of *Uncle Tom's Cabin*; and Melville too, like Stowe, apparently echoes Rousseau's ironies. But by inverting them, he exposes them. Yes, of course, the American slave is made into a Christian, he seems to say. Yes, of course, Christian servitude is highly favourable to such tyranny. The captain of the *Pequod* (himself part caricature of the slave-owner, John C. Calhoun) is even revealed in his crazed dependence on his little Alabama Pip, exclaiming: 'There is that in thee, poor lad, which I feel too curing to my malady.' But far from profiting as individual Christian, the bell-boy is wholly desolated by such a régime. Melville's ironies form an exact counterweight to Stowe's: as against Tom's uplift to glory, he presents Pip's breakdown and dissolution; as against the father as martyr he presents the piccaninny as castaway; as against Uncle Tom's cabin, he presents Captain Ahab's cabin. There Pip pleads: 'No, no, no! ye have not a whole body, sir; do ye but use poor me for your one lost leg; only tread upon me, sir; I ask no more, so I remain a part of ye. . . . Oh good master, master, master!'

Such ironies are all naïvely literal. Literally Melville transforms the doomed negro as an eternally grinning boy to this tender-hearted child-martyr. Just as literally he had transformed Isaiah's sacrificial lamb into Old Fleece, summoned to Stubb's supper. That grizzled 90-year-old black cook pines for his hammock. Deaf, recalcitrant, withdrawn, he nurses a deep-felt resentment. Goaded by a world of white sharks, he stops mumbling at last to issue his shrill challenge: 'Cussed fellow-critters! Kick up de damndest row as ever you can; fill your dam' bellies till dey bust—and den die.' It is a revolutionary challenge. His sermon to the sharks is a radical address on social charity preached to the shark-like indifference of his gluttonous, cannibal 'Massa Stubb'. But little Pip, the docile, musical Sambo, is grounded neither in pagan self-reliance (of a Daggoo), nor in sexual self-assertion (of a Queequeg), nor in Christian transcendence (of a Starbuck). 'Oh, thou big white God aloft there somewhere in yon darkness,' had been his prayer, 'have mercy on this small black boy down here; preserve him from all men that have no bowels to feel fear!' Cast adrift, he cannot even mumble Old Fleece's sullen challenge. Inexorably he moves, like Uncle Tom, to the stage centre of his maddened world, to die enthroned in Ahab's sinking cabin.

For the whole intractable black problem of antebellum America stands at the very centre of *Moby-Dick*, whose prologue opens with the 'great Black Parliament' of New Bedford. As Ishmael stumbles in,

> A hundred black faces turned round in their rows to peer; and beyond, a black Angel of Doom was beating a book in a pulpit. It was a negro church; and the preacher's text was about the blackness of darkness, and the weeping and wailing and teeth-gnashing there. Ha, Ishmael, muttered I, backing out, Wretched entertainment at the sign of 'The Trap!'

Ishmael, in his search for personal salvation, joins first a cannibal rover, then a band of warrior Pequots, to evade the profoundest social evil of his time. But he could not evade it. What had opened in 'a negro church' is soon transformed to the joint worship of a 'little negro'. The whole voyage of the *Pequod* is to confront this issue in the most personal (that is, in sexual as well as social) terms. Whatever its metaphysical inversions, the voyage of the *Pequod* is a voyage into the very heart of America's 'blackness of darkness'.

The course is set to the surreptitious refrain of T. D. Rice's well-known shuffle dance:

> Weel a-bout and turn a-bout
> And do jis' so
> Ebry time I weel a-bout
> I jump Jim Crow.

'Lord! how we suddenly jump.' Here Ahab wheels about and turns on deck 'with a crucifixion in his face', leading his Christy's Minstrels on their ocean tour. There stands Stubb, 'two bones stuck into a pair of old trowsers, and two more poked into the sleeves of an old jacket': for Pip (with the pip) a 'scare-crow' Judas, or Mr. Bones. Here Captains Ahab and Boomer shake 'bones together!—an arm and a leg!': caw! caw! caw! Mr. Tambo and Mr. Bones! There Ishmael performs the last solo turn in 'that slowly wheeling circle' of the closing vortex.

But it is little Pip, humming snatches of *Old King Crow*, who interprets the whole wheeling circle 'of the *Pequod*'s circum-navigating wake' as one blackface minstrel show. Elijah is Ahab's official prophet; but a bell-boy aptly becomes his officiating priest. His is the first solo turn (by leaping over-board) and solo tragedy that transforms him from Mr. Tambo, jingling his tambourine, to a sacrificial Mr. Bones. For this jolly black, in a world of white whaling jollies, must first be stripped of his missionaries' Deity, totally abandoned, crucified, drowned, and buried, to rise again 'with that unearthly idiot face'. No longer a Nigger Christ even, he is become another Jim Crow merely, pitched headlong from the crow's-nest, as it were, to turn ship's idiot for ever mouthing the spiritual:

> O Lord, keep me from sinking down,
> O Lord, keep me from sinking down,
> O Lord, keep me from sinking down,
> Jesus is dead and God's gone away.

So a New World triptych is completed. Crèvecoeur was the almost exact contemporary of Francisco Goya. It is as if Goya of *Los Caprichos* had wandered into the Carolina backwoods: 'El sueño de la razon produce monstruos' might well be inscribed below his nightmare portrait of the caged negro. What had begun with this stroll into the American forest of the subconscious was transformed by Stowe to a Methodist martyrdom, a tract for devotional and inspirational reading. 'Ye poor miserable critter! . . . I forgive ye, with all my soul!' is the heart-felt blessing to hang below her portrait of Uncle Tom. But this literary calvary is capped by Melville's black crucifixion of 'The Castaway': 'uncompromised, indifferent as his God'.

Richard Wright, himself a Southerner, was the first to turn the tables on this whole monstrous theme. In Bigger Thomas's words: 'They don't even let you feel what you want to feel. They after you so hot and hard you can only feel what they doing to you. They kill you before you die.' In the brothel of America all blacks are bound, literally and metaphorically, to prostitute themselves to the social, moral, political and sexual needs of the white majority. 'The Negro', in Tocqueville's words, 'has lost even the ownership of his own body.' James Baldwin was to develop the theme of the nigger as prostitute. Wright celebrates the Nigger Golem that runs amuck:

> For the corpse is not dead! It still lives! It has made itself a home in the wild forest of our great cities, amid the rank and choking vegetation of slums! . . . By night it creeps from its lair and steals towards the settlements of civilization! And at the sight of a kind face it does not lie down upon its back and kick up its heels playfully to be tickled and stroked. No; it leaps to kill.

And Wright's example, at least among black writers, was decisive. By claiming the zombie in Bigger Thomas as his own brother, he helped to eradicate for ever all such messianic myths.

Black culture heroes were readily ranged in pairs: W. E. B. DuBois versus Booker T. Washington; Martin Delany versus

William Wells Brown; David Walker or Frederick Douglass versus Uncle Remus and the whole black minstrel show led by Paul Laurence Dunbar; Marcus Garvey of the Universal Negro Improvement Association versus James Weldon Johnson, the quisling who sanctioned the rôles of darky entertainer and docile child; Richard Wright versus Ralph Ellison; Eldridge Cleaver versus James Baldwin; Malcolm X versus Martin Luther King. Even champions, however, could be misled into false alliances: Frederick Douglass with white abolitionists and congressional radicals; W. E. B. DuBois with the dominantly western ideology of the Communist Party; Malcolm X with the Arab slave-traders. But by and large it was the prophets of rebellion and revolution who were seen to overcome those who favoured integration and assimilation. Violence was a cathartic force. In literary terms the need was for black men to acknowledge the Bigger Thomas in their character; only then could the novelist truthfully explicate the world of black folks. Imamu Baraka (Leroi Jones) was hailed as the ultimate prophet, like DuBois before him claiming the right for Blacks to define themselves. The most serious problem, he wrote in *Home* (1966), 'that faces any Negro is that for so long now the white man has told him that his, the Negro's version of America and the world, is shameful fantasy'.

That was one recurrent theme of the 1960s. The other was the symbolic warfare with white writers from Harriet Beecher Stowe to Vachel Lindsay and Gertrude Stein. Again the dialectic was readily expressed in pairs: Jean Toomer or Claude McKay versus Carl Van Vechten's *Nigger Heaven* (1926); Imamu Baraka versus William Styron's *Confessions of Nat Turner* (1966), condemned as 'the copulative theory of revolution'. The New York Jewish literary establishment was dismissed outright for its perpetuation of Van Vechten's Jazz Age vision of Blacks as sexual pariahs enslaved by drugs and promiscuity or violent bucks for ever caught in the brutalizing trap of their own aggression. Especially Mailer's essay on 'The White Negro' (1959), drawn by the glamour of black depravity and perversion, seemed fair game. The drawing of lines was nevertheless complex. Ralph Ellison had already attacked Irving Howe's 'Black Boys and Native Sons' (1963), while

111

Eldridge Cleaver and Julius Lester, for example, championed 'The White Negro'. James Baldwin enthusiastically greeted *The Confessions of Nat Turner* as the dawn of 'our common history'. While both Baldwin's *Another Country* (1961) and Cleaver's *Soul on Ice* (1968), otherwise natural antagonists, were contemptuously paired as black versions of the same white myth—that of Blacks as self-hating copulative apes.

For writers were confusingly drawn into the middle (or mulatto) class, with its vested interests in caste and colour and respectability, that traditionally concerned itself with élitism and 'passing'. James Weldon Johnson's *Autobiography of an ex-Coloured Man* (1912) was the early prize exhibit of a 'white coconut'. The Harlem Renaissance was mainly a middle-class movement, neither truly Black nor American. Even Martin Luther King, despite his martyrdom, remained to the end a product of the black middle class. So too Ellison's 'Invisible Man' had opted for a middle ground *between* Harlem and white Manhattan. For as DuBois said almost eighty years ago in *The Souls of Black Folk*:

> It is a peculiar sensation, this double consciousness, this sense of always looking at one's self through the eyes of others, of measuring one's soul by the tape of a world that looks on in amused contempt and pity. One ever feels his twoness—an American, a Negro; two souls, two thoughts, two unreconciled strivings: two warring ideals in one dark body, whose dogged strength alone keeps it from being torn asunder. The history of the American Negro is the history of this strife—this longing to attain self-conscious manhood to merge his double self into a better and truer self.

Take Charles W. Chesnutt (1858–1932), one of the few outstanding Black intellectuals of the Reconstruction generation. Both Booker T. Washington and Chesnutt wrote biographies of Frederick Douglass. Both saw themselves as isolated Moses figures to lead their race, if not to a promised land exactly, through the snares and complexities of White supremacy, White sexuality, White cultural hegemony. Yet as a distinctly prosperous, bourgeois figure of a light-toned skin colour, holding himself aloof from most civil rights organizations, he has always proved difficult to fit into the hurly-burly radical tradition of Black protest. He felt himself to be doubly

112

isolated: first, as the son of 'free colored' parents who had fled North Carolina in 1856 to settle in Cleveland; secondly, by his complexion. If his 'free issue' and pale skin made him seem uppity to local Blacks, he was too dark for local Whites. As a sensitive Negro intellectual he was cut off from just about everyone in the nineteenth-century South.

Nevertheless Chesnutt was an early member of the National Association for the Advancement of Colored People as it developed in 1909 and 1910, though always on his own terms. He constantly differed with Booker T. Washington, even if he never went over to the public attack. He operated independently as a liberal Black spokesman, protesting against 'Jim Crow' railway cases, working for a Social Settlement house in Cleveland, denouncing Thomas Dixon's *The Birth of a Nation* to the Governor of Ohio, attacking Harvard University for attempting to exclude Black students from its dormitories and dining halls.

He might have passed for White, that is, but he never tried to duck his racial responsibilities. William Dean Howells's warm review of his stories, in any case, made his 'African descent' wholly explicit. In fact, as early as 1891 he had been conscious of his opportunity as a pioneer Black writer. In writing to Houghton Mifflin, he emphasized:

> There is one fact which would give this volume distinction. It is the first contribution by an American of acknowledged African descent to purely imaginative literature.
>
> In this case, the infusion of African blood is very small—is not in fact a visible admixture—but it is enough, combined with the fact that the writer was practically brought up in the South, to give him knowledge of the people whose description is attempted.

It had taken many years of teaching in rural Black communities (near Spartanburg, South Carolina) and of business ventures as stenographer on his return to Cleveland, before he could launch on that proud boast. For the *fin de siècle* period was one of White militancy and Black disfranchisement, culminating in the Wilmington 'massacre' of 1898. Black authors—unable, at first sight, to live up to the more radical expectation of their heirs—were pitting themselves against the

Ku Klux Klan. A high moral vision drove Chesnutt to authorship. His was to be 'a moral revolution' to elevate the conscience of Whites and support the Blacks. As he wrote of *The Marrow of Tradition*: 'The book was written, as all my books have been, with a purpose . . . the hope that it might create sympathy for the colored people of the South in the very difficult position they now occupy' (1905). But his dream, like that of the Colonel of his last novel, failed. The Colonel, acknowledging defeat, moved back North, even if his creator could still insist: 'I have faith in humanity, and if that faith is justifiable, the problems involved in the Southern situation will in time be worked out in a number for the best happiness of all concerned.' Yet he too was to give up. He gave up fiction altogether in 1905, acknowledging final defeat.

His clearly stated aim had been to stem the sentimental stereotypes of the Plantation Nigger School, led by Thomas Nelson Page, with the creation of genuine Blacks and genuine Mulattos. Page himself was generously quick to recognize the achievement. But the ultimate target was none other than the White press, North and South, that fostered such stereotypes. Torn between his professional White (invariably Northern) narrators and Black (usually Southern) actors, the literary stance no doubt often seemed ambiguous. But only from the shallow view that equated the sly Uncle Julius of *The Conjure Woman* with Uncle Remus rather than Brer Rabbit. However cautious, Chesnutt was deeply committed to the Black man's rightful place in American society.

For Blacks, in that sense, the cross had never been redemptive. Though imbued with Christian values they transformed the experience of slavery with metaphors drawn from two pre-Christian sources: the Old Testament and West African folklore. The myth of Israel's captivity in Egypt, above all, supplied an emotional and intellectual charge. Presented in America's first white tract against slavery, Samuel Sewall's *The Selling of Joseph* (1700), it also lay at the heart of its first black manifesto, David Walker's *Appeal* (1829). That appeal, in effect, was to a syllogism: as Joseph and Moses were to Pharaoh and the Egyptians, so today's Egyptians (African slaves of North America) were to the President of the United States and 'Christian Americans'. In an elaborate Hebrew parable Walker demonstrated that 'the enlightened Christians of America' were the negroes' 'natural enemies', resisting ownership of property, denying racial intermarriage and political and administrative posts.

A generation earlier, a negro witness of Gabriel Prosser's abortive march on Richmond had casually referred to fellow slaves as 'Israelites in service to King Pharaoh'. A generation later it was left to William Wells Brown to cap even Sewall and Walker by noting that the Pharaohs were now selling their own children! But other myths competed with the Egyptian for transcending black experience, such as Nebuchadnezzar's fiery furnace or the lion's den. All counselled *trust*, the trust of Moses or Daniel in a God who helped his beleaguered people. In the words of the spiritual:

> Go down, Moses,
> Way down in Egypt land,
> Tell ole Pharaoh,
> Let my people go.

Or with the faith of the prophet Elijah:

> Swing low, sweet chariot,
> I gwine to heaven on a eagle's wing.

Such was the world of black revivals and camp meetings. But matching the trust of the Hebrew prophets there lurked a deep, native, African *mistrust*, expressed by their own black champion, who had emigrated across the Atlantic with them, the trickster hero of the Brer Rabbit cycle. He is the lone ranger, the black entrepreneur in the ever pressing contest for status and females and food. Though gregarious and relaxed, he is an unscrupulous cynic in his undermining of all social codes. 'Sassy ez a jay-bird', Uncle Remus calls him. With a more recent change of animal metaphor, he reappears as the modern hipster or 'cool cat'. For the spirituals may express the black man's 'soul', but Brer Rabbit reveals his 'cool'.

Yet Africa, for Wright, turned out to be a land of charlatans and clowns. Wright's journey to Ghana (*Black Power*, 1954) raised in him 'associations of hatred, violence, and death'. He felt not merely an outsider, in his own terms, but an outcast. Africa might be some kind of 'homeland', either idealized or debased; but for neither DuBois nor Wright nor Ellison was it an active political force making its own moral and aesthetic demands. All move to an extreme feeling of boredom or discomfort or outright aggression on involvement with the concept of Africa. For theirs was a twofold inheritance, or rather twofold robbery by both physical and conceptual assault. Despite Martin Delany and Marcus Garvey, despite the significance of the emigration movement in the nineteenth century and 'Pan-Africa' in the twentieth, American Blacks, until the recent rise of Black Studies, remained the tools and victims of white propaganda. Not only the technological but also the moral standards of the West were held up as an example to Africa, regardless of the system of slavery and racism which the black nationalists condemned. That was the final paradox: that the image of Africa among the majority of Blacks, until the publication of *Roots*, did not differ appreciably from that of Whites.

Over a million copies of *Roots* are now in print. The publication turned out to be the literary event of the Bicentenary. It was the year of Haley's comet. Previously known only as the ghost who devised *The Autobiography of Malcolm X*, Alex Haley had pulled off another coup unrivalled since *Gone with the Wind*, possibly rivalling even that first of all American bestsellers, *Uncle Tom's Cabin*. What Harriet Beecher Stowe achieved at a time of unprecedented racial crisis, Haley had repeated today. A West African village was specially constructed near Savannah, Georgia; another slave ship was launched. Shown on eight successive nights on A.B.C. television, the twelve-hour programme was watched, it is calculated, by some 130,000,000 people.

What, then, is *Roots*? It is a colossal myth of naturalist documentation, whose cultural godfather is Emile Zola, whose logical goal is the television screen. Neither a novel exactly, nor history, its overwhelming purpose is to provide an identity to an alienated people whose roots are in Africa, as everyone knows, but as no one before Haley has succeeded in tracing across the barbarous anonymity of the slave traffic by disentangling a single clue of heredity back to its transatlantic source. That was Haley's triumph, a triumph of patient detective work, culminating in his return to his great-great-

great-great-grandfather's Gambia. Such is the book that black America has taken to its heart as a sort of family bible. At last, like any fellow Swede or Pole or Jew, the black American has been restored in all the dignity of his individuality to the Old World. For black Americans notoriously were a people without a history. Haley managed to throw a lifeline to the past by means of clues that consisted of little more than the words '*Ko*', '*Kin-tay*', and '*Kamby Bolongo*', heard from his maternal grandmother on her front porch in Henning, Tennessee. The miracle was that these words could recover their source in the Mandinka tongue; that Henning, Tennessee, could be linked with the village of Juffure on the Gambia River; that the black American oral tradition could be matched by an identical African oral tradition.

But Alex Haley was not alone in his inheritance. W. E. B. DuBois too, for example, could recall such mumbo-jumbo, as he tells in *The Souls of Black Folk*:

> My grandfather's grandmother was seized by an evil Dutch trader two centuries ago; and coming to the valleys of the Hudson and Housatonic, black, little, and lithe, she shivered and shrank in the harsh north winds, looked longingly at the hills, and often crooned a heathen melody to the child between her knees, thus:
> 'Do ba-na co-ba, ge-ne me, ge-ne me!
> Do ba-na co-ba, ge-ne me, ge-ne me!
> Ben d'nu-li, nu-li, nu-li, nu-li, ben d' le.'
> The child sang it to his children and they to their children's children, and so two hundred years it has travelled down to us and we sing it to our children, knowing as little as our fathers what its words may mean, but knowing well the meaning of its music.

It is Alex Haley's achievement to have traced his word-hoard back to a 17-year-old, Kunta Kinte (born in 1750, son of a Moslem holy man) who on 29 September 1767 was brought ashore from the hold of a British slave ship at Annapolis to be auctioned for the price of 'ten strong mules'. He compared ship registers at the Admiralty with slave auction lists in Charleston. At Lloyd's of London he pinpointed the *Lord Ligonier* as the only slave ship to sail from the Gambian coast to Maryland in 1767. He found that Kunta was one of ninety-eight survivors from a batch of 140 captives who had set out on the three-month crossing. He even found Kunta's £70 bill of sale.

Yet all that he had originally to work on were his grandmother's tales of 'the African' who was landed at 'Naplis', was bought by a 'Mas' John Waller' and taken to 'Spotsylvania County, Virginia'; who escaped so often that finally he had a foot chopped off with an axe against a tree-stump by a slave catcher; that his life was saved by 'Mas' William Waller', a doctor, 'Mas' John's' brother, who bought him and called him 'Toby'. But he was not 'Toby', he told his daughter Kizzy; he was '*Kin-tay*'; he came from the '*Kamby Bolongo*' (pointing to the river near the plantation) and that was his '*Ko*' (pointing to a banjo). As he learned more English, he told Kizzy how he had been captured; he had not been far from his village, he said, chopping some wood to make himself a drum, when four men had overwhelmed and kidnapped him. At 16 Kizzy herself was sold away to 'Mas' Tom Lea', a North Carolina planter, who promptly raped her. Her first-born she named George, who eventually had seven children. One of his sons, Tom, had seven children too; and he in turn passed on the family story to Grandmother Cynthia Murray Palmer from whom little Alex first heard it in Henning.

The journey back to Africa proved a long one. A Belgian scholar recognized the Mandinka tongue. Gambian officials at Bathurst noted the 'Kinte' clan, whose villages of Kinte-Kundah and Kinte-Kundah Janne-Ya still lay along the river. They also contacted *griots*, epic narrators of clan genealogies, whose oral repertoire was to transform Haley's quest. Finally at Juffure, opposite the old British fort on James Island, the American met his *griot*. After hours of recitation to the sound of the *kora* and *balafon*, the 73-year-old clan poet reached the offspring of Omoro and Binta: 'They had four sons', recited the *griot*. 'About the time the king's soldiers came, the eldest of those four sons, Kunta, when he had about sixteen rains, went away from his village, to chop wood to make a drum, and he was never seen again.' As Haley was to realize: 'Grandma, Aunt Liz, Aunt Plus, and Cousin Georgia also had been *griots* in their own way.' The prodigal son had returned and was welcomed back to the clan and mosque of his forefathers.

118

Research in London revealed that 'Colonel O'Hare's Forces', dispatched in mid-1767 to protect James Fort, exactly corroborated the *griot*'s account. From the Gambia River he traced the *Lord Ligonier* (commanded by Captain Thomas Davies) to Annapolis on her eighty-six-day crossing. The unwilling emigrant had arrived in the New World. His distant descendant could now trace his ancestry back through eight generations of forbears, from Omoro and Binta to Kunta to Kizzy to Chicken George (the greatest gamecocker in North Carolina) to Blacksmith Tom to his grandmother, and beyond that to the remote clan history in Mauretania and Old Mali. It remains an unmatched feat of which any Anglo-American might be proud with all the help of his national archives and British parish records.

Nor was Haley content to leave it at that. He needed to relive in his imagination every moment of that new life in the New World. Yet his learning was simply not wide enough. Otherwise he could hardly have invented the pastoral Eden for the African genesis of his first parents (Omoro and Binta) at a time when Juffure was a trading centre of possibly 3,000 people, chief city of the powerful king of Ñomi who tightly controlled through customs all the traffic of the Gambia River. Haley's description of the capture of Kunta Kinte, under the very nose of Ñomi and his war fleet, is inconceivable. No white men could have risked it; indiscriminate retribution could have been exacted from any ship that sailed as far as James Island. Anthropological lessons are fastened on Kunta, just as historical lessons are woven into the sketch of the plantation community. Even in the American sections Haley is capable of the wildest errors: cotton picking in northern Virginia before the Revolution, for example, or the use of wire fencing in the eighteenth century.

In fact, Haley had a precursor, though he never seems to have looked into 'The History of Job ben Solomon' in Francis Moore's *Travels into the Inland Parts of Africa* (1738). There he would have found a parallel capture, a generation earlier, of the son of the High Priest of Bundo, in Foota. Job was a Fula, or a Fulani, also from the Gambia, who was captured by his hereditary enemies, the Mandingos, on the banks of the river in 1731 and sold to a British trader. Job too was a Moslem and literate in Arabic. Having been shipped to Maryland and sold to a planter, he managed to write a letter to his father, appealing for ransom. The letter fell into the hands of the famous colonist and philanthropist, James Oglethorpe, who had it translated at Oxford. Redeemed from slavery by Oglethorpe, Job eventually reached London. There he translated Arabic manuscripts for Sir Hans Sloane and was fussed over by the Duke of Montague, who even introduced him to the Royal Family. When Job sailed home, he took back with him 500 pounds' worth of presents. His reappearance on the Gambia was wholly unexpected. He astonished his people as much as Alex Haley over two centuries later was to astonish the men and women of Juffure. Echoing Job, Haley might have said: 'I was gone to a land from whence no *Pholey* ever yet returned.'

That tale would have made both a poignant contrast and guide. For a sense of history is missing. It was missing in DuBois; it is still missing today. Yet it is precisely history, as Harold Cruse argued in *The Crisis of the Negro Intellectual*, in the sense of awareness of historical continuity, of which each new generation of black artists stands most in need. 'Black' is a political word and the mere assimilation of spirituals and blues is not enough to win the accolade of 'soul'. A sense of cultural continuity is needed which *Roots*, for all its inherent nonsense and vulgarity, has so effectively urged.

7

Models of Virtue

It is an old conundrum to distinguish what children actually read from what is expressly written for them. 'James Bond' is passed round in tattered copies today, no doubt as Cooper's *The Pilot* or *The Prairie* or *The Red Rover* were eagerly swapped in the 1820s, or Poe's tales in the 1830s. Such books were long remembered by a Richard Henry Dana or Herman Melville, both children of those decades. England too supplied some exciting new imports: translations of German folk tales by the brothers Grimm, and of fairy-tales by Hans Christian Andersen, and Edward Lear's *Book of Nonsense*, and Charles Dickens's *A Christmas Carol*, and a whole range of fiction from Maria Edgeworth to Captain Marryat, R. M. Ballantyne and Thomas Hughes. Not until after 1860 were Americans able to match such talent with the appearance of *Little Women* in 1868 and *The Adventures of Tom Sawyer* in 1876.

But the careers of Louisa May Alcott and Mark Twain belong to the decades after the Civil War. What of the decades before? Who were the heroes then? Most striking today is simply what is missing, the absolute void on the juvenile map of American experience: hardly a pioneer or an immigrant in sight; seldom a foray into the wilderness; no encounter with Indians, or bears; rarely even a backward glance to the heroic past of the Revolutionary War. Instead merely fables and more fables of temptation resisted, anger restrained, disobedience punished, and forbearance learned. Not a sense of adventure, in a word, but idealism was to be fostered; not spontaneity or high spirits, but a pervasive and rational self-restraint. These were not literary experiences to be

121

absorbed, but moral cameos rather for studious contemplation.

The children's fiction market itself was confined, ranging from 6-, say, to 12-year-olds. Adolescence (that middling status for the middle-class child), as Tocqueville observed, had not yet been invented in antebellum America. But lack of range and quality can have its sociological compensations. This masquerade proves a treasure-trove of parental attitudes. The overriding need in those rapidly changing decades—of Jacksonian democracy and war with Mexico—was to inculcate personal moral responsibility. The aim was to achieve an early maturity, an early sense of purpose and self-control. In an expressly American context the ambition was to replace Maria Edgeworth, as it were, with homegrown products for domestic consumption.

The urge was didactic, therefore, indebted largely to the American Sunday School Union. Fiction as fiction was considered dangerous to the morals of children. 'Books of light reading', warned one author, 'are as numerous and injurious as the plagues of Egypt.' Nevertheless, even the American Sunday School Union published fiction of moral instruction to form the character. For stress had shifted from right *knowledge* to right *feeling*. These nationalists were no longer moved by a Jeffersonian faith in education to guide a republic of yeoman farmers; theirs was an earnest moral mission to young and pliant minds.

For this was also the first age of 'the almighty dollar'; and the most pressing task must have seemed that of dividing the moral from the aggressive drives. Both instincts were needed. But they were now to be kept rigorously in tandem for the separate needs of business life and home life, of the public and the private sector: one the peculiar preserve of the male, the other of the female. A woman's rôle meant the mother's rôle. The maternal stereotype as domestic saint was pursued with a baroque intensity. The indoctrination was relentlessly passionate:

> With eyes uplifted to a protecting Heaven, she must walk a narrow path of right—a precipice on either hand—never submitting, in her lowliness of soul, to the encroachments of the selfish, and eager, and clamorous crown—never bowing her own native nobility to the dictation of those whom the world

styles great. . . . Her children revere her as the earthly type of
perfect love. They learn, even more from her example than her
precept, that they are to live not to themselves, but to their
fellow-creatures, and to God in them.

She must be both mystic and martyr, as women like Maria
McIntosh and Catherine Maria Sedgwick and Lydia Maria
Child tirelessly stressed. For it was mainly women authors
who filled the breach, though Samuel Goodrich proved the
most prolific and successful, beginning with his *Peter Parley's
Tales of America* (1827). He was to be the Enid Blyton of the
juvenile trade, eventually publishing some 170 volumes of
which 7,000,000 had been sold by 1856. The greater part of
this vast output was nonfiction—geographies, histories,
botanies, readers—but even his *Peter Parley's Juvenile Tales* and
Peter Parley's Fables were mainly compounded of factual
information and moral exhortation (on the model of Hannah
More's *Cheap Repository Tracts*). At the very time of the folk-tale
revival, he mockingly opposed the nonsense of *Mother Goose* as
much as the fantasy and violence of such 'old monstrosities' as
Little Red Riding Hood. His was an instructional market. 'Had it
not been for the constant teaching of rectitude', he recorded in
his *Recollections*, 'by precept and example, in the conduct of my
parents, I might, to say the least, have been seriously injured.'

Was it true? That was the key question. Or if not true, as
fiction by definition could not be, was it morally useful? The
age of utilitarianism for American children inevitably meant a
spate of adult propaganda. We can easily preen ourselves on
our superiority to such sterile blueprints, yet our gain may also
be our loss. Death, disease and despair were visible then as
they have rarely been in children's books since. 'They were not
so much a mirror of their time', writes Anne Scott MacLeod,

> as a composed picture of what the writers believed children
> needed to know about the world in order to survive in it, to
> impose order upon it, to take moral responsibility, and to cope
> with whatever life brought them by way of success or failure.
> They were less a factual than an emotional portrait of an era.

The minds of boys and girls were deliberately bent away
from frivolity. Jefferson's yeomen were still the model of
pastoral virtue, but imbued with a new moral self-awareness.

They were to live in a pastoral utopia, it seems, undefiled by alcohol, by field work, or by muck. Earnestness went hand in hand with simplicity (in food and clothing) as two sides of the same moral coin. It is curious that no one questioned such superior examples, or wondered how or why they should unfailingly spur others to emulation. Was not that archetypal American, 'first in the hearts of his countrymen', George Washington himself praised not for his military achievements or his presidential administrations but for his 'noble character'? The influence of such superior excellence applied equally to the little fictional heroes and heroines. Not only would they influence fellow children but even adults. Dickens's Little Nell and Harriet Beecher Stowe's angelic Eva St. Clare are the commonplaces of children's fiction.

Their saintly qualities could most immediately be exercised on alcoholic fathers and selfish or indolent mothers. Fathers in particular might desert their families or take to drink or simply die. Huck's 'Pap', last of a long line of vicious fathers, manages to combine all three rôles. For these children were usually marooned inside their narrative frames, without grandpas or grannies, without uncles and aunts, often even without brothers and sisters. Large families are exceptional; typically there were one to three children at home, seldom more. Social institutions too were all but invisible. Yet within these airless echo-chambers the great themes of poverty, child mortality, widowhood, orphancy, again and again are sounded, from which modern children, for all their myths and adventures, are almost wholly protected.

For children had to learn to confront death with composure. Home was not proof against sickness or poverty; and drunkenness was horrifying precisely because it destroyed family and home. All the more important then, in this unpredictable and unreliable universe, was the lesson to seek security not by wealth but a pair of skilled hands and an upright heart. The undoubted key was the self-discipline of restraint. Spontaneity must always be curbed in the interest of careful moral calculation. Again and again these heirs of the Puritan tradition preach the ingrained habits of self-scrutiny and self-denial. Above all, children owe a constant debt of reverence and gratitude to their parents. 'The obligation on

the side of children to their parents can never be acquitted',
wrote the author of *Filial Duty Recommended and Enforced, by a
Variety of Instructive and Amusing Narratives.*

The great betrayer of this family idyll was the disobedient or
spoilt child. Good children can invariably be recognized by
their docility and submissiveness. Expressions of anger or envy
or pride were taken very seriously, not because authors
expected perfection in children, but because such outbursts
were indicative of wrong feelings which had to be checked
before they grew overwhelming. Even when passion had been
checked, a moral inquisition must still be faced. 'Let us
examine our MOTIVES before we say we have DONE
WELL', suggests one typical Mama. Self-denial is the
ultimate lesson. Selfishness, whether in breadwinner, house-
keeper or child, is the universal enemy. As if the go-getting
ethos of the mid-century were at some lunar remove, these
children are constantly warned against all foot-loose, restless,
enterprising activity. The rabid search for El Dorado, that
found contemporary expression in the Gold Rush of 1849, is
nowhere reflected in children's fiction. True wealth was of the
spirit, preached American mothers and ministers, not of this
world. A servant with this clause made drudgery divine. Or
rather, in this utilitarian context, virtue was likely to bring its
own reward of a prosperous marriage or successful business.

If the realities of American society in that thrusting,
belligerent, capitalist age are ignored, its republican ideals at
any rate are celebrated. Merit, not money, rules supreme;
industry, rather than talent, wins the race; snobbery has a fall.
There sounds the true Jacksonian note of the period: that any
task whatever was within reach of one willing to work at it.
Though enterprise was discouraged, enterprise paradoxically
brought its own rewards. Lawyers, doctors, ministers—unlike
their British counterparts—are nearly invisible; the ideal
fathers are inevitably merchants. Urban commerce was the
source of income, even if pastoral landscapes were the source
of morality. Enterprising boys rarely entered college, but built
up their own business. For behind all the egalitarian talk of the
work ethos a sense of 'station' persisted. If snobbishness is
rightly scorned, the deserving poor are everywhere patronized
as grateful pets. Though the class structure was far more fluid

than in England, a condescending charity is the mark of the virtuous.

Yet this was hardly surprising in an immigrant society facing tide after ragged tide of new arrivals. It was the poverty of the Irish that most shocked the sensibility of established families. It was the Irish, those illiterate and papist new-comers, who formed the first great proletariat of North America. But children's authors were uniformly sympathetic. Their most frequent epithet for the Irish is 'warm-hearted'. For it was not Irish servants or labourers who destroyed their families and homes. It was that iniquitous trinity: war, drunkenness and slavery. The reply from New England was the counter-trinity of Pacifism, Temperance and Abolitionism, not explored in their political context but in the cause of Christian progress. The horror stories of war or rum could be treated as openly as the cause of slaves. Abstinence, above all, seemed a perennially suitable theme. Anti-slavery after 1830 was gradually dropped as socially too divisive.

After 1850 more humour and melodrama began to creep in. Serene mothers are choked in tears; ineffectual fathers rebuke their unruly offspring. Moral fantasy and daily reality were clearly splitting apart. But only now, too, did those submissive children become sentimentally smudged and blurred. No wonder *Huckleberry Finn* was banned from the Concord library! It offended not only the new gentility—and Transcendental optimism—of the middle-aged but the patient didacticism of the older generation. But a new talent was waiting in the wings. His very name has become a byword for phenomenal success, for a rise from rags to riches conceivable only in America. For three decades, from the 1860s to the 1890s, some 110 books, with such alliterative titles as *Brave and Bold*, *Sink or Swim*, *Strive and Succeed*, *Strong and Steady*, *Try and Trust*, *Fame and Fortune*, tumbled from the press at the rate of three or four a year. Their alliterative heroes (Frank Fowler, Ben Barclay, Tom Temple, Mark Mason, Paul Prescott, Ralph Raymond) ruled the minds and imaginations of all who grew up in the United States between the Civil War and the Depression.

Never had there been such a surefire bestseller as Horatio Alger. His estimated sales range from 20,000,000 to 400,000,000, beating Mark Twain and Louisa May Alcott and Booth

Tarkington—even Dickens—hollow. He was neither as didactic as school primers, nor as lurid as dime novels, nor as terrifying as Grimm, nor as exhortative as *Peter Parley*, nor as woebegone as Andersen. His were spunky tales in which the town bully was whipped and newsboys became bankers, farmboys senators, rail-splitters President of the United States. The bootblacks and messenger boys were mostly 15 years old and usually orphaned. If country boys, they had lost their family farm to some unscrupulous villain. All had enemies: swaggering snobs, drunken swindlers, ex-convict stepfathers, who slugged or kidnapped or framed them. But they met disaster head-on—literally, in the shape of oncoming vehicles, runaway horses, or speeding trains—surviving against all odds. So by luck and pluck they rose to be clerks and invested their rewards in real estate or Erie Railroad shares. By the time they were 18 they were well on the way to wealth and bourgeois respectability.

But these honest, enterprising lads were not altogether pi. There was a foretaste of Emil and the detectives about them as they crisscrossed from Lower Broadway to the East River clearing up the mystery of their identity or recovering their lawful legacy. They puffed penny cigars, tossed down whisky at three cents a shot, and attended Bowery theatres. But they also studied at night and were resolved to better themselves. The implicit motto was: 'If Ragged Dick can do it, so can you!' Country lads, still in the vast majority, could imaginatively roam the teeming streets of Manhattan; city lads could set out on hazardous exploits to the Great Plains or Rocky Mountains. All showed the immigrant masses that the native virtues were initiative and shrewdness; that America, above all, was the land of opportunity and prosperity.

But Alger's name has also been hedged round by salacious gossip. In 1864, after graduating from Harvard and the Cambridge Divinity School, Alger was ordained as minister of the First Parish Unitarian Church of Brewster on Cape Cod. Sixteen months later, accused of 'unnatural familiarity with *boys*', he was dismissed from his pulpit. The church wrote to the American Unitarian Association in Boston that

> on the examination of two boys (and they have good reason to think there are others) they were entirely confirmed and

127

unanimous in the opinion of his being guilty to the full extent of
the above specified charges.

Whereupon the committee sent for Alger and to him specified
the charges and evidence of his guilt, which he neither denied or
attempted to extenuate but received it with the apparent
calmness of an old offender—and hastily left town in the very
next tram, for parts unknown—probably Boston.

But what Horatio Alger actually did remains unclear.
Maybe he was just another Wing Biddlebaum, the school-
master in Sherwood Anderson's story *Hands*, who was
hounded from a Pennsylvania town. The committee was all in
a froth with charges of an abominable, heinous crime 'which is
too revolting to think of in the most brutal of our race—the
commission of which under any circumstances, is to a refined
or christian mind too utterly incomprehensible'. The 34-year-
old Alger at least retired with dignity. But the charge, in
retrospect, has stuck. He never married and lived for years in
the Newsboys' Lodging House on Fulton Street where he
found much of the material for his stories.

In fact, Alger had written for adults before turning to
teenage fiction. As many as nine dime novels were serialized
while he was still at Divinity School. But after the runaway
success of *Ragged Dick* in 1868 he was discouraged by his
publisher from confusing his readership and was forced to
issue adult novels surreptitiously. *A Fancy of Hers* was
published anonymously in 1877 and never promoted lest it
hurt Alger's juvenile market. But he was fond of the book and
kept tinkering with it until it was reprinted in *Munsey's
Magazine* seven years before his death in 1892. The attraction
must have been due, in part, to the autobiographical touches
from his own childhood in the impoverished manse of the
Rev. Horatio Alger, Sr. *The Disagreeable Woman* was first
published in 1895 under the pseudonym Julian Starr. They
make a finely contrasted pair of New Hampshire and
Manhattan life.

Both are mysteries of a kind in which a wealthy lady,
incognita, inhabits the humdrum world of a New England
village or New York boarding-house in order to test the
generosity and decency of a homespun American community.
It is a device familiar from Haroun-al-Raschid's Baghdad to

Measure for Measure, cast here in female guise. Alger's customary formula is flipped upside down. It is the benefactress now, not the ragged youth, who concerns us; it is her moral scrutiny, piercing through pomp and sham, that confronts us with the knowledge of ever-present, divine aid. Trite as it may seem, these fictions are saved by Alger's absolute faith in their fairy-tale convention; they are enhanced by his ironic delight in the hypocritically shabby societies which his slumming divinities (descending like Zeus in a shower of gold) expose.

The Lady Bountiful in *A Fancy of Hers* is a wealthy orphan who, instead of visiting Newport or Bar Harbor, like a proper Jamesian heroine, opts for schoolteaching in remote New England. The world of Edith Wharton's *Ethan Frome* or Harold Frederic's *The Damnation of Theron Ware* is opened up to the discerning gaze of a social butterfly who can dance rings round the rural oafs with their sewing circles and donation parties and school committees and ecumenical (part Methodist, part Congregational) Sunday School outings. Soon she is adored by all the children and finds true love. Her 'experiment' brings its own reward. So does that of the blunt, brusque 'disagreeable woman' of a Manhattan boarding-house who cuts through all humbug and pretension, but seems less and less disagreeable as she moves stage-centre, longing to be tapped of her wealth for true heart-felt charity. At the melodramatic crisis she rediscovers her lover whom she had once rejected from pride and obstinacy. The ending is fatuous. The first-person account, by a young doctor, may seem *jejune* compared to a Jamesian or Proustian command of such narratives. But there is no need to read it with the arch gaze of a Daisy Ashford. Alger's magazine style, with its rapid notation and generous use of dialogue, had plenty to teach the generation of Hemingway and Scott Fitzgerald. Even its easy acquaintance with town scenery—with Macy's and Palmer's Theatre, the Dime Museums and visits to Delmonico's for ice-cream—had only recently been naturalized by William Dean Howells for a more ambitious type of novel.

But, for all their realistic detail, it is as fairy-tales that these novellas demand to be read. Horatio Alger was a master of that oldest of all fictional forms, Greek New Comedy, with its poor little rich girls, its villains, its lovers, its disguises, its range of prototypes (the niggardly wife, the blustering husband, the elderly inamorato), its ultimate reversals and revelations. What is peculiar to Alger is that such traditional ceremonies of love must invariably be blessed by money. This is the sacred fount that can heal all ills, supplying proper sustenance or a proper roof or a proper education. Decent instincts were for Alger, as for Whitman, the precondition of American existence so that it needed only the blessing of cash to foster their potential to a radiant presence.

Yet there was a clash, which his fables never tried to resolve, between such idealism and everyday pragmatism. It was a clash, inherent in American ideology itself, between salvation by positive thinking and salvation by managerial control. The individual had both to make a personal decision to invest his talents for his neighbours' benefit and to subject himself to the impersonal forces of a market economy. In an increasingly utilitarian world, Horatio Alger plugged the old American values. The largesse of both benefactresses comes from invested capital. In an age of conspicuous consumption, as Veblen called it, the lesson of self-improvement by charity is all these fables ultimately teach. The Manhattan heiress bequeathes her funds to a needy pastor, but apparently has enough left to marry a poor artist and embark for Italy on a two-year honeymoon.

It is only in this light that the grotesque explosion of the Civil War can be measured. As with Vietnam, a century later, there had been nothing to prepare American adolescents for its horror. With some, post-war disillusionment set in and moral certainties collapsed. Others, like Horatio Alger, were ready to supply a new sentimental and romantic fiction. Others again, like Stephen Crane, zigzagged between epic enterprise and personal humiliation, only to retreat at last to the paradise of boyhood. By 1900 the cleft between high art and 'pop' art was complete. It opened a chasm between serious fiction and fun, or escapist uplift, of which we are the inevitable heirs. For it was in this generation that the moral rewards of capitalism were first subverted; that Horatio Alger's call of 'rags to riches', 'Log Cabin to White House', were simultaneously undercut by the new Naturalist Novel. The hero of self-improvement, U.S.-style, was shown, for good or ill, to be a mere victim of circumstances and/or his own illusions.

By the late nineteenth century the heroic ideal, though noisily encouraged in romantic fiction and by the popular press, had become harder and harder to sustain. For the myth of heroism was dependent on free will. But what Mendel and Ricardo and Marx and Darwin and Freud and Malthus had seemingly taught was that man was trapped; that he was the unsuspecting victim of genetic and economic and political and evolutionary and psychological forces, including an ever-spiralling population growth. The myth of heroism, moreover, depended on a vision of an integrated society with its own economic and sexual hierarchies, its own natural and super-natural controls. But, by the end of the century, the whole universe, it seemed, had disintegrated into a chaos of com-peting and anarchic forces, receding ever faster to a state of entropic collapse. Such forces, by definition, were beyond human control. No counter-attack, however defiant, could be waged by an individual alone.

By collective action, perhaps. 'The mode of production of material life', Marx had written in his preface to *The Critique of Political Economy* (1859), 'conditions the general process of social, political and intellectual life.' Or, as the American Henry George put it, 'the idea that man mentally and physically is the result of slow modifications, perpetuated by heredity, irresistibly suggests the idea that it is the race life, not the individual life, which is the object of human existence.' Such was the gospel of *Progress and Poverty* (1879). But the authorship of books was hardly ever collective; it was indifferent to progress; and by the late nineteenth century had become even more inturned, if anything, to individual 'human existence'. The overriding task remained, as always, one of composition. That alone, in a decomposing universe, made the writer's rôle potentially heroic.

Stephen Crane was among the most self-conscious of this new breed of heroic writers. 'We picture the world', he wrote in *The Blue Hotel*,

> as thick with conquering and elate humanity, but here, with the bugles of the tempest pealing, it was hard to imagine a peopled

earth. One viewed the existence of man then as a marvel, and conceded a glamor of wonder to these lice, which were caused to cling to a whirling, fire-smote, ice-locked, disease-stricken, space-lost bulb. The conceit of man was explained by this storm to be the very engine of life.

Henry Adams, his fellow American, chose to confront the *intellectual* responsibility of opting for anarchy. Crane chose to confront the *moral* responsibility (amid 'the bugles of the tempest pealing') of reeling through the blizzard. For it was as if a blizzard had struck the old American certainties. The new forces of Hegelian idealism and Darwinian biology and economic determinism—of evolution, class warfare, and heredity—were peculiarly stacked against the old Jeffersonian belief in personal self-control. Romantic individualism quickly soured, in the decades after the Civil War, to a documentary pessimism. Even before 1860 a brilliant minority of American writers, that included Hawthorne and Melville, had opted for pessimism. But now there were mass deserters.

One native response was to ask: 'So what?' 'What, in short', in the words of William James, 'is the truth's cash value in experimental terms?' But pragmatism was of little use to men who felt already doomed; for whom both Christianity and the promise of the Greek Revival had failed; who felt excluded from both the old religious and the Homeric appeals to personal glory. Like Dante, the young Stephen Crane awoke to find all confused, all lost. 'He had long despaired of witnessing a Greeklike struggle.' He aimed to fight his way out of that modern *selva oscura*, or Darwinian jungle. *The Red Badge of Courage* was to be his report from the jungle.

It appeared in 1895, a year after Kipling's *The Jungle Book*, four years before Conrad's *Heart of Darkness*. Crane was still only 24 years old. His subject was that of the hunters and the hunted, of the predators and the victims (much as that of Joel Chandler Harris's *Uncle Remus* tales) in a savagely destructive world. But his literary talent lay far from vernacular or folk tale. It comprised, above all, a split-second marksmanship in stalking his prey, nicknamed by contemporary photojournalists the 'snapshot'. This new heroic style was to rival Homer's for clarity. This new American *Iliad*, too, was subdivided into twenty-four parts. Had not the war, which it commemorated, been won by Ulysses S. Grant? Had not the artist, who first commemorated it, himself been called Winslow Homer? Like that American Homer's, Crane's theme was to be read as neither the romance of heroism, nor the triumph of heroism, but the quandary of heroism in an unheroic age, or rather (to use the title of one of his own later stories) the 'Mystery of Heroism'.

For the Darwinian metaphor, red in tooth and claw, had been miraculously turned inside out on that battlefield to become a scenario for this 'naturalist', or reportage-like, fiction. Here Crane could study the human condition, in all its turbulence, with the most exacting details of historical research. In this, too, he proved himself to be profoundly American. However realistic his setting, or his tone, he was still writing 'romances', like his great contemporary, Henry James. What Puritan New England had been for Hawthorne, the Virginian landscape of the Civil War was to be for Crane. Instead of the meeting-houses and custom-houses, the colonial wilderness and the Indians of the North, he would present the pine barrens, in mist and gunsmoke, of the South. Instead of a *Scarlet Letter*, he would depict a *Red Badge* of shame. Only the meaning shifts. Hawthorne's 'letters of guilt' would here turn to 'red letters of curious revenge'. For the theme was no longer that of lust, or some Faustian perusal of sin on a black-and-white frontier, but the psychological backlash of fear.

Just as Hawthorne, furthermore, had studied John Mason and William Hubbard and Cotton and Increase Mather (his seventeenth-century sources for the Indian wars), so Crane pored over the *Battles and Leaders of the Civil War*, Harper's *History*, the drawings of Winslow Homer, and the photographs of Mathew Brady. Their battle scenes became for him a kind of ritual test, a crisis of identity even. He had missed the Great War. He belonged to a post-war generation, guiltily hankering for some extreme engagement in a commercial and prosaic age. He studied the plans of the attacks and counter-attacks of the battle of Chancellorsville (2–4 May 1863). He mentally reconstructed that wilderness, ten miles west of Fredericksburg on the Rappahannock River, in which Sedgwick and Hooker were forced back across the river by Lee's bluff, and the brilliant fifteen-mile flanking attack, in which Stonewall

Jackson was mortally wounded. This was Lee's last great victory, leading to his invasion of the North in the Gettysburg Campaign. It became the visual and tactical source for *The Red Badge of Courage*.

For the fictional exercise came first. The emotional rehearsal came first. As with many young writers, Crane's career seems curiously inverted, though what began as a purely literary experience eventually took him to Mexico, and to Cuba and Greece to cover the Turkish War as a war-correspondent. Later, when he came to write *The Open Boat*, his text recreated the context of his own life. But when he wrote *The Red Badge of Courage*, his text had to follow another's text. It was from Stendhal's *Le Rouge et le Noir*, from Tolstoy's *Sevastopol Sketches* and the great Borodino scenes, as viewed by Pierre in *War and Peace*, that Crane learnt to use his single incoherent angle of vision. For the confusion of soldiers and cavalry charges, the roar of guns and crackle of rifles, the whole mad inconsequence of war were for Crane hugely symbolic of all terror, all uncertainty, all ultimate loneliness. Everything is questioned: the battle, the wound, the heroism, the resolution and self-respect reassembled out of doubts and lies. Crane's Chancellorsville is revealed as a cosmic trap, an absurd non-event. In the final chapter, the regiment finds itself winding back to the river it had originally crossed a few days earlier, as if nothing had happened.

For nothing, in a sense, had happened. Nothing ever happens. Everything becomes part of the antics of non-communication, which was to become Crane's final symbol (in *The Open Boat*) for the existential void in which his actors prate and strut and cower and flee; and sometimes survive; and sometimes face death with a steady dignity and calm. Battle lust is directly compared to a mad religion; the Civil War, to a sectarian conflict—as if fought by lapsed Methodists to the tune of:

> Fight the good fight with all thy might,
> Christ is thy strength, and Christ thy right;
> Lay hold on life, and it shall be
> Thy joy and crown eternally. . . .

Faint not nor fear. His arms are near,
He changeth not, and thou art dear;
Only believe, and thou shalt see
That Christ is all in all to thee.

'Well, God reigns, and in his hands we are safe, whatever awaits us', was his father's habitual refrain. Again and again (in *Maggie*, in *George's Mother*, in *The Blue Hotel*, in *The Bride Comes to Yellow Sky*) Stephen Crane seems to confront his father's snug Methodism, while simultaneously questioning the American demand for aggression, the American pride in the predatory tough guy, the Bowery kid with patent-leather shoes 'like weapons', or Westerners with guns on their hips. The attack is two-pronged.

For *The Red Badge of Courage* is charged with religious imagery: the *Ecce Homo* of the 'dead man who was seated with his back against a columnlike tree'; the notorious red sun 'pasted in the sky like a wafer'. Yet the communion of modern warfare proves a camaraderie of the absurd. The sacrifice of Jim Conklin (another J.C.) turns to a pointless *danse macabre*, like the 'devotee of a mad religion, blood-sucking, muscle-wrenching, bone-crushing'. The red badge of courage itself proves to be panic-stricken and self-inflicted. Self-discovery and personal salvation turn out inevitably to be a patched lie in a meaningless war. Even to bear the colours, that sacred trust, is merely to feel 'the daring spirit of a savage religion-mad'. All attempts to shape a moral vision are ultimately reduced to madness in an amoral universe. For 'secular and religious education had' by no means 'effaced the throat-grappling instinct', nor 'firm finance held in check the passions'. From Crane's desperate vision runs a direct line to Hemingway's nihilist litanies.

H. G. Wells was right when he wrote that Crane's writings suggested not so much Tolstoy, or Conrad's *Lord Jim*, as Whistler. Wells praised him for his 'impressionism'. We might prefer to use 'expressionism' for those suns and wounds entangled in a single obsession, like Van Gogh's *Sunflowers*, or Edvard Munch's *The Scream*. Brown, red, yellow, blue, grey, green, are laid on with a pointilliste discretion, learnt from the emotive spectrum of Goethe's *Colour Lore*. Even in his titles:

The Red Badge of Courage; *The Black Riders*; *The Blue Hotel*; *The Bride Comes to Yellow Sky*. His snapshot vision has the terrible, often hallucinatory, clarity of dream:

> Once he found himself almost into a swamp. He was obliged to walk upon bog tufts and watch his feet to keep from the oily mire. Pausing at one time to look about him he saw, out at some black water, a small animal pounce in and emerge directly with a gleaming fish.
>
> The youth went again into the deep thickets. The brushed branches made a noise that drowned the sounds of cannon. He walked on, going from obscurity into promises of a greater obscurity.
>
> At length he reached a place where the high, arching boughs made a chapel. He softly pushed the green doors aside and entered. Pine needles were a gentle brown carpet. There was a religious half light.
>
> Near the threshold he stopped, horror-stricken at the sight of a thing.
>
> He was being looked at by a dead man who was seated with his back against a columnlike tree. The corpse was dressed in a uniform that once had been blue, but was now faded to a melancholy shade of green. The eyes, staring at the youth, had changed to the dull hue to be seen on the side of a dead fish. The mouth was open. Its red had changed to an appalling yellow. Over the gray skin of the face ran little ants. One was trundling some sort of a bundle along the upper lip.

Concentrate. Focus. Advance. After the 'pounce', a 'trundling': and the 'gleaming fish' re-emerges a 'dead fish', while those primary reds and blues are dissolved, in alliteration, to a foggy yellow and pervasive green.

Such shifts of mood and their ironies constitute the pattern of Crane's work. Though capable of explication, like the symbolism of Van Gogh's canvases, they ultimately resist—must resist—a reductive interpretation into patterns of moral and spiritual significance. In this Crane is not like Hawthorne, nor fundamentally, I think, like Melville. Henry Fleming ('the youth' of *The Red Badge of Courage*) can never be wholly educated out of his illusions, his fantasies, his flickering shifts of mood. Crane did his best to impose an ending.

> Yet gradually he mustered force to put the sin at a distance. And at last his eyes seemed to open to some new ways. He found that

he could look back upon the brass and bombast of his earlier gospels and see them truly. He was gleeful when he discovered that he now despised them.

With the conviction came a store of assurance. He felt a quiet manhood, nonassertive but of sturdy and strong blood. He knew that he would no more quail before his guides wherever they should point. He had been to touch the great death, and found that, after all, it was but the great death. He was a man.

But that seems rather pretentious, strained. He tried rewriting it several times. For just as Henry had fled from battle, in pursuit of a squirrel skittering into the trees, so the blind rage that turns him into a hero, a flag-bearer in the end, is mere animal rage. Man is out of control: that is the burden of Crane's message. Far from reason or courage, it is illusion and impulse, again and again, that twitches and throws us.

The Red Badge of Courage reads like some zany inscrutable allegory of *non-sense*. Crane's soldiers are seldom named: 'the youth' (Henry Fleming), the 'tall soldier' (Jim Conklin), the 'loud soldier' (Wilson), the 'spectral soldier', the 'tattered man', the man with 'a cheery voice', the man with a shoeful of blood who 'hopped like a schoolboy in a game', who 'was laughing hysterically'. A decade earlier, in *Specimen Days*, Whitman had written of the unknown dead, 'The Million Dead':

> (In some of the cemeteries nearly *all* the dead are unknown. At Salisbury, N.C., for instance, the known are only 85, while the unknown are 12,027, and 11,700 of these are buried in trenches. A national monument has been put up here, by order of Congress, to mark the spot—but what visible, material monument can ever fittingly commemorate that spot?)

It was Crane who composed that 'visible, material monument'. Long before the multiplication of Tombs of Unknown Warriors throughout the world, Crane had revealed that warrior, with his schoolboy hop and hysterical laugh, as the scared and impotent victim. Long before Wilfred Owen and Siegfried Sassoon, Crane had confronted the chauvinism, the imperialism, the patriotic humbug of a bellicose decade that gloried in the honour and self-sacrifice of war. In modern wars, he taught, it is the victims who are greeted as heroes.

137

For death, he realized, *exposes* man. It is the final betrayal of lives mercifully protected by shame, concealment, lies. Like the paper-thin torn soles of the shoes on the feet of a fallen soldier: 'it was as if fate had betrayed the soldier. In death it exposed to his enemies that poverty which in life he had perhaps concealed from his friends.' Wounds, however, may strangely glorify a man. As he declared in 'An Episode of War':

> A wound gives strange dignity to him who bears it. Well men shy from his new and terrible majesty. It is as if the wounded man's hand is upon the curtain which hangs before the revelations of all existence—the meaning of ants, potentates, wars, cities, sunshine, snow, a feather dropped from a bird's wing; and the power of it sheds radiance upon a bloody form, and makes the other men understand sometimes that they are little.

Crane himself, throughout his short career, seems a wounded man, a suicidally haunted man, in his far-ranging quest for wars from Cuba to Turkey. At the time of writing *The Red Badge of Courage* he had come no closer to war than Philoctetes. Like Hemingway, his heir, he seems a ready-made case-book study for Edmund Wilson's *The Wound and the Bow*. All his fiction, whether set in the Bowery or in the Virginian or Western wilds, seems to fashion his own psychological skirmish, in tougher and tougher engagements, with the amoral, aggressive, commercial, bourgeois jungle of the 1890s.

How does one plot a meaningful life? How plot a meaningful life in such a meaningless universe? Men cannot be wholly predetermined, he seems to say. Economic and social and hereditary environment cannot be all. Men *must* be seen as first movers. Men *must* retain the illusion of free will, to operate in spite of their environment. Against the sins of pride and self-delusion, the sycophantic faith in society's codes and the dogmas of God, must be asserted the moral responsibility of self-definition. 'In a story of mine called "An Experiment in Misery" ', he wrote, 'I tried to make plain that the root of Bowery life is a sort of cowardice. Perhaps I mean a lack of ambition or to willingly be knocked flat and accept the licking.' Crane viewed the bums of the Bowery flophouses uncompromisingly. Cowards are those who cannot confront the question of self-definition. Heroes can and do. Cowards are those who fall prey to social delusions, from whom Crane abdicates all responsibility as a writer. Cowards are those who fail to stand up against the 'collaboration of sin', like the Easterner in tacit alliance with the card-sharper (of *The Blue Hotel*) versus an outsider. The iron bars of tradition and of the law in which man travels Crane called 'a moving box'. The problem is that of living without bars, without order, outside dogmas or codes, in a blizzard of whirling and competing forces. The question is one of decomposition with dignity in a decomposing universe. Not only the rôles but the writing must be disintegrated to reassert our inherent worth and dignity as men.

The ultimate question is that of heroism: not the passionate heroism of Crane's pseudo-heroes—rushing to save, to kill, to prop the flag—but the stoic restraint of a Jim Conklin (in *The Red Badge of Courage*) or the correspondent (in *The Open Boat*). Neither the Swede fuelled in Scully's whisky (in *The Blue Hotel*), nor black Henry Johnson rushing into a blazing laboratory (in *The Monster*), nor Fred Collins recklessly crossing no-man's-land for some water (in 'A Mystery of Heroism'), nor Henry Fleming in his final berserker fury, is a hero. All are 'blindly led by quaint emotions'. All, even at best, are masters merely of their own visionary worlds. As Emily Dickinson once put it:

> A coward will remain, Sir,
> Until the fight is done;
> But an *immortal hero*
> Will take his hat, and run!

True heroes act with a nervous integrity: 'as deliberate and exact as so many watchmakers', as Crane wrote of the Cuban conflict. In his final writings (in 'The Veteran', 'The Price of the Harness', *Wounds in the Rain*, the Spitzbergen tales) Crane dealt increasingly with such cool deliberation. Theirs is the dignity of self-possession. Heroes are those who can go forward, alone; who accept moral responsibility for themselves and others; who can accept isolation; who remain committed to life; who stand up to the 'collaboration of sin'. Though they too, of course, must die. They too, like Jim Conklin, may at any moment collapse with an animal-like kick of death.

Crane's heroes cradle their wounds in careful self-support, grabbing their left arm with their right hand, or holding their right wrist tenderly as if it were 'made of very brittle glass'. For Crane saw through the dignity to the fragility and the pathos of self-possession. He was still only 28 years old when he died. It was of tuberculosis that he died. Within a generation his fragile dignity was reduced to a mere code, a moral shorthand for stoic self-definition and self-control. That is often called Hemingway's code. Yet Hemingway also delivered Crane's finest epitaph. 'What about the good writers?', asks a German in *Green Hills of Africa*. 'The good writers are Henry James, Stephen Crane and Mark Twain', Hemingway replies. 'That's not the order they're good in. There is no good order for good writers.' And what happened to Crane, the German asks. 'He died. That's simple. He was dying from the start.'

8

Theatrical Models

Those iron bars of tradition Crane called 'a moving box'. The best work by Dreiser and Norris, his contemporaries, was one of moral dismantling, hacking away at those iron bars. The most dated aspects of Naturalism are those insisting on reintegration, whether by means of socialism (an in Upton Sinclair), or a quasi-religious force (like Dreiser's 'chemisms'), or a belief in the perfectibility of man (as in Steinbeck's later fiction), often just by daydreaming, by escaping into illusion, turning the whole commonplace world of America (and, by extension, Paris, Cuba, Alaska) to a gigantic stage show.

In the 1900s Broadway still ruled supreme. Thirty years later it was the 'talkies'. In one generation there emerged the mighty illusionists of American fiction, literary Barnums and Houdinis, who transformed the most unlikely scenarios (the Chicago lake-front, the Klondike, the San Fernando Valley, or Fifth Avenue) to theatricals. The last age of popular prose fiction, whose heroes (Hemingway, Wolfe, Fitzgerald, Dos Passos, James T. Farrell) became household names, was exactly matched by the rise and fall of Hollywood. Compare a trio of American Edwardians—such as Theodore Dreiser, Jack London and Henry Miller—with their counterparts today: John Barth zestfully rewriting his own reading (in *The Sotweed Factor*) as well as his writing (in *Letters*); or Hunter S. Thompson invading the communal world itself as an *agent provocateur*, baiting the traps he feeds on, provoking the very hysteria he is engaged in reporting. Such is the link between *The Red Badge of Courage* and *The Great Shark Hunt*. Stephen Crane had turned the Civil War battlefields into a scenario for his reportage-like fiction; Hunter S. Thompson, as reporter, inspires his own zany theatre of incoherence.

Dreiser lacked confidence in his own procedures. As he wrote to his secretary, Sally Kusell, while at work on *An American Tragedy* in 1923:

> The trouble with me when I set out to write a novel is that I worry so over the sure even progress of it. I start and start and change and change. Have done so with nearly every one. What I really ought to have is some one who could decide for me—once and for all when I have gotten the right start—when I am really going ahead—or one who would take all the phases I pen down and piece them together into the true story as I see it. That is what I eventually do for myself—but all the struggles and the flounderings.

He did, of course, decide for himself, especially when writing his masterpiece. He wrote and rewrote *An American Tragedy*: 'Sometimes I write enough to make two chapters or three in a day and yet ⅓ of one chapter that is eventually O.K.' But by the time a final typescript was ready a whole committee of editors had been involved, his 'editorial staff', as Dreiser called them. First Sally Kusell would suggest changes and cuts. Then Louise Campbell in Philadelphia, who had been helping Dreiser since 1917, would edit the revised manuscript. Last T. R. Smith of Boni and Liveright would make a third set of suggestions. As Dreiser himself annotated a late typescript of Book II: 'Finally revised and cut copy—with cuts by myself, S.K., L.C. and T. R. Smith. From this the final typed copy for the printer was made.'

The whole procedure smacks almost of the film lot, as if some script were being passed from cubicle to cubicle among the writers. But his last books were not merely edited, they were wholly rewritten. Maxwell Perkins's relation to Thomas Wolfe, that prototype of an American editor's relation to his author, is as nothing to Dreiser's pathetic capitulation in his final years. Dreiser had worked on *The Bulwark* from 1914 to 1920 and picked the task up again in 1942, enlisting the aid of Mrs. Marguerite Tjader Harris, who had helped him with the 'editorial preparation' of his *Gallery of Women*. Mrs. Campbell too was again involved and his editor, Donald Elder at Doubleday. Even James T. Farrell was roped in; he wrote a twelve-page letter with suggestions for further revision (duly sent on to Mrs. Campbell). The result of this collaboration, as it can only be called, was a castration of Dreiser's lumbering, prolix, atmospheric style. Such 'simplification' merely stripped and highlighted Dreiser's essential clichés.

Those clichés have also from the start been a matter of controversy. For the art of the cliché lies at the very core of Dreiser's art. Almost all his plots have their origin in popular literature: the plight of the seduced country or working girl in *Sister Carrie* and *Jennie Gerhardt*; the Horatio Alger myth of success in the Cowperwood trilogy; the romance of the artist in *The 'Genius'*. In each instance, however, Dreiser reverses the basic moral assumption of the popular myth. In *Sister Carrie* Carrie is not redeemed, unless it be by her restless search for success and pleasure; she rises not because she is honest or courageous but because she is shrewd enough to allow others to carry her in the direction she wishes to take. With stereotype plots, however paradoxical in the execution, go stereotype characters with whom Dreiser identifies to every nuance of their hackneyed diction. His women wear little tan jackets that are all the rage that fall; his men gather in really gorgeous saloons, or temples of gastronomy. Even his images or symbols are those of the commonplace; Carrie is a boat adrift on troubled waters or a small craft in search of a safe harbour. It is in their repetition, as when Carrie's Chicago rocking-chair becomes Hurstwood's in New York, that their gathering strength is developed. The theatre as a form of escape, of the art of illusion that itself becomes a source of income (as much for Dreiser as for Sister Carrie), is the ultimate metaphor. It is the salesman, Drouet, who first introduces Carrie to amateur theatricals. Both are meretricious players, supported solely by their social rôles, whose stage set is the city, whose mirror the popular theatre. For it is these stage sets and their appurtenances (clothes, apartments, bars, flophouses) which supply Dreiser's most basic commonplaces, at once the raw material and symbolic patterning of his art.

Hurstwood's decay is the decay of his clothes, his room, and his appearance. Such physical patterns do more than communicate a moving psychological and emotional reality; in most ways they *are* Hurstwood's sole psychological and emotional reality. Once worn beyond the point of no return, they reach inevitably to Hurstwood's death. He moves from warmth into the cold. In larger terms, all Dreiser's scenes in their cyclic rhythms move from sexual heat to lone frigidity, or from cool to heat, within alternating scenarios of snug retreats and inhospitable chill. Even *An American Tragedy* (though its period setting was shifted from 1906, the year of the Chester Gilette case, to the 1920s) is autobiographical, not merely in its opening sequences but in its theme. Its ultimate aspiration was Dreiser's. For Clyde Griffiths, like Fitzgerald's 'Great Gatsby', is victim of that archetypal American myth in which sex and prosperity unite in the image of a beautiful young girl. Like Fitzgerald, his successor, Dreiser served both as celebrator of such American illusions and critic of all such small town aspirations that associate man's noblest dreams with a wealthy girl.

Unlike Hemingway or Fitzgerald, however, Dreiser needed to deploy the commonplace, the hackneyed theme in whatever paradoxical form. He produced murals, never miniatures. In late 1923, while at work on *An American Tragedy*, Dreiser told an interviewer that a major fault of contemporary American realism was that most of its adherents were attempting the impossible task of presenting life on a 'ten-inch canvas'. Thus spoke the surviving heir of the naturalist era, still attempting works on the grand scale of Frank Norris's *The Octopus* and *The Pit*. Yet Crane was always the miniaturist, while aiming at epic size. So too was Jack London.

Though it is difficult to take Jack London seriously. The Russians still read him. Youngsters may still read him. But the reputation of this Californian adventurer, war correspondent and self-styled socialist has steadily dwindled since the heady days of his world-wide sales sixty years ago. He made more than a million dollars by his writing. He was the last pulp author of genius, before the rise of Hollywood, to feed the dreams and passions of the literate masses. A crude disciple of Kipling, he fathered a hollow archetype: the virile American as man of letters, perpetuated over two further generations by Hemingway, Kerouac and Mailer.

The Kipling of the Klondike they called him, or the Bret Harte of the Yukon. For it was the Alaskan foray of 1897–98 that provided the pay-dirt for the rest of his literary career. Yet it was his experience as an 18-year-old hobo that provides far more telling clues. In the spring of 1894 he had jumped the freight cars out of Oakland to follow Kelly's army of the unemployed. The aim was to join Jacob Coxey's army in their march on Washington. Arrested for vagrancy in Buffalo, however, he landed thirty days in jail. That was his first contact with what he was to call the 'Social Pit' or, in his sketch of London's East End, the 'Abyss'. 'I was no spring chicken in the ways of the world', he recorded thirteen years later,

> and the awful abysses of human degradation. It would take a deep plummet to reach bottom in the Erie County Pen . . . filled with the ruck and the filth, the scum and the dregs, of society—hereditary inefficients, degenerates, wrecks, lunatics, addled intelligences, epileptics, monsters, weaklings, in short, a very nightmare of humanity.

Cleverly he befriended an old lag who became (in the slang) his 'meat'. This old lag had him appointed a trusty within two days, one of thirteen 'hall men' who exploited the 500 prisoners. Sexuality, as always in Jack London, is veiled. But his record of that time, *The Road* (1907), is dedicated to Josiah Flynt; and Flynt did reveal the truth about hobo life for Havelock Ellis's *Studies in the Psychology of Sex: Sexual Inversion*, bought by London for his library. In 'Homosexuality Among Tramps' Flynt declared that one in ten of the 60,000 professional tramps was an invert. Such men would pick up slum boys between the ages of 10 and 15 and seduce them into travelling the road. The boys were called 'prushuns'; their masters, 'jockers'. Jack London was careful to dissociate himself from such trade. In his chapter on 'Road-Kids and Gay-Cats' he states:

> I was never a prushun, for I did not take kindly to possession. I was first a road-kid and then a profesh. . . . And be it known, here and now, that the profesh are the aristocracy of The Road. They are the lords and masters, the primordial noblemen, the *blond beasts*.

What London was claiming surreptitiously is that he was never a sexual underdog, never a pariah, never part of this sterile wasteland, but a blond aggressor, the primordial beast. The image is determinedly butch. As it will remain, whether snooping in Whitechapel among the tarts and muggers of the Commercial Road or roistering in the South Seas. The macho Californian speaks for the misfits, the oppressed; the protofascist for the scavengers of the jungle. Though superficially akin to George Orwell's *Down and Out in Paris and London*, Jack London's descent into the Abyss (equipped with camera and housed with a police detective) is more like a photo-journalist's search for copy. For he knows what awaits the sluggish, drab, stunted dross of the capitalist machine. Again and again, from *The Call of the Wild* to *The People of the Abyss*, Jack London rehearsed his parables of oppression, of domestication, and of retrogression to the wilderness. In his Wellsian fantasy, *The Iron Heel*, his rôle switched to that of blond superman as terrorist. But it is typical of his vision (and his most potent legacy) that for him the golden age of socialism could dawn only 300 years after a successful fascist revolution.

Jack London, on a later visit to the Marquesas, made a point of riding out to Melville's valley of the Typees. Like Melville, he too had lived among sailors, tramps and prisoners. But unlike Melville he had turned that experience into nothing but adventure stories and socialist lectures. Tramps for him were the sterile organic waste, like prostitutes, of a capitalist society. Yet his heroes (Wolf Larsen and Burning Daylight), as Maurice Magnus observed as early as 1911, were themselves curiously innocent of women: brute force is translated to brutes, or deserts human culture altogether for the wolf pack. Multiple killings and sadistic deaths are a hallmark of his fiction. He married twice: first, a loveless match as 'Daddy-Boy' to 'Mother-Girl'; next a comradely romp as 'man-boy' with 'mate-woman'. Charmian, who fenced and boxed and tumbled with him in the surf, became his Eternal Kid. It was to her that he confessed his dream of the 'Man-Comrade' who 'should love the flesh, as he should the spirit'. That man was the whimsical poet (of *A Wine of Wizardry* and *The House of Orchids*), George Sterling. Sterling was 'Greek' to London's 'Wolf'. 'There's no question', Kenneth Rexroth decided, but that his relations with George Sterling were as homosexual as could be. Whether they found overt expression is of no moment. They were sufficiently comprehensive in their only moderately covert form. Similarly, his relations with women, both in life and in fiction, have been described enough times as persistent refusal to accept woman as anything but a deformed boy. London practically invented the heroine as Good Chum. The homosexuality is not the point but the immaturity is. There are simply no adults anywhere in London's fiction. It is impossible to take seriously sea captains, goldminers, entrepreneurs, revolutionary leaders who behave like newsboys, playground bullies and Eagle Scouts.

Jack London's cult was that of the male body—his own perfect body. He had pictures taken of himself in bathing costume, flexing his muscles. He wrestled and boxed in the nude. He took naked snapshots of George Sterling. The posing, the sadism, the masochism—down to the final suicide—are all too reminiscent of Yukio Mishima. Though doubts have been cast on the legitimacy of the verdict, that injected overdose of morphine was more than accidental. London believed that he was in the tertiary stage of syphilis; That he had a tumour on the brain. Aged 40, he was disgusted with his impotent body, bloated by drink and arsenic poisoning, racked by piles and psoriasis. His alcoholism he had broadcast bravely in *John Barleycorn* (1913); the suicide was prefigured at the end of *Martin Eden* (1909). George Sterling committed suicide ten years later.

Lycanthropic to the end, London sat gobbling raw fish and two blood-red wild ducks a day. For he never resolved the tension between his cult of virility and married love; nor that between his pose of Nietzschean superman and Marxist revolutionary. He believed in socialism through natural selection. He wanted to be both the lone wolf, that is, and the leader of the wolf pack. Lecturing at Harvard in 1905, he declared: 'I speak, and I *think*, of these assassins in Russia as "my comrades".' Yet it was not London but Harvard's own John Reed who rode with Villa's guerillas across Chihuahua; it was Reed who was to be buried under the walls of the Kremlin. London remained the blond beast, preaching imperialism as the vanguard of the proletarian revolution: for him 'the survival of the fittest race must precede the victory of the fittest proletariat'; and white was fittest. His racism was unabashed, aimed at 'black' and 'brown', 'red' and 'yellow' aboriginals alike. Himself a bastard, he boasted of his Nordic blood. Kipling's *Plain Tales from the Hills* was debased to such racist formulas as *Adventure* and *South Sea Tales*.

Life and letters for Jack London had long mingled in confusion. Henry Miller's most personal experience, from the start, was turned to a self-parading fiction; his fictional progress, to a literary legend. Just fifteen years younger, Henry (Valentine) Miller was born into the same age—before Dreiser's *Sister Carrie* or the trial of Oscar Wilde even—of German immigrant parents, in Manhattan's Yorkville, in 1891. He only spoke German at home until he went to school. At least half his life, until he was well into his forties, was to be spent manoeuvring out of sight of his mother's prim ambitions, backing away both from the codes of the genteel age and the drudgery of his father's tailoring shop in Brooklyn. He too was a young runaway to California. But, unlike London, he remained hopelessly, abjectly, dependent on women. Far from an American satyr, he was a sexual clown, all of whose five marriages broke up in various ragged disasters. His first marriage went early off the rails when he was caught bedding his mother-in-law.

Nel mezzo del cammin, by his thirty-fifth birthday, he had achieved nothing; married to June Mansfield, he was living (between occasional jobs as a grave-digger or encyclopedia-salesman) essentially as a pimp off her earnings. June was a bar hostess with literary ambitions. It was years before Miller could detach himself from her scheming. His first novel was written in her name, to ingratiate her with an admirer who might send them both to France. This coup came off and sent them both to Paris in 1928. But back in New York he relapsed into inertia as her ghost, writing a novel about her and daily journalism for her. In one desperate catalogue he listed her lovers, totalling forty-two men and sixteen women. Yet it was June who finally despatched him back to Europe, to clear him out of New York. It was also June who financially kept him there. His sole assets on arrival in Paris in 1930, aged 38, were his suits, made by 'Henry Miller, Gentleman's Tailor', and a copy of Whitman's *Leaves of Grass* (his fellow author from Brooklyn).

It was in Paris, haunted by June, that he turned memory to rhapsodic fiction.

> He thought of her silky, squirming crotch with its reddish brown lips and the little fluttering ridges in its upper channel and he remembered everything they did, how salty she tasted, and how she would moan.

It was the first time that he had ever been truly independent with no mother, nor older mistress, nor efficient wife, to fall back on. He was an American innocent abroad. When the cheques ceased, he slept in cinemas or under the Seine bridges. He sold his father's suits. It was the degro zero of his existence, cadging from Russian emigrés or wealthy Yale graduates. In his fortieth year, he began his slow ascent to ambiguous stardom as the King of Smut.

By then he had met Anaïs Nin and begun *The Last Book* (later to be called *The Tropic of Capricorn*, and finally *The Tropic of Cancer*). 'It's like a big, public garbage can,' he wrote to a New York friend. 'Only the mangy cats are missing. But I'll get them in yet.' For it was to be a great pot-pourri of his experiences—spun out of fantasy, digression ecstasy—in a Proustian recall of his early poverty and despair in Paris. It was also to be a Book of the Dead and of resurrection: 'The essential thing is to *want* to sing. This then is a song. I am singing.' By the time *Cancer* was published, in September 1934, he was no longer supported by June. It was Anaïs who raised 600 dollars to alter the Obelisk Press contract to more favourable terms. But success, when it came, was immediate and overwhelming. Marcel Duchamps was enthusiastic. Blaise Cendrars climbed Miller's stairs. Ezra Pound declared that Miller had out-Ulyssesed Joyce. Havelock Ellis praised its psychological truth. T. S. Eliot wrote to assert the unquestionable superiority of *Tropic of Cancer* over *Lady Chatterley's Lover*.

Miller had invented a new kind of epistolary novel—the confession as fantasy. A prose-Whitman, he addressed his most intimate letters to his readers. As Emerson had written (in passages marked by Miller): 'Life consists in what a man is thinking all day';

novels will give way, by and by, to diaries or autobiographies— captivating, if only a man knew how to choose among his experiences, that which is really his experience, and how to record truth truly.

The draft of *Tropic of Capricorn* was finished by 1938, acclaimed by Miller as 'a thousand times better than Joyce or St. Augustine'. His explorations in the 'Land of Fuck' proved part autobiographical, part Dionysiac, and part Dada or Surrealist. Masquerading as a *Divina Commedia*—ascending from civilization (*Inferno*), through sensuality (*Purgatorio*), to the liberated imagination (*Paradiso*)—its Beatrice was June. June even now remained his hero's confusion, his beckoning mystery and salvation.

These were Miller's great years. He was the only true expatriate left in Paris; all the rest (Hemingway, Fitzgerald, Cowley), by comparison, had been tourists. But by 1938 the party was over. The Nazi terror was encroaching. Miller departed for Greece. (Out of that experience, and his meeting with George Katsimbalis, came *The Colossus of Maroussi*.) On his return to the States, he criss-crossed the country by car until he settled in Hollywood to finish *The Air-Conditioned Nightmare*. Aged 50, he was back in America: 'a desert in which the sensitive man or woman spills his unwanted seed' (he wrote to Osbert Sitwell) '—like camels pissing in the dark somewhere in Arabia.' Yet there he stayed, now on the coast in Big Sur, now near Sunset Boulevard in Pacific Palisades, to become a Californian sage. What the English Lawrence had begun in New Mexico, the native Miller was to perpetuate: part Blake, part pornographer, part Hieronymus Bosch, in a mystic triad.

By the post-war period, he had become both a target for right-wing abuse and a tourist attraction. Though he promoted new authors from Jack Kerouac to Erica Jong, he felt increasingly out of tune with the new age, marooned by the sexual revolution. To an interviewer, who praised him for his influence in 1976, he replied:

> Sexual revolution? Linda Lovelace? Oh I consider it a misfortune for us that we have created these things. . . . Really, I am amazed and disgusted. . . . There's such a gap between me and the younger generation. Maybe I'm just an old man, too

old to appreciate and understand them, but I don't see any *reverence* in the young.

He was wounded by Kate Millet's attack on him in *Sexual Politics* and even more disliked Norman Mailer's defence in *The Prisoner of Sex*. Though Mailer eventually won him round with his anthology, *Genius and Lust*. He had become a classic.

For, well into his seventies, he remained an Edwardian Valentino, a great lover. 'Marriage kills love', he said wrily in 1976. Just as he had waited for June outside the clip joints of lower Manhattan, so half a century later he was still waiting for the 27-year-old Japanese singer Hoki (his fifth wife) outside the Grand Star Restaurant in Chinatown. That marriage too, like all the others, was not to last. But the endearing innocence of his adoring obsessions has endured. *Crazy Cock*, in that sense, remains as theatrical an illusion as *White Fang*. For it was the free play of fantasy he was ultimately after. It was ecstasy and illumination, not sex. He flinched from the blasphemies of the post-war generation and its jokes. His were visionary quests, not cartoon balloons like *Giles Goat-Boy* with its new catechism of heaven and hell: 'Who neglects his appetites suffers their pangs; Who presumes incautiously may well be butted; Who fouls his stall must sleep in filth.'

Henry Miller had never been near a university. For John Barth the whole universe could be turned into a university and Giles Goat-Boy, stepping out of a Houyhnhnm land (of goats) into a Laputa (of computer technology) was to be its new Messiah. He is the Grand-tutorial Ideal Laboratory Eugenical Speciman, a 22-year-old 'horned human student' from the School of Animal Husbandry, knight-errant in search of his identity. His heroic exploits, his struggles to be accepted as new Grand Tutor, form the basis of an allegory in which *Gulliver's Travels*, *Alice in Wonderland*, *The Pilgrim's Progress*, *Nineteen eighty-four*, Kafka and the *Kama Sutra* are shaken and mixed. But this *Après-Midi d'un Faune* is strictly for American kids, a camp *Lord of the Rings* (turned *Lord of the Reels*), a book of doom, a dream in a science-fiction landscape whose grail is no longer Mordor but the Automatic Implementation Mechanism or AIM of the university computer's tapes. Even the randy gusto of the copulative sequences, in all their variety of hard thrusting, remains curiously unpornographic: scene after scene with stud-males humping, laying, tupping, servicing, swiving, mounting, clipping, screwing their females (or fellow males on occasion), this endless strip-cartoon comedy for sexual members expresses neither joy nor pain but utter indifference.

So the iron bars of law and tradition disintegrate. What began with masquerades of sex ends with a political masquerade: first writers as victims, then the victim himself as reporter. *Facit indignatio Gonzo.* Juvenal did not glut his loathing for the Emperor Domitian with more glee than Hunter S. Thompson for President Nixon. Nor did Nixon, as the dedication of *The Great Shark Hunt* acknowledges, ever let him down. A more predictable title might have been *Fear and Loathing of Richard Milhous Nixon.* A pun on Thompson's own name, however, suggested the title. For Gonzo is journalism of the hunter on the hunt. The technique consists in avoiding the spectacle at all costs by fastening on the spectators instead. It is the spectators who must be turned into the event: 'thousands of people fainting, crying, copulating, trampling each other and fighting with broken whisky bottles'. It is Thompson's crazed need to contact, or whip up, the spectators that constitutes the event. Or rather, it is the frenetic stampede of his address as it raves and stumbles and vomits in hot pursuit of his fellow Americans. The idea is to saturate each page with a verbal debauch, as he simultaneously combines the rôles of decoy and victim. For the failed dreams of America are his. The nightmare is his. The terminal identity crisis, as he calls it, is his.

The aim, far from comprehending events, is to lose control of events, to turn every assignment into a drunken spree of sleepless nights, scrambled memories and whisky-sodden notes. The end is nervous prostration. Every story—whether devoted to the Kentucky Derby, the McGovern campaign trail, or Watergate—turns into an hysterical stampede:

> The rest of that day blurs into madness. The rest of that night too. And all the next day and night. Such horrible things occurred that I can't bring myself even to think about them now, much less put them down in print. Steadman was lucky to get out of Louisville without serious injuries, and I was lucky to

152

get out at all. One of my clearest memories of that vicious time is Ralph being attacked by one of my old friends in the billiard room of the Pendennis Club in downtown Louisville on Saturday night.

The expressionist prose radiates fearful vibrations. Wave on wave, they distort the landscape, verbal equivalents of Munch's *The Scream*. Not unlike the nightmares that haunt Huck after the Grangerford feud:

> I ain't a-going to tell *all* that happened—it would make me sick again if I was to do that. I wished I hadn't ever come ashore that night to see such things. I ain't ever going to get shut of them—lots of times I dream about them.

Yet, as with Huckleberry Finn, the final effect is not one of horror. Rather *The Great Shark Hunt* seems to be celebrating some peculiarly American form of carnival—some holocaust without tears. Searching for a mirror image of his own hallucinations, the face Thompson finds in the end is naturally familiar:

> a puffy, drink-ravaged, disease-ridden caricature . . . like an awful cartoon version of an old snapshot in some once-proud mother's family photo album. It was the face we'd been looking for—and it was, of course, my own.

Such is Gonzo journalism, whose visual correlatives Ralph Steadman's caricatures supply. (Its political correlatives, Thompson claims, were the student massacre at Kent State and Nixon's bombing of Cambodia.) In all this there is something of a revivalist preacher howling his prophetic malaise at the world,

> raving and screeching about all those who would soon be cast into the lake of fire, for a variety of low crimes, misdemeanours and general ugliness that amounted to a sweeping indictment of almost everybody in the hotel at that hour.

For *The Great Shark Hunt* has a good deal in common with the black cook's sermon to the sharks in *Moby-Dick*: 'Cussed fellow-critters! Kick up de damndest row as ever you can; fill your dam' bellies till dey bust—and den die.' Hunter S. Thompson might so easily have become yet another American sports columnist in the tradition of Ring Lardner and George

Plimpton. He covers fishing and yachting, horse-racing and football and boxing, as well as the motorcycle gang of the Hell's Angels. But writing for *Rolling Stone*, he developed into the laureate of *angst*. His prose often sounds meaningless, larded with expletive 'goddams' and 'bastards', 'dingbats' and 'bitches' and 'geeks'. Kerouac, in comparison, seems a mother's boy, Ginsberg a cop-out, Warhol phoney. Even if, in the end, he writes off *Fear and Loathing in Las Vegas* as a failure, it was 'a rare goddam trip for a locked-in, rent-paying writer to get into a gig', he admits, 'that, even in retrospect, was a kinghell, highlife fuckaround from start to finish . . . and then to actually get *paid* for writing this kind of manic gibberish'.

For Gonzo was the Joker in Tom Wolfe's prestigious New Journalist pack. Hunter S. Thompson did not merely structure his journalism as fiction (in the manner of Truman Capote), he allowed the spirit of fiction to *dictate* his journalism (in the manner of Norman Mailer) by starring himself in the lead rôle. His contribution was to push reportage beyond analytic realism, beyond impressionism even, to those wilder shores where the drug-crazed, boozed-up, horror-stricken reporter is king. As he says of Ralph Steadman:

> His best drawings come out of situations where he's been most anguished. So I deliberately put him into shocking situations when I work with him. I always found that that's when he does his best stuff.

Or again:

> He gives me a perspective that I wouldn't normally have because he's shocked at things I tend to take for granted. Photographers just run around sucking up anything they can focus on and don't talk much about what they're doing.

But then Steadman had what Thompson calls 'that King-George-III' notion of America. He probably thought it was doomed from the start. Thompson's own loathing, as he half realizes, is the far side of a thwarted innocence that drives him back repeatedly to his rural retreat. He sides with Sitting Bull in a desperate effort to salvage the American Dream. He had driven to Las Vegas in 1972 'to find the American Dream'. 'The trial of Richard Nixon, if it happens,' he wrote in 1974, 'will amount to a *de facto* trial of the American Dream.' He was

154

a McGovern man and a McCarthy man on the long haul from the Haight-Ashbury in the mid-1960s to Aspen, Colorado; and in Aspen, during the Nixon trauma, Thompson built his final hedge against despair and alienation.

But never *apathy*. His famous trip to Las Vegas, he was at pains to emphasize, had been

> a classic affirmation of everything right and true and decent in the national character. It was a gross, physical salute to the fantastic *possibilities* of life in this country—but only for those with true grit.

His journalistic essays on political themes from McGovern to Carter and popular themes from Marlon Brando to Muhammad Ali, form a hymn of hate to everything for which the United States were heading when it broke with the British connection—above all, Nixon. Again and again he returns to that

> monument to all the rancid genes and broken chromosomes that corrupt the possibilities of the American Dream; he was a foul caricature of himself, a man with no soul, no inner convictions, with the integrity of a hyena and the style of a poison toad. The Nixon I remember was absolutely humourless; I couldn't imagine him laughing at anything except maybe a paraplegic who wanted to vote Democratic but couldn't quite reach the lever on the voting machine.

That is pure Gonzo. Unadulterated Gonzo. Or as Muhammad Ali once put it: 'My way of joking is to tell the truth. That's the funniest joke in the world.'

9

The Big Splash: Hemingway and Scott Fitzgerald

Hemingway was long revered for his style. But there were two Hemingway styles. Behind the clipped control of his published work lurked a compulsive chatterbox and gossip. Only on the publication of his letters did this vulnerable, expansive, essentially isolated side of his character fully emerge. For Hemingway fell victim to a peculiarly Puritan insistence on a split between work and play, tension and relaxation. His fiction was assessed by daily word counts. Days of 1,200 or 2,700 were something that made him happier than you could believe; if he had only 320 he felt good. The ideal was trim and spare. Epic, he informed Maxwell Perkins in 1945, was usually false; for an epic note was impossible for anyone to sustain. It was no accident, he claimed, that the Gettysburg address was so short. The laws of prose writing were as immutable as the laws of flight.

But letters were a by-product; so they could be as voluminous as he liked. For he conflated the Puritan ethos with that of the romantic or creative artist. He agonized over his work in the tiniest homoeopathic doses. Yet with all the emphasis on artistry and workmanship and professionalism, he could not spell and had difficulties with his grammar. 'His position', Carlos Baker writes, 'was that one could always hire people to correct such minor slips. There was also a suspicion that unreined language might just possibly have a life of its own beyond accepted rules.' The spontaneous artist, in other words, was above such details. Yet even the spontaneity was a pose. His laconic avoidance of grandiloquence became notorious. 'Hemingway Choctaw' they called it. Lillian Ross gave some examples in her *New Yorker* profile of Hemingway on vacation in Manhattan. On being ushered into a hotel room he said, 'Joint looks okay.' After a visit to the Metropolitan Museum of Art, he muttered, 'Was fun for country boy like me.' At lunch, chewing vigorously, he asserted, 'Eat good and digest good.' His habitual speech became that of a messenger boy who had read too many telegrams.

It was a confused, self-contradictory performance of which he was all too aware. From his earliest years he had toyed with German or Jewish parodies of his name. 'The greatest of the Hemingsteins' (1918) he called himself, 'Jeremiah Hemingstein the great Jewish Prophet' (1929), 'Ernst von Hemingstein' (1952), just as in the 1920s already he had adopted the name 'Papa'. He needed such nicknames not merely to bolster his ego, but to distance himself from himself. Another way was to reduce everything to numbers. His word counts, his fish catch, his weight, his blood-pressure, his sales, his royalties, his bank balance, his taxes, were plotted in log books, cheque books, or on bathroom walls. The whole performance became a parody of his own youthful self. His boyish attitudes to honour, honesty, courage, ossified to a code. To use a favourite phrase, picked up (he claimed) on the Wind River reservation:

> 'You Indian Boy?'
> 'Sure.'
> 'Cheyenne?'
> 'Sure.'
> 'Long time ago good, now heap shit.'

For he loved the low-down, sneaky, malicious detail. 'Am always a perfectly safe man to tell any dirt to', he wrote John Dos Passos, 'as it goes in one ear and out of my mouth.' He was no duffer at backbiting himself. He was so often lonely, bored, stuck in isolated places: Idaho, Cuba, Pamplona, Key West. People who specifically got his goat in later years included Franklin D. Roosevelt, Field-Marshal Montgomery, General Jacques Leclerc, André Malraux, Cardinal Spellman and Senator Joe McCarthy. They were all 'jerks'. Literary jerks included Lionel Trilling, Saul Bellow, Truman Capote, Jean Stafford, Wyndham Lewis, and eventually Edmund Wilson and Gertrude Stein:

> Sherwood [Anderson] was like a jolly but tortured bowl of puss turning into a woman in front of your eyes. Stein was a nice woman until she had change of life and opted for fags and fags alone. . . . Faulkner gives me the creeps.

Frogs, wops and kikes abound. Many contemporaries, like E. M. Forster and Virginia Woolf, he simply could not understand.

Yet he wrote to be liked, as if his letters were pleas for understanding. Assiduously he played the rôle of family man. Anyone married to him (he claimed) ate regularly, got fucked when they wished, and had a fairly interesting life. But he needed male friends to *share* that life. He needed to show off as the insider who knew the answers, the James Bond stuff: how to win at roulette or horse racing or poker; how to get from Paris to Montreux, from Chicago to Horton Bay, from New York to Nairobi; how to make a Bloody Mary, outbox an adversary, outfox a customs officer. He had the 'dope' or (in an R.A.F. term which he preferred) the 'gen'. 'The *true* gen is what they know but don't tell you. The true gen very hard to obtain.'

He himself liked to spin yarns. His letters comprise a vast epistolary fiction, as he declared to Bernard Berenson:

> Writers of fiction are only super-liars who if they know enough and are disciplined can make their lies truer than the truth. If you have fought and diced and served at court and gone to the wars and know navigation, sea-manship, the bad world and the great world and the different countries and other things then you have good knowledge to lie out of. That is all a writer of fiction is.

The voracity and self-conviction are endearing. From his earliest days as cub-reporter he was having 'a swell lot of fun' with 'a dandy bunch of fellows'; he always had a clear idea of his merits, though his mind became increasingly clouded by paranoia about pederasts and Lesbians. By his fiftieth birthday he had really hit his big-headed, pushy stride. Herzog-like, he began composing vitriolic letters (probably

158

never sent) to distinguished contemporaries. 'Am very snobbish Charley', he wrote to Charles Scribner.

> Always try not to be and hate all false snobs. But the true snobbery of fighting people and gambling people and people who do not give a shit is what makes White's fun and Boodle's faintly chicken shit and all the others just beautifully run imitations of where the gentry go. The gentry has always been those who didn't give a god-damn. It has nothing to do with where you went to school (the poor bastards suffer and sweat that out). Jerks get into White's. But everybody knows they are jerks and they are tolerated, snubbed, or ignored. The real gentry are almost as tough as the really good gangsters.

There were streaks of crudity and cruelty about him. Even fiction became a punch-up, trying for 'Mr. Turgenieff', trying for 'Mr. Maupassant (won't concede him the de) and it took four of the best stories to beat him'. But he knew quite well that he was outrageous. It was both bragging and a send-up of bragging. *The Wound and the Bow* upset him. He flinched from Edmund Wilson's 'shit about hidden wounds'.

> Why doesn't he say what the mysterious thing is? Could it be that my father shot himself? Could it be that I did not care, overly, for my mother? Could it be that I have been shot twice through the scrotam (*sic*) and through the right hand, left hand, right foot and left foot and through both knees and the head?

For even in his lifetime he had become a subject of academic study in the United States, joining Washington Irving, Hawthorne, Poe, Mark Twain, Henry James and Sherwood Anderson into school anthologies. A particular focus was *In Our Time* (1925), Hemingway's third publication but first real book. The model, he informed Scott Fitzgerald, had been Anderson's *Winesburg, Ohio*: in other moods he gestured vaguely in the direction of Cézanne. By that time, of course, he was sitting at the feet of Gertrude Stein and it was none other than Pound who originally introduced him to *The Little Review*. Uncle Ez's tutorial pencil links *The Waste Land* to *In Our Time*. But an older mentor, surely, was Tolstoy. From Tolstoy he learnt that loose correlation of war and peace which, for a post-war generation, he transposed to rituals of public violence (of Chicago gangsters, Spanish bullfighters and prison executions) juxtaposed with the feuds, shifts and evasions of domestic life.

But there are basically three collections of Hemingway stories: *In Our Time, Men Without Women* (1927) and *Winner Take Nothing* (1933), together with 'The Short Happy Life of Francis Macomber' and 'The Snows of Kilimanjaro'. All were written in two great creative surges, from 1923–27 and 1933–36. But the heartland of Hemingway's storytelling is the Nick Adams saga. Hemingway eventually published sixteen stories with Nick Adams as the protagonist; eight others were published posthumously; and half a dozen more could be placed in the Nick Adams chronology. When in 1972 Philip Young collected the complete *Nick Adams Stories* into a single volume, it became clearer than ever that the controlling centre of all Hemingway's work was missing. Nick Adams is the first avatar of a series of fictional spokesmen who resemble their creator: Jake Barnes, Frederic Henry, Richard Cantwell and Thomas Hudson. All these, as Philip Young pointed out, were to have 'part of Nick's history' behind them and 'correspondingly, part of Hemingway's'.

But Hemingway never composed this key book of autobiographical fiction. All that remains is a debris of charged fragments. This may seem odd for a self-avowed professional who despised all colleagues—both journalists and athletes—who had never bothered, as he put it, to learn their trade. What he achieved were marvellous one-act sketches. The larger architecture was lacking. Perhaps his professional base was too limited. 'Watch what happens today', he told a young writer on a fishing trip in 1930:

> If we get into a fish see exactly what it is that everyone does. If you get a kick out of it while he is jumping remember back until you see exactly what the action was that gave you the emotion. Then write it down making it clear so the reader will see it too and have the same feeling that you had.

Perhaps the emotional seeds of self-doubt and self-pity from which he developed his fictional dramas were too slight. What is clear is that the seed-bed remained obstinately in the past—in the experiences of his young manhood before the final break with Michigan.

Then in 1921, on his return to Europe, questions of

technique became uppermost. But as Frank O'Connor pointed out:

> The real trouble with Hemingway is that he so often has to depend upon his splendid technical equipment to cover up material that is trivial or sensational. For much of the time his stories illustrate a technique in search of a subject. In the general sense of the word Hemingway has no subject.

Or again:

> Hemingway . . . is always a displaced person; he has no place to bring his treasures to. There are times when one feels that Hemingway, like the character in his own 'A Clean Well-Lighted Placed', is afraid of staying at home with a subject. In his stories one is forever coming upon that characteristic setting of the café, the station restaurant, the waiting room, or the railway carriage—clean, well-lighted, utterly anonymous places. The characters, equally anonymous, emerge suddenly from the shadows where they have been lurking, perform their little scene, and depart again into shadows.

For Hemingway shirked his American testament, his 'Education of Nicholas Adams', his first authentic book. Though obsessed with his mother, he could not confront his mother. She had soured him. It was Grace Hemingway who was the prototype of Mrs. Adams in 'The Doctor and the Doctor's Wife' and 'Now I Lay Me'. It was Grace who had dressed her little Ernest in gingham dresses as a twin for Marcelline. It was Grace who dismissed her son's first novel, *The Sun Also Rises*, with 'I can't stand filth!' As Philip Young noted: 'Almost nothing Hemingway ever wrote could be set in Oak Park; it is extremely doubtful that he could have written a "wonderful novel" about the place. . . . In the overall adventure, life became an escape to reality'—away from Michigan to Italy, to France, to Spain, to East Africa, Cuba or Florida, each another and more desperate variant of what Huck Finn called 'the territory' beyond matriarchal civilization.

Male comradeship in the hunt implied relaxed self-fulfilment: female partnership of sex implied tense male abnegation. 'Once a man's married', as Bill put it in 'The Three-Day Blow', 'he's absolutely bitched. He hasn't got anything more. Nothing. Not a damn thing. He's done for.' Everything of value lies in independent, dominant virility—in that world of 'Men without Women'. For Hemingway from the start played the frontier hero, neither Indian exactly nor Indian-lover, but a pioneering mock-Indian. Thus his edgy oblique view from the sidelines on the making or marring of any brand of Americanism. In *The Torrents of Spring* he flirts with, but refuses to surrender to, Indian lore and sexuality, just as elsewhere he flirts with, but refuses to surrender to, its complement: the all-male communion of the Indian hunter. He remained the eternal boy scout, drawn to the bean-feast and beyond to the pastoral utopia of the prairie or the literary utopia of Paris, but with his own tensions undermining any social or political resolution outside the camp-fire circle of his temporary and ever-shifting bivouac.

Lloyd Arnold, guide and tracker for Sun Valley Lodge, Idaho, knew him as well as anyone. Hemingway visited Sun Valley off and on for twenty years. In 1959 he finally bought his own home on Big Wood River to the north of Ketchum. What clinched his loyalty—more than the elk and antelope, partridge and mallard duck—was a warm and increasingly intimate friendship with Lloyd Arnold. It brought out the best in Hemingway as sportsman and comrade, far from literary editors and academic critics. 'Pappy' Arnold, in his turn, did more than store Papa Hemingway's Model 70 Winchester, old Springfield and Colt target revolver, he became his shadow. From the start he was aware that the big man was watching him as much as he was watching the big man. In a way each was consciously using the other.

Even their use of publicity was mutual. Hemingway promised an article on Idaho's shotgunning for *Esquire*; Robert Capa came over to do a photographic story for *Life*; and Arnold himself eventually joined the Los Angeles public relations office for Sun Valley. *For Whom the Bell Tolls*, from typescript to movie, in a sense was a product of local promotion. Movie locations were a lucrative business for the resort; and Hemingway himself suggested that Adams Gulch, west of Big Wood River, be photographed for a possible Hollywood deal. It was at the Trail Creek Cabin that Gary Cooper and Ingrid Bergman were first suggested for the rôles of Robert Jordan and Maria. 'There was no bigger sucker for fine leather than Papa Hemingway', reports Pappy Arnold; and the man who loved the ancient hunting range of the Shoshoni was aware of his own ambivalence as sportsman-journalist-novelist. He was startled, nevertheless, when an old-time mountain man looked him up and down, from battered Stetson, worn Afrikaner style, to round-toed cowboy boots, and asked: 'Ernie, you write Westerns?' Or on another occasion, in a local bar, when a loud-mouthed dude turned and asked whether 'he had high-altitude, dry-air trouble, or did he wear the beard for effect?' Pappy Arnold must have represented some kind of Western ideal: brought up on a ranch in the Oklahoma-Texas panhandle, not Oak Park, Illinois; with older brothers, not sisters; without the need to apologize for a domineering mother or a father's suicide. 'True, it was a cowardly thing for my father to do', Hemingway told him in 1939,

> but then, if you don't live behind the eyes you can't expect to see all of the view. I know that part of his view, and I suppose he was mixing it up some . . . and you do such a thing only when you are tortured beyond endurance, like in war, from an incurable disease, or when you hasten a drowning, because you can't swim all of the sea.

'You get over everything but death', he told Charles Scribner in 1949, 'and death is shit too.'

James Aldridge, in *One Last Glimpse*, probed that torture, that endurance, that point of view. By juxtaposing Hemingway and Fitzgerald, he posited a morality of two contrasted and interlocking types: the literary prize-fighter, aiming always for the kill, and the literary drunk, aiming for failure. On it he constructed a whole theory of literature:

> 'You know the weakness in your theory, Ernest?'
> 'What theory?' Hemingway said. 'I don't believe in theories.'
> "You're teaching Kit observation, but you're wrong. It's what you bring to things that counts. Not what you actually see.'
> 'You're crazy', Hemingway said. 'You have to see what you see, don't you?'

163

'No', Scott said. 'You're telling him to start with the obvious, which is like telling him to stare like an ape at a blank brick wall.'

'Don't even listen to him, kid', Hemingway said to me. 'Just look for the obvious. It's the skin of the world.'

Thus runs this modern battle of the books: of Hemingway-type observation versus the Fitzgerald-type observer; of the professional hunter versus the priest as saviour; of the thick skin versus moral fibre. What Aldridge was exploring is that crisis of creativity when the public performance threatens to stifle the private, the invention to strangle the inventor. The Hemingway answer, in this equation, is one of self-conscious repression; the Fitzgerald answer, one of self-conscious expression. Both are based on fear; and both, he argues, are suicidal.

Fitzgerald was a loyal man—loyal to his publisher, his friends, his literary passions from Conrad to Gertrude Stein's *The Making of Americans*, all of which he freely shared with his editor, Maxwell Perkins. It was Fitzgerald who first introduced Radiguet to Scribner's in 1924; and this education continued to his last extant letter (13 December 1940): 'Kafka was an extraordinary Czechoslovakian Jew who died in '36. He will never have a wide public but "the Trial" and "Amerika" are two books that writers are never able to forget.' (Perkins admitted he knew nothing about Kafka, but would look him up.) The introduction of one 'Ernest Hemmingway' with a 'brilliant future' was part of that same education. What Fitzgerald could not have realized in 1924 was how closely his own life's graph was to be interlinked with his. As usual, though, Fitzgerald was wholly percipient:

> One time I had a talk with Ernest Hemingway, and I told him, against all the logic that was then current, that I was the tortoise and he was the hare, and that's the truth of the matter, that everything that I have ever attained has been through long and persistent struggle while it is Ernest who has a touch of genius which enables him to bring off extraordinary things with facility. I have no facility. I have a facility for being cheap, if I wanted to indulge that. I can do cheap things. (March 1934)

But to trace the upward curve of the hare and the downward spiral of the tortoise is like witnessing some medieval morality, presided over by Fortune. With that wounding jibe in 'The Snows of Kilimanjaro' and jeers at Scott's alcoholism, Hemingway's star continued in its ascendant to the final triumph of *For Whom the Bell Tolls*.

'There are no second acts in American lives', Fitzgerald had written; yet he himself had gone west in 1937 not just for the money—like Faulkner and Nathanael West, and most of the English colony for that matter—but to write movies. In Hollywood perhaps he could begin a second, lucrative, glamorous act, achieving on screen the golden moment that had failed him in fiction. There had been earlier visits to Hollywood—in 1927 with Zelda, and again alone in 1931. Yet not until 1968, when a research student penetrated the 'morgue' below Metro-Goldwyn-Mayer, where cardboxes the size of coffins had lain undisturbed for three decades, was it possible to asssess Fitzgerald's true rôle in the Californian film capital. Legends of party-going, drunken sprees, of Sheilah Graham and *The Last Tycoon*, had obscured the real day-to-day work on screen plays whose notes, endless memos and letters now came trundling up to the Thalberg Building.

Aaron Latham went on to interview Fitzgerald's daughter, his agent, and some contemporary Hollywood stars and writers, returning east to the Princeton rare-book room to mull over the rest of Fitzgerald's scripts written for Selznick International, Twentieth Century-Fox, United Artists, etc. The effect is sobering—the contemplation of a melancholy waste. Those last precious years, from 1937 to 1940, like his earliest years at Princeton, were again more noteworthy for promise than for achievement. The scripts he worked over sound resonant enough—*The Women, Madame Curie, Cosmopolitan* (years later made into *The Last Time I Saw Paris*), and a last verbal manicuring of *Gone with the Wind*. But in all those years Fitzgerald received only one screen credit, for a verbose treatment of Erich Maria Remarque's *Three Comrades*, and then two-thirds of his script had been cut. Yet it was voted one of the ten best pictures of 1938 and Fitzgerald got a raise from $1,000 to a fabulous $1,250 a week.

But only the money was fabulous. That golden dream-lot, like any industry, was agog with in-fighting and Machiavellian intrigue and counterplot. At which the Irish Prince Charming

proved pathetically innocent. When he got his one genuine
chance at a film, for which he cared as deeply as he had cared
for *The Great Gatsby*, he ran slap into the brick wall of sexual
prurience and propriety known as the Hays Office. The film,
to star Joan Crawford, was to be called *Infidelity*. It had an
almost wordless sound-track. The vogue for restored silence
had recently grown in response to the constant jabbering of
the new 'talkies'. Fitzgerald's treatment of a husband's
adultery against a backdrop of expensive New York houses
and Long Island estates might have seemed modern in the
post-war cinema dominated by French and Italian directors;
but Hunt Stromberg was no Antonioni. This dream-landscape
of infidelity—originally sparked off by Zelda's 1924 affair with
a French aviator—sounded like fantasy; and photography was
a realistic art. That was Hollywood's golden rule: fantasies
don't make money. Stromberg also knew the Hollywood code:
even a coy change of title to *Fidelity* could not slip it past
Joseph Breen's 'Legion of Decency'. After three months
Fitzgerald was taken off the story. Yet again the legendary
slob, bum, drunk had overrated the creative intelligence of
Hollywood, as in *The Last Tycoon* he was to overrate its
commanding genius, Irving Thalberg. Not that Fitzgerald was
too good for Hollywood; it was only that Hollywood cared
nothing for Conrad or Thackeray. Though Fitzgerald tried, it
could not usefully employ him.

Yet Fitzgerald's fiction really has surprisingly little to do
with the bedroom. For all his emancipation he seems closer at
times to the nostalgic conservatism of Edith Wharton—even
the gentility of Booth Tarkington—than to most of his other
contemporaries. Everything he wrote was autobiographical in
one way or another. His whole fiction was an imaginative
extension of himself. Like *Walden*, like *Moby-Dick*, Fitzgerald's
oeuvre may be claimed as archetypally American in two
respects: it was fathered by an extreme romantic ideology of
self; it was conceived as literature of yearning quest whose goal
is unreached and unreachable. Anthony and Gloria Patch,
Gatsby, Dick Diver, Monroe Stahr—all are doomed. The
American dream is inevitably turned to nightmare. For what
is doomed is precisely that search for values.

There is something sweet-and-sour about Fitzgerald. He

himself argued (against Hemingway) for his 'composite' characters: part calculating, part naïve. First comes the romantic innocent, the dreamer, Gatsby, 'Mr. Nobody from Nowhere', who is also Scott, the spoiled playboy. Linked to him, as Eng to Chang, is the moral commentator, Nick Carraway of *The Great Gatsby*. Blurred to a single entity he is Dick Diver of *Tender is the Night*, as well as Fitzgerald, the dedicated artist, essayist, salon Marxist. The single object of their joint obsession is the Golden Girl, the belle, the flapper, the flirt, the 'baby vamp'. As Bitch Goddess of the Golden West, she embodies the white, virgin emptiness of a virgin land. She is Ginevra King; she is Zelda, arrogant, careless, irresponsible, pampered. She is the ideal prize, combining Beauty, Health, Youth and Wealth. Metaphors abound of vampire and prey, of candle and moth. For this Golden Girl of the American Dream is La Belle Dame Sans Merci—both Morgan le Fay and Fata Morgana, both hunted enchantress and mirage. ('The Beautiful Lady Without Mercy' was among the early rejected titles of *The Beautiful and Damned*. Daisy Buchanan, née Fay, became the heroine of *The Great Gatsby*.)

Thus a whole line of temptresses can be drawn, from Henry James's Daisy Miller and Edith Wharton's Lily Bart (those flowers of American girlhood) to Fitzgerald's Fay and Nabokov's Lolita. These daisies are all bright and laundered white around a sun's golden eye. Now pinnacled skyscrapers, rather than castle penthouses, cradle their slumbering beauties. But it is never the naïve Adam who awakens and wins them. It is a Tom (fleshy, virile, ex-football-star of *The Great Gatsby*) whose *droit de seigneur* over Daisy is ironically crowned by the Olympic Myrtle (his sentimental, tasteless whore). Thus the Fitzgerald plot is one of betrayal. The innocent is betrayed by his own naïvety and the girl to whom he has dedicated his whole identity. Such was the national experience of the United States. The entire history of America, concludes Nick Carraway in the final paragraphs of *The Great Gatsby*, is the history of doomed dreams 'borne back ceaselessly into the past'. 'Gatsby believed in the green light, the orgiastic future that year by year recedes before us.' But 'orgastic' is what Fitzgerald had really intended. 'Orgastic', he explained to Maxwell Perkins, 'is the adjective for "orgasm" and it

expresses exactly the intended ecstasy. It's not a bit dirty.'
The *idea* of America, he wished to indicate, was an infinitely
extended sexual trauma, whose martyr he was, whose wounds
he bore. Not for nothing had he been named after the author of
'The Star-Spangled Banner', his great-great-great-grand-
uncle, Francis Scott Key. The title he really wanted for *The
Great Gatsby*—though too late to change the plates—was
'Under the Red, White, and Blue'.

The riskiest years had been those spent with Gerald and
Sara Murphy, expatriates extraordinary in Paris, France, and
at the Villa America on Cap d'Antibes. Tragedy was to strike
later when a tubercular son and mental breakdown were to
reunite the Murphys and Fitzgeralds in Switzerland. But for a
few golden years of Irish-American hospitality the whole
contemporary bandwaggon (Picasso, Cocteau, Hemingway,
the Fitzgeralds, Léger, Dos Passos, Archibald MacLeish)
passed through the Villa America. There sat Picasso's mother
in black amid the beaded swim-suits; there posed her son with
a fig-leaf pinned to his swimming trunks; Cole Porter jostled
Rudolph Valentino; and Hemingway was giving his son
'Bumby' a piggy-back on the beach. But the most vulnerable,
uneasy partners were Zelda and Scott. Their escapades that
summer of 1926 are now notorious; they had rented a villa in
Juan-les-Pins and the two couples were often together. But out
of that self-destructive, tormenting bravado was to grow *Tender
is the Night* and Zelda's *Save Me the Waltz*.

Zelda, New York's *prima* flapper *assoluta*, in all else felt
herself to be a failure. As a novelist's wife she desperately
sought success in painting, ballet, and finally, during a
nervous breakdown in the Johns Hopkins Hospital in
Baltimore, in fiction, too. But 'by the time a person has
achieved years adequate for choosing a direction,' she wrote,

> the die is cast and the moment has long since passed which
> determined the future. We grew up founding our dreams on the
> infinite promise of American advertising. I *still* believe that one
> can learn to play the piano by mail and that mud will give a
> perfect complexion.

She was to learn not by mail, as it turned out, but from her
husband. The Fitzgeralds' courtship, from the start, had been

under fictional pressure. If Zelda's favourite character was Becky Sharp, Scott's certainly was to be Zelda. Her words, her letters, her actions all supplied his 'copy'. As she wrote, reviewing *The Beautiful and Damned* under her maiden name:

> It also seems to me that on one page I recognized a portion of an old diary of mine which mysteriously disappeared shortly after my marriage, and also scraps of letters, which, though considerably edited, sound to me vaguely familiar. In fact, Mr. Fitzgerald—I believe that is how he spells his name—seems to believe that plagiarism begins at home.

She herself, in 1922, published a *Eulogy on the Flapper*. For she *was* the original flapper, the southern belle from Montgomery, Alabama, transported by her fairy prince (first lieutenant in the 67th Infantry) to 'all that glamour and loneliness' of New York. New York itself was a fictional sphere where her Midwestern prince (from St. Paul, Minnesota) had proved his royal estate—proved it to the tune of $50,000 spent, with reckless Irish abandon, in two years.

But if 'Zelda' was so much 'raw material' for Scott, what of Zelda herself? 'What shall *Zelda* do?' became the refrain of their early marriage. Obviously she could not write—obviously to Scott, that is; for she was *his* literary property. But could she paint? Could she act? Could she dance? What could a gay, daredevil, spoilt, eternal 'Baby' of the family *do* once she had married her handsome lover? She could still be a feminist perhaps of the kind, less common today, who dislikes most women. She could still, she hoped, be a flapper. 'I refer', she wrote,

> to the right to experiment with herself as a transient, poignant figure who will be dead tomorrow. Women, despite the fact that nine out of ten of them go through life with a death-bed air either of snatching-the-last-moment or with martyr-resignation, do not die tomorrow—or the next day. They have to live on to any one of many bitter ends.

Das Ewig-Weibliche was to be linked to her own self-promotion campaign.

So the dangerous years in Manhattan or the Riviera, in Paris or Baltimore, began. A golden youth—riding astride the hoods of taxis or diving into the fountain at Union Square—

turned rapidly to a gilded charade. Who was afraid of Zelda Fitzgerald? While Scott was writing *The Great Gatsby* in St. Raphaël, Zelda flirted with the young French aviator. After his departure and her first suicide attempt the romance itself became a turn, a joint recital, one of their acts together. As Hemingway's first wife, Hadley, recalled:

> Scott would stand next to her looking very pale and distressed and sharing every minute of it. Somehow it struck me as something that gave her status. I can still see both of them standing together telling me about the suicide of Zelda's lover. It created a peculiar effect.

The shocking young couple, dressed in matching white knickerbocker suits, had begun to shock each other. Both needed the limelight; both needed an artistic outlet; both settled for the same romantic credo: 'You took what you wanted from life, if you could get it, and you did without the rest' (*Save Me the Waltz*). As early as 1922 Scott had recognized, in a letter to Edmund Wilson, that 'the most enormous influence on me in the four and a half years since I met her has been the complete, fine and full-hearted selfishness and chill-mindedness of Zelda.'

Rebecca West, oddly, remembers her as 'very plain' with a 'certain craggy homeliness'. The photographs and later self-portrait confirm the haunted look of the strange eyes, almost masculine in their directness. Gerald Murphy compared her to an American Indian. She ruminated, rather than conversed, aloud: 'Gerald, don't you think that Al Jolson is just like Christ?' Or, more perversely, when introduced: 'I hope you die in the marble ring.' For the crack-up was Zelda's before it was Scott Fitzgerald's. She became tense, watchful, withdrawn. The long, self-destructive dive began in the 1920s only to end in 1948, in that ordeal by fire in an Asheville asylum.

Whatever American quest was theirs, fact and fiction had become inextricably entangled. A flight to stardom had become a contest for personal survival. The parties, the drinking bouts continued. Scott invited a Paris taxi-driver and ex-boxer to be his chauffeur; Zelda indulged her Pavlova complex, her untiring need to prove herself a ballerina. Up on the stage she seemed taller, more muscular, almost grotesque in her intensity. In this new version of 'Modern Love', the wife seemed betrayed by the creative act, her literary husband by his 'model', and neither was content to play cuckold or avenger. It was a dual failure; and in all their suffering and resentment both, at heart, knew this. Beneath the bitter self-torment, they needed and loved one another. For it was not only his identity, his laughter that became unhinged. It was Zelda who grabbed the steering-wheel of their car along the Grande Corniche and tried to put them over the cliff. It was Zelda who was finally offered a solo rôle in *Aida* with the San Carlo Opera Ballet Company in Naples (and turned it down). It was Zelda who first collapsed, to be removed for extensive psychiatric treatment on the shores of Lake Geneva. It is in those strange, intense letters from the asylum that Zelda at last seems to come into her own. Some hidden element is revealed, beyond the most Jamesian construct of art:

> Then the world became embryonic in Africa—and there was no need for communication. The Arabs fermenting in the vastness; the curious quality of their eyes and the smell of ants; a detachment as if I was on the other side of a black gauze—a fearless small feeling, and then the end at Easter. . . .

That was 1930. Wall Street had crashed; the jazz decade was finished. The diagnosis: schizophrenia.

The Swiss asylum appeared a resort hotel. But here the Alabama belle—the eponymous gypsy queen of her mother's dreams—was stripped of husband, child, career. Like some female Job, she developed a severe eczema that covered her face, neck and shoulders. As Scott was trapped, she was trapped. Alcoholism or madness: they seemed two sides of a single complex, demanding a joint diagnosis. But Scott was on the outside; she, on the inside. As he asserted himself, she began a softer pleading:

> I believed I was a Salamander and it seems that I am nothing but an impediment. . . . *Please* help me. Every day more of me dies with this bitter and incessant beating I'm taking.

Or later from Baltimore:

> The only message I ever thought I had was four pirouettes and a fouetté. It turned out to be about as cryptic a one as [a] Chinese laundry ticket, but the will to speak remains.

What Scott had loved, what many had sensed in her, now swells and blooms into myriad disturbing details. For all her outward inferiority, there is a growing self-confidence in her verbal, visionary powers:

> I want to fly a kite and eat green apples and have a stomach-ache that I know the cause of and feel the mud between my toes in a reedy creek and tickle the lobe of your ear with the tip of my tongue.

It is the world of Sylvia Plath's *The Bell-Jar*; and out of it grew her one completed novel.

On seeing *Save Me the Waltz*, Scott exploded. Zelda had invaded his literary dream. For four years, he wrote to her doctor, he had been forced to work on his novel (*Tender is the Night*), 'unable to proceed because of the necessity of keeping Zelda in sanitariums'. Zelda had heard 50,000 words of his novel and

> literally one whole section of her novel is an imitation of it, of its rhythm, materials ... there are only two episodes, both of which she has reduced to anecdotes, *but upon which whole sections of my book turn*, that I have asked her to cut.

He was now living in a state of 'mild masturbation and a couple of whiskeys to go on'. On his visits he grew insulting when Zelda refused to show him a story. She was exploiting her relation to do him harm. He grew hysterical, obsessive in his resentment, writing to her doctor:

> I will probably be carried off eventually by four strong guards shrieking manicly that after all I was right and she was wrong, while Zelda is followed home by an adoring crowd in an automobile banked with flowers, and offered a vaudeville contract.

By 1933 Scott felt the marriage had destroyed him. A 114-page clinical transcript of one of their wounding word-battles makes terrifying reading:

SCOTT: It is a perfectly lonely struggle that I am making against other writers who are finely gifted and talented. You are a third rate writer and a third rate ballet dancer.

ZELDA: You have told me that before.

SCOTT: I am a professional writer, with a huge following. I am the highest paid short story writer in the world. I have at various times dominated . . .

ZELDA: It seems to me you are making a rather violent attack on a third rate talent then.

SCOTT: Everything we have done is my . . . I am the professional novelist, and I am supporting you. That is all my material. None of it is your material.

Long ago, in Paris, Zelda had accused Scott of a homosexual liaison with Ernest Hemingway. She had called him a 'fairy'. Now he hit back. Yet their polarities—of male intuition and female watchfulness—continued to reach out for one another. Their nerves remained entwined like roots and branches of two trees. Zelda needed Scott to shape her life and art, though his ambitions undermined hers; Scott needed Zelda for a zest that gave meaning to his life, though her restlessness undermined him. Not till he met Sheilah Graham (another Zelda in looks and vitality) could he begin his last major novel. Though Zelda's stage intermittently continued to shrink and darken, an inward illumination, a mature calm began to appear.

But Scott, of course, went on to further successes, whereas Zelda's novel was a flop, her farce was a flop, her paintings seemed a flop. She was never confined, 'committed' in a legal sense; she had always gone to hospital of her own free will and so had to be released on request. For four years a continent divided them; for a final six Zelda outlived him, writing, painting—herself a grandmother now—in a small white-frame bungalow shared with her mother. Now no collegiate beaux, but admirers of F. Scott Fitzgerald visited her from college. Life had come full circle, bringing the fairy-tale princess back to Alabama, the 'Baby' home.

They were buried side by side; but from beyond their grave the chorus of marital pleading and recrimination still resounds. Was Scott 'her great reality, often the only liaison agent who could make the world tangible to her', as he claimed in 1936? or was he reversing their rôles, as he had admitted three years earlier?

> In the last analysis, she is a stronger person than I am. I have creative fire, but I am a weak individual. She knows this and really looks upon me as a woman. All our lives, since the days of our engagement, we have spent hunting for some man Zelda considers strong enough to lean upon. I am not.

To their daughter, the fruit of their marriage, he paradoxically announced:

> The mistake I made was in marrying her. We belonged to different worlds—she might have been happy with a kind simple man in a southern garden. She didn't have the strength for the big stage—sometimes she pretended, and pretended beautifully, but she didn't have it.

10

A Southern Diptych: Faulkner and O'Connor

William Faulkner's life, in retrospect, seems singularly uneventful. What was lacking in adventure or high drama, however, was more than compensated for by a sly, secretive, devious, often absurd and unexpected fantasy. His very life style as Southern gentleman farmer was part of that fantasy. With the mounting pressure, even assault, on his personal privacy, he resisted prying critics as much as peeping Toms. PRIVATE was the notice literally and metaphorically posted round his real and literary estate. Poachers and other unwary trespassers in his woods confronted a flinty squire.

Faulkner kept them fooled. A potted biography, sent to *Forum* in 1930, ran:

> Born male and single at early age in Mississippi. Quit school after five years in seventh grade. Got job in Grandfather's bank and learned medicinal value of his liquor. Grandfather thought janitor did it. Hard on janitor.

Hard on his readers too. For if this self-proclaimed cross between a negro slave and an alligator reckoned to keep peeping Toms at bay, his novels were equally contrived to confound literary carpetbaggers from up North and overseas. Even his correspondence proves no revelation. It was not meant to. The wily novelist made sure of that. From his early days as postmaster at the University of Mississippi he resented the task of sorting and pigeonholing the mail that kept him from more creative work. 'I reckon I'll be at the beck and call of folks with money all my life', was his parting shot on

175

dismissal, 'but thank God I won't ever again have to be at the beck and call of every son of a bitch who's got two cents to buy a stamp.' That resentment was never forgotten. In 1944 he wrote to Malcolm Cowley:

> My mail consists of two sorts: from people who dont write, asking me for something, usually money, which being a serious writer trying to be an artist, I naturally dont have; and from people who do write telling me I cant. So, since I have already agreed to answer No to the first and All right to the second, I open the envelopes to get the return postage stamps (if any) and dump the letters into a desk drawer, to be read when (usually twice a year) the drawer overflows.

In his later years, admittedly, Faulkner somewhat relented. In 1956 he gave Jean Stein a celebrated interview for the *Paris Review*. Ten years earlier he had opened up to Cowley at work on *The Portable Faulkner*. More recently Oxford (Mississippi) folk have given close-up diverting glimpses of Faulkner as neighbour, hunter, balky local character and sage. Especially from his post-Nobel Prize years—when Faulkner made himself more openly available through the State Department to foreign audiences and at home to reporters or universities—speeches and tape-recordings and reminiscences accumulate in heaps that threaten to choke the living man, let alone that canny fabrication of myth and memories at his hidden centre.

For Faulkner's South was the old South. Caroline Barr, his 'mammy' (and his grandfather's and father's before him) to whom *Go Down, Moses* is dedicated, and whose funeral sermon he himself was to deliver, had been born a household slave: 'free these many years', he wrote, 'but who had declined to leave'. Such patriarchal relationships of affection, mutual welfare and trust he understood. He loved Mississippi, recording her history as an extension of his own family and personal biography: a completion in ever-widening circles of time and space—west to Old Man River, north to Memphis, south to the Delta (hunting country)—of his inmost self. He loved his state, despite the lynchings, the narrow folkways, the ever louder 'ringing of a cash register bell'—'loving all of it even while he had to hate some of it because . . . you love despite; not for the virtues, but despite the faults'. As an

18-year-old dandy, with an eye for clothes and a taste for drink, Billy Falkner was nicknamed 'the Count', or sometimes 'Count No 'Count'; and one consistent trait from those early days, when he was immersed in Keats and Swinburne and *The Shropshire Lad*, is the transcription of fact to fiction, identity to alibi, finally Oxford to Jefferson, Mississippi to Yoknapatawpha, in his single-minded career. Like a youthful parody of his own grandfather, Colonel William Falkner, with ramrod back and out-thrust jaw, he would outface the world.

The first metamorphosis was to an R.A.F. officer, returning from Canada after five months' training with trench-coat and officer's swagger-stick and British accent overlayering his Southern drawl. As well as a limp. He had flown his Sopwith Camel 'halfway through the top of a hangar' in one version; in another, 'landing upside down'. No evidence for such a crash, let alone his even flying, exists: self-dramatization and catastrophe were early linked. It was as Cadet Faulkner, no longer Billy Falkner, that he first grew that distinctive trademark of a moustache. His second metamorphosis to an aspiring poet, obscurely serving at the Doubleday bookstore in Fifth Avenue, New York, was more traditional. Still, it had to be done with Southern style. This new *persona* too—part hard-drinking planter, part wounded war ace—was no more successful in launching a career; and when he again retreated to Oxford as scoutmaster and postmaster to the University of Mississippi, he still had published nothing outside his home town. As 'Count Wilhelm von Faulkner, Marquis de Lafayette (County)' at the age of 26 he appeared in the pages of the *Mississippian*, a leisured bohemian who could draw in the style of Beardsley and write with a touch of Pater or Verlaine. A glass and a bottle of 'white lightning' might be produced from under the shirt of this elegant figure with the memorable line: 'There is no such thing as bad whiskey; some are just better than others.'

Hamilton Basso later recalled 'his beautiful manners, his soft speech, his controlled intensity, and his astonishing capacity for hard drink'. He was drinking so heavily that he had to be removed from the scout troop and finally from his sinecure at the post office. It was then, in December 1924, that his first book of poems appeared with the resounding title *The Marble Faun*. When it was pointed out that this was already the title of Nathaniel Hawthorne's novel, 'Who's Hawthorne?' was the reply. 'The title is original with me.' Meanwhile Elizabeth Prall, manager of the Doubleday bookstore, had married Sherwood Anderson and moved to New Orleans. There Faulkner joined her, armed with 'some six or eight half gallon jars of moon liquor' stowed in the pockets of his tweed overcoat. No longer a bohemian layabout, he reappeared as the ex-R.A.F. pilot and air-crash victim, sometimes limping with a cane, sometimes without; sometimes speaking in his Mississippi drawl, sometimes in clipped English-English. 'You can't expect much of Bill', was the general view, Anita Loos recalls, 'because he has that silver plate in his head and he isn't very smart.' The war-hero's drinking, it was said, alleviated the pain from his wounds.

Apart from side trips to Memphis, he had never been further afield than Greenwich Village and British Canada. It was in the Vieux Carré that Faulkner perfected his disguise as the complete Southerner: the dreamy, poetic, elegant, aristocratic, bellicose, hard-drinking, ambitious youth with Tom Sawyerish pretensions of quixotic gallantry. This also involved a new *persona* as boot-legger, supposedly running a launch from New Orleans across Lake Pontchartrain into the Gulf to pick up raw alcohol from Cuba. In July 1925 this bearded, bohemian, ex-R.A.F. boot-legger at last made his Grand Tour to Europe; and the following year *Soldier's Pay* was published. His father refused to open his son's first novel, while the library of the University of Mississippi declined a gift copy. Back at home, Mississippi had remained Mississippi: the success of the Oxford season being a fashion show of burial shrouds, modelled by a local gym instructress in a reclining posture. At least a generation's time-gap separated Europe from the American backwoods, still foundering in Celtic Twilight.

Flags in the Dust (retitled *Sartoris*) and *The Sound and the Fury* followed, evoking comparison with Dostoevsky, Joyce and Euripides. The stock market crash and the rise of William Faulkner's star were simultaneous. The young man with the boot-leg gin and jars of Crosse and Blackwell's marmalade in his capacious pockets became a celebrity. Richard Hughes was so excited that he persuaded Chatto and Windus to bring out Faulkner's first three titles in England. For the *Evening Standard* Arnold Bennett wrote:

> Faulkner is the coming man. He has inexhaustible invention, powerful imagination, a wondrous gift of characterisation, a finished skill in dialogue; and he writes generally like an angel. None of the arrived American stars can surpass him in style when he is at his best.

Two days later another reviewer for the *Evening Standard* ranked Faulkner above D. H. Lawrence and Hemingway. As early as 1931 Maurice Coindreau had introduced Faulkner to French readers in *La Nouvelle Revue Française*; Valery Larbaud and André Malraux contributed prefaces to *As I Lay Dying* and *Sanctuary*. While Jean-Paul Sartre, who had published an important essay-review of *The Sound and the Fury* before the war, was shocked, on visiting eastern colleges in America in 1946, to find so many students who had never so much as heard his name. In South America Jorge Luis Borges translated *The Wild Palms* shortly after its appearance in the United States.

Literary fantasy, however, was only one aspect of his essentially private needs, his inner shyness. Another was escape into drinking bouts, his 'collapses' as he called them. 'The bouts were usually deliberate', Joseph Blotner considers.

> Faulkner would ensure a sufficient supply of liquor. He would plan when he would start, and he would often plan when he would stop. John Faulkner thought these sessions were merely faked drunkenness—when Bill was bored, when he wanted to avoid work or to be waited on. On many occasions, however, they were not fakes but rather serious, prolonged, and debilitating illnesses.

These bouts would usually occur in reaction to intense creative effort. They might occur from two to four times a year, lasting maybe a week, a fortnight, or even a month and a half. Sometimes he was able to taper off; more frequently he needed to be dried out in hospital. He was 'not an alcoholic', as Robert Coughlan was later to remark, so much as 'an alcoholic refugee, self-pursued'. Like his fellow Southerner, Poe. 'A small head, very dark brown eyes', Cowley remembered later:

> One eyebrow goes up, the other down, and perhaps that is what
> gives him the resemblance to Poe. Hair lies close to his head
> and is ringleted like a Roman gentleman's. Very small hands
> and feet.

The bouts continued over a period of thirty years. Later in
Hollywood even his wife Estelle began to suffer from
alcoholism. Again and again he collapsed into comas on his
literary visits to New York. Again and again he suffered all the
withdrawal symptoms of insomnia, hallucination, delirium
tremens, with convulsive spasms and retching. But he had a
strong constitution. His appetite never failed; and even more
remarkable was his memory. He retained an acute awareness
of what was happening to him and was later able to remember
all his conversations during a period of intense drinking.

Sometimes fantasy merged with fact. By 1931 he was able to
write proudly home from New York:

> I have created quite a sensation. I have had luncheons in my
> honor by magazine editors every day for a week now, besides
> evening parties, or people who want to see what I look like. In
> fact, I have learned with astonishment that I am now the most
> important figure in American letters. That is, I have the best
> future. Even Sinclair Lewis and Dreiser make engagements to
> see me, and Mencken is coming all the way up from Baltimore
> Wednesday.

Or fact merged with fantasy. At home, at Rowan Oak, he was
able to take visitors round on local walks, pointing out the
road where Lena Grove had travelled, 'looking for the father of
her child'; stopping before an old barn 'where Popeye came to
life'; indicating a stream 'where the folks dropped the coffin in
As I Lay Dying'. Southeast lay Frenchman's Bend. That, he
said, 'is where Christmas hid for a while from those white folk
that were after him'. Or again, fantasy merged with fact when,
recalling the death of his week-old child Alabama, he claimed
to have fired at the doctor—either outside his office (in one
version), or outside his home when the doctor arrived too late
(in another).

But one fact could not be eased into fantasy. *Sanctuary*
continued to make money; he expected royalty cheques from
$4,000 to $6,500; but he never received a cent in cash. In

1931–32 his publishers went broke. At the height of the depression mounting debts confronted him. But then came his lucky break: a contract with Metro-Goldwyn-Mayer of Culver City at a salary of $500 a week. He was obliged to Howard Hawks for his *entrée* to Hollywood. There is a story Hawks liked to tell of a dove-shooting expedition when he and Faulkner were discussing contemporary literature. Their companion, Clark Gable, asked Faulkner whom he considered the best living writers. 'Ernest Hemingway, Willa Cather, Thomas Mann, John Dos Passos, and William Faulkner', Faulkner replied. 'Do you write, Mr. Faulkner?' asked Gable. 'Yes, Mr. Gable', Faulkner drawled. 'What do you do?' After twenty-two years in Hollywood and work on about forty-eight films, even Clark Gable could hardly have remained ignorant of the Nobel Prizeman in their midst. Faulkner worked at one time or another with Jean Renoir, Irving Thalberg, Derryl F. Zanuck, Nunnally Johnson and Jules Furthman. He even reworked a project first tackled in 1930 by Sergei Eisenstein. He collaborated, among other things, on *The Big Sleep, To Have and Have Not, The Southerner, The Road to Glory* and *Air Force*.

So began a long, yet profitable, labour in the Augean stables of Hollywood. Faulkner cleared $6,000 on the sale of *Sanctuary* to Paramount as *The Story of Temple Drake*. In July 1934 he accepted a salary of $1,000 a week from Universal Studios. In 1935 he shifted, at the same salary, to Twentieth-Century-Fox. *The Unvanquished* was sold to M.G.M. in 1938 for $25,000. Commuting annually back and forth between Southern California and Mississippi, he bought a farm near Oxford. A proud father at last, he had achieved his boyhood dream of landed property. But for most of the year, perforce, it still remained a dream. Nor did all go well in Hollywood. He was far too aloof, too idiosyncratic for that. In 1942 he signed a seven-year contract with Warner Bros., which increasingly weighed on him like a judicial sentence. He had had to settle for $300 a week, rising to $500. By 1944 he was deep in a script treatment of *To Have and Have Not*, working now for Jean Renoir, now with Humphrey Bogart and Ginger Rogers.

Those years with Warner's mark the end of his great creative phase. Never before had he truckled to a regular job or social discipline. The loner, the aloof observer had succumbed at last. As he had casually remarked in 1937 in an Irish bar on Third Avenue:

> Nothing will come if yo' haven't got the stuff. . . . It comes natural yo' know, or it doesn't come at all. Everything comes; the people, the place, the story, and yo' just act like the fella feeding the corn shucker. Keep moving about and filling.

The Hollywood stint must otherwise seem sheer madness for a writer who had astutely skirted most academic contacts in his impressionable years and still refused to have a wireless in his house. But that career raises further questions of the chicken-and-egg variety: which came first, an interest in cinematic techniques from the writings of Joyce, Eliot and Dos Passos, or an interest in literary techniques through the silent cinema? He had been a regular moviegoer as a child and still admired D. W. Griffith's *The Birth of a Nation*. Yet his reported words on arrival in Hollywood were: 'Newsreels and Mickey Mouse, these are the only pictures I like. How about my writing newsreels?' (He had an idea for Mickey Mouse, he told M.G.M.) While Faulkner's fiction remained highly cinematic, his screenplays for whatever reason were based on traditional fiction. Even his treatment of his own fiction, like *Absalom, Absalom!* (*Revolt in the Earth*, 1942). Maybe Faulkner learned his lesson from Hawks all too well: to distrust fancy cutting, refuse to use flashbacks, and just 'tell a good story'. On the other hand, maybe, Faulkner never considered film to be a serious medium at all. It was after writing *Revolt*, Faulkner told Cowley, that he managed to lock movie work 'off into another room'.

It was Faulkner's fiction, then, that secured his place in film history. His influence on fellow film-makers remains that of his stories, not of his scripts. At a time when the coming of sound rendered montage unfashionable and the economics of the film industry militated against experiment, Faulkner's fiction acted as a kind of incubator for the techniques of the silent screen. Faulkner's novels kept the traditions of a radically subjective vision and montage alive. It is through Faulkner, above all, that the New Wave film-makers (Alain Resnais, Alain Robbe-Grillet, Marguerite Duras and, most significantly, Jean-Luc Godard) rediscovered the cinema's own narrative rôle.

What the New York customs-house had been for Melville,

the Hollywood film lot was to be for Faulkner. Both men were burdened with family responsibilities. Neither had made a go of life as gentlemen farmers. Neither was written out. The turn of his fortunes came after the war with the appearance of *The Portable Faulkner*. Malcolm Cowley has published his own 'file' on that vital collaboration. Faulkner himself, with a nod at Edgar Lee Masters, called it 'Spoonrivering my apocryphal county', with a single phrase pointing to the attractive but potentially misleading heart of Cowley's work. But as Robert Penn Warren added in a review: 'Perhaps it can mark a turning point in Faulkner's reputation.' Which certainly came true. Faulkner's books now rapidly came back into print. With reputation followed financial security. In 1948 film rights of *Intruder in the Dust* were sold to M.G.M. for $40,000. The sentence of Hollywood drudgery was broken.

The rest is history. The final scenarios were played out under the arc-lights of world-wide publicity: first, as Southern country boy, up from the farm, receiving the Nobel Prize in Stockholm; then as cultural ambassador to Japan or Europe or South America; last as fully accredited man of distinction to the University of Virginia. For much of his time abroad he felt cornered, in his own phrase, 'as a treed coon'. But in Virginia he blossomed. That was to be his final avatar: as bowler-hatted Virginian gentleman-scholar-huntsman riding to the hounds with the millionaires and First Families of Albemarle County. 'I like snobs', he told a press conference. 'A snob has to spend so much time being a snob that he has little left to meddle with you, and so it's very pleasant here.' Even back at Oxford 'Count No 'Count' had finally made it: the Nobel Prize was clearly a feather in his cap; the filming of *Intruder in the Dust* with local extras had sealed his reputation. Yet he remained somewhat withdrawn, even misunderstood and alienated, to the end—as political trouble-maker, branded 'nigger-lover', during those crucial years of the Civil Rights crisis in the late 1950s.

A pile of jumbled photographs and descriptions (by John Malcolm Brinnin, Robert Coughlan and Donald Hall) evoke the man: compact, wiry, erect, with close-cropped, pepper-grey hair; a pipe in his lips, a glass at his elbow perhaps; turning the beaky curve of his nose with bird-like curiosity; his deep-set, brown eyes steady, concentrated, almost expressionless; his slurred voice bourbony; 'like a somnolent cat who still in the wink of an eye could kill a mouse'; like a river-boat gambler, turned farmer, who had studied Plato; courteous, speculative, aloof, yet somehow stern; a 'rigid, stony figure—delicate and stony at the same time'.

Only two correspondents broke through his immense reserve. One was Malcolm Cowley. The other was Joan Williams, a college girl who in 1949 had just won a short story competition. To her Faulkner was to expound his art of fiction—a solitary, romantic art of emotional travail and painstaking parturition. Putting words together was a 'form of anguishment'. 'You must expect scorn and horror and mis-understanding from the rest of the world who are not cursed with the necessity to make things new and passionate; no artist escapes it.' Craft too was necessary. 'Start off', he advised her, 'by seeing if you can tell the story orally to me, for instance, in one sentence.' A writer must learn from other writers the best point from which to approach a story, to milk it dry.

> How else can a young carpenter learn to build a house, except by helping an experienced carpenter build one? He cant learn it just by looking at finished houses. If that were so, anyone could be a carpenter, a writer.

But the power, the source of inspiration, was a mystery: 'a fine ecstatic rush' like an orgasm. 'I listen to the voices', he told Cowley, 'and when I put down what the voices say, it's right. Sometimes I don't like what they say, but I don't change it.' Will power, concentration alone, was never enough:

> You have got to break your wall. You have got to be capable of anything, everything, accepting them I mean, not as experi-ments, clinical, to see what it does to the mind, like with drugs or dead outside things, but because the heart and the body are big enough to accept all the world, all human agony and passion.

The profoundest mystery, however, was his own perennial possession by such genius. Not that Faulkner called it genius. In good cracker style he merely called it 'stuff'—stuff from the barrel:

> And now I realize for the first time what an amazing gift I had: uneducated in every formal sense, without even very literate, let

alone literary companions, yet to have made the things I made. I dont know where it came from. I dont know why God or gods or whoever it was, selected me to be the vessel. Believe me, this is not humility, false modesty: it is simply amazement. I wonder if you have ever had that thought about the work and the country man whom you know as Bill Faulkner—what little connection there seems to be between them.

But he had always seen himself as a split personality: part farmer, part writer; or rather 'merely a writer and never at all a literary man'. So he was neither a man of letters nor a letter-writer: in his eyes the two were interchangeable. There was only William Faulkner the novelist (all fiction) and Bill Faulkner the correspondent (mostly fact) who drove his jeep, loaded his mules, and stowed the hay into his barn 'all chaff and dust and sweat, until sundown'. The novelist invariably came first. It was only the fiction that mattered:

> I dont care much for facts, am not much interested in them, you cant stand a fact up, you've got to prop it up, and when you move to one side a little and look at it from that angle, it's not thick enough to cast a shadow in that direction. . . . I would have preferred nothing at all prior to the instant I began to write, as though Faulkner and Typewriter were concomitant, coadjutant and without past on the moment they first faced each other at the suitable (nameless) table.

This divorce between fact and fiction, this Siamese bond between the writer and his text (made a writer only by means of his text), lies at the root of Faulkner's insistence on total, personal privacy. Of course, he wanted letters, as he needed the reviews from New York. The Mississippi stores, he complained in 1929, carried nothing without 'either a woman in her underclothes or someone shooting someone else with a pistol on the cover'. But that did not mean strangers could drive into his yard and pick up books or pipes as souvenirs; these strangers in his later, more affluent, years as likely as not were prowling journalists from *Time* or *Life* or *Look*. As he wrote to Cowley:

> I will protest to the last: no photographs, no recorded documents. It is my ambition to be, as a private individual, abolished and voided from history, leaving it markless, no

refuse save the printed books; I wish I had had enough sense to see ahead thirty years ago and, like some of the Elizabethans, not signed them. It is my aim, and every effort bent, that the sum and history of my life, which in the same sentence is my obit and epitaph too, shall be them both: He made the books and he died.

His ambition had always been 'to put everything into one sentence—not only the present but the whole past on which it depends and which keeps overtaking the present, second by second'. His novels live in the memory not so much as isolated, disparate fragments, but as parts of a vast, unfolding saga, whose one prodigious, ever twisting and turning sentence embraces everything, past, present and future: the work not of this Mississippi farmer (or aviator, boot-legger, script-writer, squire) but of an anonymous bard, as he had hoped—who made the books and who died. Faulkner insisted all his life on the frustrating isolation of all human beings 'who for all the blood kinship and everything else, cant really communicate, touch'. Art alone can hope to transmit and bridge their passions. If a writer, for all his sacrifices, fails in that transcendent touch, then why bother with letters from him, or photo-journalism about him, or the prying gossip of mere 'facts'. 'Mr. Faulkner', a gushing Hollywood matron once said to him, 'I understand that an author always puts himself in his books. Which character are you in *Sanctuary*?' 'Madam', Faulkner replied, 'I was the corncob.'

It was Faulkner who allegedly remarked: 'The few times I tried to read Truman Capote, I had to give up. His literature makes me nervous.' Yet both are Southerners, self-engendered out of their fantasies; both share a penchant for gothic horror; both like to keep us fooled. Only the means have changed: Capote's first roman à clef ('Old Mr. Busybody', written at the age of 9 for the *Mobile Press Register*) brazenly served up local scandal as fiction; *Handcarved Coffins* (1980) more engagingly served up fiction as local scandal. The facts of his own life he kept equally confused. 'I don't care what anyone says about me', he told David Frost in an interview, 'as long as it isn't true.' But far from avoiding fame, Capote from the start has courted every kind of literary and non-literary attention. He has always seemed a glamorous writer, a sort of literary Oliver Messel or Cecil Beaton: a renegade Southerner as dandy. Like any *soigné* designer or fashion photographer, in fact, he has designs on us. His most casual talk and offhand arrangements are intended to take possession of other people. That is what drew him so obsessively, in the first place, to scenes of crime. That is what fascinates him about criminals. For writers, too, dispose of the living for their own designs. They too, like criminals at large, are irresponsible predators. They too fashion 'handcarved coffins'.

Such are the limitations of the artist as chameleon constantly changing his protective colouring to suit his art. Flannery O'Connor, his exact contemporary, never confined herself in this sense. She was never a predator. Though equally drawn to violence and criminals, she never conceived of her fiction, like Capote's, in cold blood. Nor did she dispose of the living for her own designs. Her art had moved beyond such aesthetic masquerades since she was a Catholic writer. Though this seems a confining term. She was an artist of the most exacting and universal perception. By the time of her thirty-ninth and final year, it had become clear that she was among the outstanding writers of American fiction of the twentieth century.

Almost a dozen books and innumerable articles have been published since 1964 on her small but intense *oeuvre*: two novels (*Wise Blood* and *The Violent Bear it Away*) and two collections of stories (*A Good Man is Hard to Find* and *Everything that Rises Must Converge*). An additional volume of her prose, in the form of lectures and articles (*Mystery and Manners*, 1972), helped to locate her own concerns for the problems of the regional writer and Catholic novelist. But far the longest and most important posthumous publication was that of her letters, a collection of more than 600 pages spanning the years 1948–64. For wealth of anecdote and intellectual variety and emotional depth, *The Habit of Being* too will prove an incomparable American work.

Its keynote is joy. Confined to hospital in 1950, with what was then diagnosed as 'acute rheumatoid arthritis', she wrote, 'I have been reading *Murder in the Cathedral* and the nurses thus conclude I am a mystery fan.' But the nurses were right. She was a 'mystery fan'; and she confronted life's mystery with an extraordinary aptitude for laughter. Two years later she was told that the so-called rheumatism was really *lupus erythematosus*, the scourge that had killed her father. The red wolf was to pursue her and hem her in and tear up her short life. 'I have enough energy to write with,' she confided to Robert Lowell in 1953, 'and as that is all I have any business doing anyhow, I can with one eye squinted take it all as a blessing.' She withdrew to her mother's farm near Milledgeville, Georgia, and despite the bone disease that afflicted her, reducing her to crutches by 1956, she continued to make occasional visits to friends or to give lectures—even to join a pilgrimage to Lourdes—until an operation for a tumour in 1963 reactivated the lupus from which she died.

Not only did she write gothic fiction, she realized, but she herself had come to look comically gothic. As she explained, on first hearing of her need for crutches: 'I will henceforth be a structure with flying buttresses.' For her agony at the non-recognition and incomprehension that bedevil the world was always lit by humour—or, as she might have said, moments of grace—and it was a robust sense of humour at that:

> I have decided I must be a pretty pathetic sight with these crutches. I was in Atlanta the other day in Davison's. An old lady got on the elevator behind me and as soon as I turned around she fixed me with a moist gleaming eye and said in a loud voice, 'Bless you, Darling!' I felt exactly like the Misfit and I gave her a weakly lethal look, whereupon greatly encouraged, she grabbed my arm and whispered (very loud) in my ear. 'Remember what they said to John at the gate, darling!' It was not my floor but I got off and I suppose the old lady was astounded at how quick I could get away on crutches. I have a one-legged friend and I asked her what they said to John at the gate. She said she reckoned they said, 'The lame shall enter first'. This may be because the lame will be able to knock everybody else aside with their crutches.

Of one of the nurses, who tended her after the final operation in 1964, she wrote:

> I seldom know in any given circumstances whether the Lord is giving me a reward or a punishment. She didn't know she was

funny and it was agony to laugh and I reckon she increased my
pain about 100 per cent.

There is nothing in the least coy about her. She intensely
disliked the work of Carson McCullers. The key characters in
her life, as in her fiction, are all ordinary, plain folk, like those
nurses, or her mother who so devotedly helped her, or her
mother's farmhands. Of one such farmhand, who was actually
taking a correspondence course in Catholicism, she reported:
'He is not going to be a Catholic or anything—he just likes to
get things free in the mail.' But she bred peachicks and
surrounded herself with peacocks, since 'you can't have a
peacock anywhere' (as she wrote of 'The Displaced Person')
'without having a map of the universe'. Those radiant birds,
displaying their bronze planets hung in green, enthralled her:

> The fact is that with his tail folded nothing but his bearing
> saves this bird from being a laughing stock. With his tail
> spread, he inspires a range of emotions, but I have yet to hear
> laughter.

'Oh, look at his underwear!' cry the chorus of first-grade
schoolchildren. 'Amen! Amen!' once cried an old Negro
woman. Some whistle; some are silent. One truckdriver,
pulling on the brakes, shouted: 'Get a load of that bastard!'
Another, after coaxing a cock for minutes to make his display,
only stared intently to remark: 'Never saw such long ugly legs.
I bet that rascal could outrun a bus.'

No wonder commentators are obsessed with her symbolism,
chasing and explicating those images through her texts. For
she saw the world transfigured. Even her turkeys with the
sorehead, for which the cure was liquid black shoe polish, ran
about in blackface 'like domesticated vultures'. Her comedy is
divine; yet no one could say of her, as one Jesuit visitor said of
a Sister who wrote poetry: 'Boy, I bet she's crucified.'
Flannery O'Connor was not 'crucified' in that vulgar sense.
For it was she, of course, who quoted the remark. It was
precisely a feeling for the vulgar that was her natural talent.
She quoted the nurses, the farmers, the Southern preachers:

> Mrs. P. was telling about how her new preacher sings his
> sermons. He puts a chair out on the platform and then calls up
> various Biblical characters to testify. 'Paul,' he says, 'will you

come up and testify?' They imagine the Apostle Paul getting up and taking a seat in the chair I suppose. Then the preacher sings 'Rock of Ages'. Then he says, 'Peter, will you come up and testify?' and sings something for Peter to testify. She thinks it's wonderful. 'Evy eye is on him,' she says. 'Not a breath stirs.'

Or again, talking of a reception desk in hospital:

When I came in & gave the information about myself at the admitting place, the woman, who had carrot-colored hair & eye-glasses to match, asked me by whom was I employed. 'Self-employed,' says I. 'What's your bidnis?' she says. 'I'm a writer,' I says. She stopped typing & after a second said, 'What?'
'Writer,' I says.
She looked at me for a while, then she says, 'How do you spell that?'

Such is the bric-à-brac, the raw material of her fiction. Georgia, at least in her younger days, she considered pretty well illiterate. Southerners, as far as she was concerned, knew nothing about the literature of the South unless they had gone to Northern colleges or to 'some of the conscious places like Vanderbilt or Sewanee'. Her own 'Jawger' relatives were a philistine brood who wanted her to write about 'nice people' or 'rich folks'. A literary conversation with mother might run like this:

'Who is this Kafka?' she says. 'People ask me.' A German Jew, I says, I think. He wrote a book about a man who turns into a roach. 'Well, I can't tell people *that*', she says. 'Who is this Evalin Wow?'

It was Evelyn Waugh, in fact, who managed later vastly to insult Mrs. O'Connor, by commenting on *Wise Blood*: 'If this is really the unaided work of a young lady, it is a remarkable product.' 'Does he suppose you're not a lady?' she repeated. 'WHO is he?'

Who indeed? Evelyn Waugh would have felt altogether 'displaced' in Milledgeville. So, even, would Graham Greene. As O'Connor herself penetratingly remarked:

If Greene created an old lady, she would be sour through and through and if you dropped her, she would break, but if you dropped my old lady, she'd bounce back at you, screaming 'Jesus loves me!'

Her comic sense had something hysterical; yet her whole serene vision of that comedy lies in that remark. She felt as close to that old lady as to all her frayed and demented characters. 'You talk just like a nigger', her mother told her, 'and someday you are going to be away from home and do it and people are going to wonder WHERE YOU CAME FROM.' Maybe she did. Despite her occasional classes and visitors and the nearby location of the Georgia State College for Women—as well as of Georgia's state mental hospital— she led a fairly isolated life, surrounded by books and correspondence.

Immersed in that world, she had little patience with silly queries—even from Vanderbilt University:

> They asked me such things as 'Miss O'Connor, why did they stop at *the Tower?*'—trying to make something of the word *tower*. They try to make everything a symbol. It kills me. At one place where I talked, one of them said, 'Miss O'Connor, why was the Misfit's hat *black?*' 'Well', I said, 'he stold it from a countryman and in Georgia they usually wear black hats'. This sounded like a pretty stupid answer to him, but he wasn't through with it. In a few minutes he says, 'Miss O'Connor, what is the significance of the Misfit's hat?' 'To cover his head', I say. When the session was over they obviously thought I didn't have sense enough to have written the story I wrote.

Like all her anecdotes, this is acute. She was playing hard to get, of course. But only because art and the recognition of art—not grace, nor the symbols of grace—must always come first. Her most outraged riposte she sent to a Professor of English who had inquired about her 'intention' in writing 'A Good Man is Hard to Find'. First she explains that the story is not meant to be realistic in the sense that it portrays the everyday doings of people in Georgia. It is stylized and its conventions are comic even though its meaning is serious. Then she lets go:

> The meaning of a story should go on expanding for the reader the more he thinks about it, but meaning cannot be captured in an interpretation. If teachers are in the habit of approaching a story as if it were a research problem for which any answer is believable as long as it is not obvious, then I think students will never learn to enjoy fiction. Too much interpretation is

191

certainly worse than too little, and where feeling for a story is absent, theory will not supply it.

My tone is not meant to be obnoxious. I am in a state of shock.

That is as tough as she ever allowed herself to be. For she wrote mainly to literary friends (John Hawkes, the Fitzgeralds, the Tates, the Lowells) and personal admirers who became epistolary friends. Of the many cranks who wrote to her, she remarked: 'I get some letters from people I might have created myself.' For she loved her own work. She loved to enjoy it as if she had had nothing to do with it. 'The truth is', she admitted, 'I like them better than anybody and I read them over and over and laugh and laugh, then get embarrassed when I remember I was the one who wrote them.' The stories might be hard, but they were never brutal or sarcastic. They were hard because there was nothing harder or less sentimental than what she called 'Christian realism':

> I believe that there are many rough beasts now slouching toward Bethlehem to be born and that I have reported the progress of a few of them, and when I see these stories described as horror stories I am always amused because the reviewer always has hold of the wrong horror.

The most abiding childhood influence on her, she admits, was a volume 'called *The Humerous Tales of E. A. Poe*'. Was she some latter-day Poe, then, converted to Catholicism? In her own experience, everything funny she had written was more terrible than it was funny, or only funny because it was terrible, or only terrible because it was funny. Simone Weil's life she considered the most comical life she had ever read about and the most truly tragic and terrible. For that juncture of comedy and terror for her was naturally located in the Incarnation:

> One of the awful things about writing when you are a Christian is that for you the ultimate reality is the Incarnation, the present reality is the Incarnation, and nobody believes in the Incarnation; that is, nobody in your audience. My audience are the people who think God is dead. At least these are the people I am conscious of writing for.

Catholic orthodoxy was essential to her. 'I feel that if I were not a Catholic', she insists,

I would have no reason to write, no reason to see, no reason ever to feel horrified or even to enjoy anything. I am a born Catholic, went to Catholic schools in my early years, and have never left or wanted to leave the Church. I have never had the sense that being a Catholic is a limit to the freedom of the writer, but just the reverse.

All this puts her on the extreme edge of the American tradition. No wonder, then, claims are made to view her symbol-laden, frustrated, forced entries into the Kingdom of Heaven as maverick Protestant texts. She herself had a saner perspective. In her opinion, the only thing that kept her from being a regional writer was being a Catholic and the only thing that kept her from being a Catholic writer, in the narrow sense, was being a Southerner. As one correspondent astutely pointed out, the best of her work sounds like the Old Testament would sound if written today, since her characters' relations are more directly with God than with other people.

Not that she had submitted to orthodoxy easily. Like Jacob, she had wrestled with the angel. From the age of 8 to 12 she had regularly locked herself into a room and fiercely whirled around in a circle with her fists knotted, socking the angel:

This was the guardian angel with which the Sisters assured us we were all equipped. He never left you. My dislike of him was poisonous. I'm sure I even kicked at him and landed on the floor. You couldn't hurt an angel but I would have been happy to know I had dirtied his feathers—I conceived of him in feathers.

Having won through though, she was impatient not only with academic but all high-flown intellectuals. Some time in the early 1950s she was taken by Robert Lowell and Elizabeth Hardwick to have dinner with Mary McCarthy (then Mrs. Broadwater):

We went at eight and at one, I hadn't opened my mouth once, there being nothing for me in such company to say. . . . Having me there was like having a dog present who had been trained to say a few words but overcome with inadequacy had forgotten them. Well, toward morning the conversation turned on the Eucharist, which I, being the Catholic, was obviously supposed to defend. Mrs. Broadwater said when she was a child and received the Host, she thought of it as the Holy Ghost, He being the 'most portable' person of the Trinity; now she thought of it as a symbol and implied that it was a pretty good one. I then said, in a very shaky voice, 'Well, if it's a symbol, to hell with it'. That was all the defense I was capable of but I realize now that this is all I will ever be able to say about it, outside of a story, except that it is the center of existence for me; all the rest of life is expendable.

It is in this light that one must read her definition of fiction as 'the concrete expression of mystery—mystery that is lived'. It was almost impossible for her to write about supernatural grace in fiction. She had to approach it negatively. In the words of Matthew, taken for the title of her second novel: 'Since the time of John the Baptist until now, the kingdom of heaven suffereth violence, and the violent bear it away.' Or, as she wittily put it years later: 'In the gospels it was the devils who first recognized Christ and the evangelists didn't censor this information.' For her violence revealed those human qualities least dispensable to a man's personality, 'those qualities which are all he will have to take into eternity with him'; and since all her characters are on the verge of eternity, all are evading, or half glimpsing, or intruding on various states of grace, most urgently revealed in that final trio of stories ('Revelation', 'Judgement Day' and 'Parker's Back') written in the last year of her life.

She is never didactic. Again and again she insists that writing is a vocation; that a writer can choose his subject 'but he cannot choose what he is able to make live, and so far as he is concerned, a living deformed character is acceptable and a dead whole one is not'; that church dogma, far from straitjacketing the story-teller, sets him free to observe. Throughout her brief career, she resolutely kept herself free from being subjected to others' vision. 'When the Catholic novelist closes his own eyes and tries to see with the eyes of the Church,' she wrote, 'the result is another addition to that large body of pious trash for which we have so long been famous.' In that resolution lay her aesthetic independence. Not for a moment did she doubt her own gifts. 'Miss O'Connor, why do you write?' a student asked her. 'Because I'm good at it', came the reply. That was the one talent it was death to hide. To speak in parables—of work which borders everywhere on parable—she is like the blind man whom Christ touched, 'who looked then and saw men as if they were trees, but walking'. This, for her, was the beginning of vision.

Once she was approached by an order of Dominican nuns, the Servants of Relief for Incurable Cancer, with a request to write a hagiography for a saintly, afflicted child. The order founded by Rose Hawthorne (Mother Alphonsa in religious life), daughter of the novelist, itself seemed a link between her religion and literature. Yet she refused the request, only agreeing to vet their own manuscript. The nuns meanwhile inspected her writings. In the course of a visit one of them asked why she wrote about such grotesque characters, why the grotesque of all things was her vocation. While Flannery O'Connor struggled for an answer, another guest interposed: 'It's your vocation, too.' That was an eye-opener. 'Most of us have learnt to be dispassionate about evil,' she pondered,

> to look it in the face and find, as often as not, our own grinning
> reflections with which we do not argue, but good is another
> matter. Few have stared at that long enough to accept the fact
> that its face too is grotesque, that in us the good is something
> under construction.

'I am not interested in abnormal psychology', she long ago insisted. Nor in the finer points of theology. 'The natural comes before the supernatural and that is perhaps the first step toward finding the Church again.'

11

Eminent Bohemians

Bohemia, like Arcadia, is a state of mind, wholly detached from its roots among Peloponnesian shepherds or gipsy vagabonds of Czechoslovakia. Yet it is an ideal in constant search of geographical realization. For Americans, since the turn of the century at least, it has been located in Greenwich Village.

There are, or have been, bohemian cells in Chicago, St. Louis, New Orleans, San Francisco and Carmel from which to colonize realms of freedom from competition and exploitation, from material cares and regular employment and the sexual stereotypes of middle-class hypocrisy. But Greenwich Village— stretching from Fifth Avenue to 14th Street, and from Houston Street to the Hudson River—remains the ideal, the bohemian capital. For it was a perfect small town nucleus in the big city where a decrepit maze of eighteenth-century houses was being penetrated by Irish and Italian slums, where 'high society' in the Greek revival grandeur of Washington Square could safely mingle with prostitutes, petty criminals and bums. Its very geography is nonconformist, lying crazily oblique to the rectangular grid of uptown New York. Something of its pastoral dream was shattered with the extension of 7th Avenue in 1918. The Golden Age lay back in the years before the First World War.

It was a Golden Age that itself preached a return to the Golden Age. In Gonzalo's famous words:

> All things in common nature should produce
> Without sweat or endeavour: treason, felony,
> Sword, pike, knife, gun, or need of any engine,

Would I not have; but nature should bring forth,
Of its own kind, all foison, all abundance,
To feed my innocent people.

The ideals were those of poverty and comradeship, the Whitmanesque joys of 'loafing' in the busiest, most enterprising of all American cities, where to be conspicuously relaxed even today is the mark of the bum or the foreigner. In 1916 Floyd Dell saluted Village rebels for their intimacy, candour, and 'the aristocratic use of leisure' without money. Malcolm Cowley, in *Exile's Return* (1934), revived Dell's notion. The pre-war Villagers, he argued, 'read Marx and all the radicals had a touch of the bohemian'; the post-war Villagers tasted the fruit of psychoanalysis. Not only the roar of traffic, or of war, but that most ancient of sins, a too self-conscious sexuality, ruined their utopia.

Such pre-war idealism simply embodied the concepts of social justice and sexual equality prevalent in the Progressive era. Headquarters for Branch One of the Socialist party was in the Rand School of Social Science on East 19th Street, founded in 1905 for the study of social problems and providing free education for the poor. Here in the basement restaurant, Louis Untermeyer recalled, was 'a gathering place of all the Utopians, muck-rakers, young intellectuals, and elderly malcontents south of 42nd Street'. They would drift in from Alfred Stieglitz's '291' Gallery on 5th Avenue or the offices of Emma Goldman's *Mother Earth* or the Liberal Club in Gramercy Park. Later new field paths would connect the offices of *The Masses* to Mabel Dodge's salon and the Provincetown Players. But their programme was always wobbly (with a small 'w'): part aesthetic, part ideological, readily confusing the silk workers' strike in Paterson with the Armory Show. Most Villagers preferred the Madison Square Garden pageant to the picket line. As one local Wobbly organizer put it: 'An intellectual, huh. A writer titty-sucker to the Upper Classes.' Women proclaimed their new sartorial code of sack dresses, cropped hair, brown socks and sandals. Spaghetti and wine dinners were more compelling than a strikers' emergency fund. 'Most of the people look as if life had knocked them around a bit', Randolph Bourne reported, 'and they were trying to forget it; it took so much of their energy to be radical that they had no time left for the life of irony.' It was to this era of green innocence that John Reed was to bid his own ironic farewell in *America 1918*:

> Old Greenwich Village, citadel of amateurs, Battle-ground
>   of all adolescent Utopias,
> Half sham-Bohemia, dear to uptown slummers,
> Half sanctuary of the outcast and dissatisfied,
> Free fellowship of painters, sailors, poets,
> Light women, Uranians, tramps and strike-leaders. . . .
> Playing at art, playing at love, playing at rebellion,
> In the enchanted borders of the impossible republic.

Most were refugees from lonely childhoods and middle-class mores; they created a subculture of essentially small-town professionals in some ways as bitchy and snobby as that of their elders. Many of the most influential artists and intellectuals of the period—Walter Lippmann, William Carlos Williams, Alfred Stieglitz, even Randolph Bourne—never wholly gravitated to Greenwich Village. Bourne's *New Republic* articles, with their loathing of war and 'vision of a pluralistic fraternal society' beyond WASP hegemony, are worth a mass of Hapgoods and Dells with their feckless philandering in the age of the new Feminism. Hutchins Hapgood, George Cram Cook (who founded the Provincetown Players and first staged the plays of Eugene O'Neill) and John Reed were all three Harvard romantics from the provincial gentry, edging their way into journalism and the arts. John Reed was the archetypal bohemian as revolutionary, a proto-Hemingway celebrating the sacred triad of loafing, loving and war-corresponding. Between forays across the Mexican border, to ride with Pancho Villa, and trips to Ypres, the Balkans or revolutionary Russia, he always returned to the arms of Mabel Dodge or Washington Square. Mabel even accompanied him in a Pullman on the Mexican safari. 'I think she expects to find General Villa a sort of male Gertrude Stein', he wrote; 'or at least a Mexican Stieglitz. We hardly ever stir out of our drawing-room except at mealtimes, when we start with *caviar* and go right through to nuts.' But Reed needed heroes. Boyishly he aped the bully-boys. 'We are in the middle of things', he reported from Petrograd in 1917, 'and believe me it's thrilling. There is so much dramatic to write that I don't know where to begin. For color and terror and grandeur this makes Mexico look pale.' That eyewitness account of the Bolshevik coup was to become *Ten Days that Shook the World*. He himself died in the typhus epidemic of 1920, the only Harvard man to be buried below the walls of the Kremlin. Max Eastman revolved round the whole cycle from Bolshevik hero-worship to the vindication of Trotsky, outspoken criticism of Stalin, and ultimately McCarthyism, ending as 'roving editor' for *Reader's Digest*.

For there existed an inherent conflict between artistic freedom and ideological politics that Villagers never resolved; artists either ignored politics or subordinated their talents to political causes. Villagers advocated political and cultural reforms without heeding the contradictions in their pro-grammes. Bohemian rebels often confused their needs with those of the poor. But what was liberating for Villagers—informal personal relations, freedom of expression, sexual liberation, and an unregulated social life—was irrelevant to labouring families struggling for existence. The ease with which psychoanalysis, socialism, syndicalism, feminism, pro-gressive education, Cubism, and free love were tossed together was indicative of their confusion and sheer exultation in rebellion for its own sake.

A generation later it seemed as if sailors, poets, tramps and Uranians were playing at love, playing at rebellion, in every corner of the impossible republic. Allen Ginsberg was the first American writer openly to assert his homosexuality. He 'came out', that is, from the start as a poet whose self-declamatory rôle was part and parcel (in the traditional way) of his self-expression as lover. His first recorded message, written on a dorm window at Columbia University, ran 'Butler has no balls'. (Nicholas Murray Butler was then president of Columbia.) For this—and for sharing his room overnight with Jack Kerouac—he was suspended. That was in 1945. But so quickly have academic and social mores shifted that today there are Ginsberg Special Collections at the Butler Library of Columbia University.

Clearly there is stuff here for legend. Ginsberg has been called 'counsellor to two generations, a public conscience intense and powerful enough to be crowned King of the May, father-figure for half the world's youth'. His whole career is treated as legendary. Every dream, every epiphany is recorded. The first took place in 1948:

> Allen lay alone on his bed in his East Harlem apartment one afternoon. A book of William Blake, open to 'Ah! Sun-flower' (a poem he'd read many times before) lay next to him. He had just jacked off, and as his mind died momentarily he heard an ancient-sounding voice—which he took to be Blake's—recite the poem. Immediately, he looked out his window and saw in the old, intricately corniced buildings and the ancient blue sky above the sign of a Creator, and sensed behind each particle of being the presence of a vast, immortal, intelligent hand.

Later Ginsberg came to view the voice, if not the intelligent hand, as that of his own mature prophetic self:

> Now I'll record my secret vision, impossible sight of the face of God:
> It was no dream I lay broad waking on a fabulous couch in Harlem
> having masturbated for no love, and read half naked an open book of Blake on my lap
> Lo & behold! I was thoughtless and turned a page and gazed on the living sun-flower. . . .

No wonder he was shaken. His mother, Naomi, had been in an asylum for most of the previous decade. But soon he was to be in touch with William Carlos Williams who, by 1952, was writing to Robert Lowell: 'I've become interested in a young poet, Allen Ginsberg, of Paterson—who is coming to personify the place for me.' With the publication of *Howl* four years later he had come to personify the whole of America.

By then he had met Peter Orlovsky in San Francisco (his life-long lover, with whom he listed himself in *Who's Who* as married). But it was ten years earlier, in 1946, that Neal Cassady—rolling stone, jailbird, brakeman on the South Pacific Railroad—had appeared in New York and almost immediately Ginsberg had fallen in love with him. Cassady was to become the spontaneous bop hero (alias Dean Moriarty) of Kerouac's *On the Road* (1957). As Ginsberg put it to Carolyn Cassady, his wife, in 1952:

What *I* think about it is, Jack loves Neal platonically (which I think is a pity, but maybe about sex I'm 'projecting' as the analysts say), and Neal loves Jack, too. The fact is that Jack is very inhibited, however. However, also sex doesn't define the whole thing.

One homosexual indulgence by that otherwise heterosexual exemplar was bowdlerized by Malcolm Cowley to ease publication in that cautious decade. For Dean, like Neal, was intended to be a bisexual portrait. Kerouac's *Visions of Cody* was originally entitled *Visions of Neal.* Though twice married, Neal too continued to sleep on and off with men, the most distinguished of whom was possibly President Arthur's grandson, Gavin Arthur; and, as Ginsberg amusingly made clear, since Gavin Arthur had slept with Edward Carpenter, who claimed to have slept with Walt Whitman, for Ginsberg to sleep with Cassady was a kind of ultimate laying on of hands.

Twenty years later, their lives were still interweaving. Cassady reported an encounter in a North Beach bar to Ken Kesey in 1965:

> Who should be at the very end of the bar, all-sloppy-lips nuzzling a big floozey Blonde bar fly, but Allen Ginsberg. Who at once turned to nuzzling me in between, introducing me to the few poets all gathered there whom I didn't already know—Charles Olson, Bob Duncan—to shorten this . . . suffice that no less etc., than 30 or more young D. Moriarty admirers, old queens, serious poets from Ireland, County Cork, drunk poets from the local gentry & others all staggered down Grant to Francisco Street & carrying a full case of beer, went to a party. . . .

Yet Cassady was more than just everyone's sexual pet. His autobiographical fragment, *The First Third* (sent to Ginsberg as early as 1952), makes clear that the new spontaneous bop prosody was largely a creation of his own vagrant style. So Ginsberg argued, appealing to the San Quentin Parole Board in 1959, when Cassady was serving a two-year sentence for the possession and sale of marijuana. So Kerouac acknowledged in a letter to Cassady, which reflects the exuberantly wacky narcissism of the Beat Generation:

> You gather together all the best styles . . . of Joyce, Céline, Dusty [Moreland] & Proust . . . and utilize them in a muscular

201

rush of your own narrative style & excitement. I say truly, no
Dreiser, no Wolfe has come close to it; Melville was never truer.
I know that I don't dream. It can't possibly be sparse &
halting, like Hemingway, because it hides nothing; the material
is painfully necessary . . . the material of Scott Fitz was so
sweetly unnecessary. It is the exact stuff upon which American
Lit is still to be founded.

This flattering estimate, though, is hardly borne out by his
correspondence which jerks along somewhere between ecstasy
(induced by the internal combustion of sex or trucks or drugs)
and inarticulacy. At the lowest troughs, he pauses in sheepish
confusion with 'Ha. Ha. More shit. I'm dashing it off now—'
or, 'My god! I sound like the ladies home journal or worse.'
Carolyn Cassady is right. Neal lived on sexual subterfuges: 'In
an effort to keep everyone happy, Neal tried to juggle several
relationships simultaneously and felt it advisable to keep them
separate and secret from one another.' In one early letter to
Ginsberg, he wrote: 'You know I, somehow, dislike pricks &
men & before you, had consciously forced myself to be
homosexual . . .', proposing a *ménage à trois* with a girl. Less
than a fortnight later, however, he admits: 'I know I'm
bisexual, but prefer women, there's a slimmer line than you
think between my attitude toward love and yours, don't be so
concerned, it'll fall into line.' While in the same letter he
claims: 'In reality, Allen, I'm a simple, straight guy, and in
thinking of what I want for the next year I know that without
you I'd be lost. I feel a normal brotherly need emotionally for
you, just as with Jack. . . .' The fact is he had a giant
inferiority complex and was constantly afraid of letting
Ginsberg slip as if (in his own words) he 'were a woman about
to lose her man'. For Ginsberg was the big-city shepherd to
this intellectual sucker from Denver. Cassady was the moronic
adolescent to the Faustian father, apprentice to professional
poet, Goy to Jew, Dedalus to Bloom.

The odd thing is when Ginsberg visited the Cassady family
to claim his share of love, roles were at once reversed:

> I feel like a strange idiot, standing there among wife & children
> all to whom he gives needs of affection and attention, aching for
> some special side extra sacrifice of attention to me—as if like
> some nowhere evil beast intruding I were competing for his care

with his own children & wife and job which seems to occupy
energize bore & tire him.

Yet Cassady's frantic last message from Mexico ran: 'I'm
going to stay here until you get here . . . because you've got to
save me.' For though Cassady all his life continued to play the
Pied Piper as bisexual angel, the paradox remains that it was
Ginsberg, the constantly open homosexual, who acted as
emotional support for the aspiring straight and married Neal.
Altogether this is a remarkable glimpse of a twenty-year
relationship which transcends the usual clichés of homo or
hetero dependency, however 'hysterical or false faced or self
defeating', as Ginsberg admits, much of it now seems.

For Ginsberg's own emotional life, especially in the early
1950s, was never easy. He was either in analysis, or about to
return to analysis. 'I don't want to be just a nothing, a sick
blank, withdrawal into myself for ever', he moaned to
Cassady. The main thing his psychiatrist attempted was to
break him of his 'schizoid paranoid beliefs (metaphysical
ecstasy in place of real world of dragging necessity) and
queerness'. The Freudian queer-bashing was typical of that
decade. But the emphasis on the real world, which Ginsberg
eventually interpreted as the real *homosexual* world, proved
liberating. It still does. The more ecstatic pieces easily become
bombastic and tiresome. It is Ginsberg's humour, impudently
deflating the ecstasy and paranoia and transcendence by a
worldly tone and shifts of tone, that established his mature
style.

'I Allen Ginsberg Bard out of New Jersey take up the laurel
tree cudgel from Whitman', he concluded his first draft of the
poem 'America'. For the turbulent paradigm, of course, was
Walt:

> Through me forbidden voices,
> Voices of sexes and lusts, voices veil'd and I remove the
>   veil,
> Voices indecent by me clarified and transfigur'd.
>
> I do not press my fingers across my mouth,
> I keep as delicate around the bowels as around the head
>   and heart,
> Copulation is no more rank to me than death is.

Whitman's *Song of Myself* is translated, in Ginsberg's ironic version, to 'Ego Confession'. Both indulge their own comic persona: Whitman, 'hankering, gross, mystical, nude'; Ginsberg longing to

> Masturbate in peace, haunt ancient cities for boys, practice years of chastity, save Jewels for God my own ruddy body, hairy delicate antennae. . . .

Copulation and death reappear as 'Sweet Boy, Gimme Yr Ass' and the moving short threnody for Louis Ginsberg:

> Near the Scrap Yard my Father'll be Buried
> Near Newark Airport my father'll be
> Under a Winston Cigarette sign buried
> On Exit 14 Turnpike NJ South
> Through the tollgate Service Road 1 my father buried . . .

But it could never be said of Ginsberg, as Whitman wrote of himself to Edward Carpenter: 'There is something in his nature *furtive*, like an old hen.' For Whitman, like Wilde who visited him in New Jersey, gloried in masquerade and illusion: 'both in and out of the game and watching and wondering at it'. Ginsberg's comic bravura, like Mailer marshalling armies of the night in his three-piece suit, is wholly Jewish and self-deprecatingly assured. Ginsberg neither attempts the Western rôle of urban gamecock nor indulges in camp comedy. Whitman manages both ('there is that lot of me and all so luscious') in his endless saga of self-affirmation. Yet both share the need to leap for self-transcendence in a kind of cosmic love-affair that turns, as often as not, into a comic impasse of ecstasy foiled and rebuffed. 'I want to be known as the most brilliant man in America', 'Ego Confession' opens:

> I want to be the spectacle of Poesy triumphant over trickery of the world
> Omniscient breathing its own breath thru War tear gas spy hallucination
> whose common sense astonished gaga Gurus and rich Artistes—
> who called the Justice department & threaten'd to Blow the Whistle
> Stopt Wars, turned back petrochemical Industries' Captains to grieve & groan in bed. . . .

204

Until the steady crescendo of manic self-parody is ruptured:

> —All empty all for show, all for the sake of Poesy
> to set surpassing example of sanity as measure for late
> generations
> Exemplify Muse power to the young avert future suicide
> accepting his own lie & the gaps between lies with equal
> good humor
> Solitary in worlds full of insects & singing birds all solitary
> —who had no subject but himself in many disguises. . . .

The poet who entered howling in 1956 now exits shaking with laughter, like a great earth-bound Jewish-American Buddha: laughing with his jukebox prophecies; laughing with his pederast rhapsodies, even with his Dharma elegies; laughing on his own way to 'Guru Death', singing the 'Sickness Blues':

> Lord Lord I got the sickness blues, I must've done some-
> thing wrong
> There ain't no Lord to call on, now my youth is gone.
>
> Sickness blues, don't want to fuck no more
> Sickness blues, can't get it up no more
> Tears come in my eyes, feel like an old tired whore . . .
>
> Must be my bad karma, fuckin these pretty boys
> Hungry ghosts chasing me, because I been chasing joys
> Lying here in bed alone, playing with my toys
>
> I musta been doing something wrong meat & cigarettes
> Bow down before my lord, 100 thousand regrets
> All my poems down in hell, that's what pride begets.

Much as Sartre enshrined Jean Genet in *Saint-Genet*, so William Burroughs has been enshrined in an Anglo-American pantheon of modern seers. Enter Saint William of Tangier, mentor of the Beat generation, dedicatee of Allen Ginsberg's *Howl* and the friend of Jack Kerouac, introducing himself as 'an explorer of psychic areas', 'a cosmonaut of inner space'. For Burroughs is the *other* man from St. Louis, Missouri. Born in 1914, a generation after T. S. Eliot, he was a youngster of the depression years, who was to become the second and more authentic vernacular artist of the junk-yard waste land of St. Louis, re-created in London, Tangier, Paris. Like Eliot too he went to Harvard, followed by years of travel abroad on a trust fund. He studied medicine in Vienna and later anthropology in Chicago. The accidental shooting of his wife, Joan Vollner Adams, occurred in Mexico in 1952, while playing William Tell. He did not become a full-time writer until 1956, in Tangier, at the age of 42.

Exuberant, ruthless farce is the keynote of all Burroughs's most straightforward prose, such as *Exterminator!* This potential for the grotesque is an aspect of his poetic empathy for those grey areas of all-male urban squalor, what he calls 'the greasy black feel common to jails, orphanages, mental hospitals or other institution canteens':

> Did I ever tell you about the man who taught his asshole to talk? His whole abdomen would move up and down farting out the words. It was quite unlike anything I ever heard.

Swiftian energies are released by this Horror Show, fuelled by misogyny, a pervasive anti-feminism which underlies the obsessive all-male anal orgasm. As in the exorbitant demise of Mrs. Worldly:

> Her face gets blacker and blacker and starts to swell. Her face neck and arms swell like balloons splitting the skin. A scream seals shut in her throat with a muffled sound as scalding shit spurts from her boiling intestines. Diamonds pop all over the lobby. . . . Mrs. Worldly falls in a heap of shitty mink screaming like a ruptured sausage.

In *The Wild Boys* female child-bearers are altogether eliminated by cloning from 'a cell lining a man's intestine [which] contains all the information needed to produce an identical twin'. There the gospel according to Burroughs is neatly set out: that love is 'a fraud perpetuated by the female sex'; that sexual relations between men are not love but 'what we might call *recognition*'; that sexual fear originates in the female-dominated family, in parents whose state function is to cripple children in the continuation of what they themselves suffered.

Yet even this is not to reach the controlling centre of Burroughs's vision. Again and again, repeated amid the frenzy of his Dionysian imagery, the movement draws compulsively to one vital moment: the death of a beautiful boy. Call him Johnny Adonis, Narcissus, or St. Sebastian. From *The Naked Lunch* onwards this movement is always to some urban recreation of *The Bacchae*, mingling the blood rites of Thessalian maenads with homosexual cannibalism. Sparks explode, legs twitch: 'the orgasm of a hanged man when the neck snaps'. With his usual ghoulish humour Burroughs calls this 'The Orgasm Death Gimmick' (*Nova Express*). For he is concerned with sexual dependence (on orgasm and 'junk'), not with the sacrificial victim humiliated by absolute power, whether of God, the state, money, or police. In a word, totalitarianism is a metaphor for junk, not junk for addictive totalitarianism.

Yet the climax of *The Naked Lunch* has been called by Eric Mottram:

> a strictly non-pornographic satire against capital punishment, exposing the perverted sexuality of those who execute or witness or condone it. This scene will appear pornographic only to devotees of execution. It is in fact a necessary enaction of the central sexuality of power in the nation state.

It simply does not read that way. The pornography is part of the fun. The fun is obsessive, like a busily variegated burlesque of Housman's *A Shropshire Lad*. Burroughs himself has admitted as much:

> Speaking for myself, the one thing I find sexy is creation, to create on paper a sexy person—sexy to me, that is. And if it is a real creation, it will be interesting to other readers as well and I will say that any writer who has not masturbated with his own characters will not be able to make them live on paper.

Allen Ginsberg from the most intimate experience has attested that:

> In fact, the cut-ups were originally designed to rehearse and repeat his obsession with sexual images over and over again, like a movie repeating over and over and over again, and then re-combined and cut up and mixed in; so that finally the obsessive attachment, compulsion, and preoccupation empty out and drain from the image. . . . Finally, the hypnotic attachment, the image, becomes demystified. . . .
>
> He can finally look at it at the end of the spool; he can look at his most tender, personal, romantic images objectively, and no

longer be attached to them. And that's the purpose of the cut-ups: to cut out of habit reactions, to cut through rehearsed habit, to cut through conditioned reflex, to cut out into open space, into endless blue space where there is room for freedom and no obligation to repeat the same image over and over again, to come the same way over and over again.

So obsessions, it is hoped, will be purged by mechanical repetition. Pornographic satire is paradoxically aimed at release from pornography—from rehearsed habit, dependence, the conditioned reflex of what Ginsberg calls Burroughs's 'favourite and tenderly sentimental images'. The cut-ups snap the umbilical cord of fascinated attraction. They open up the way to a possibility of withdrawal, of floating free in mystic transcendence. Beyond homosexual addiction even. For it is Burroughs's concern, as it was Poe's, to push beyond the limits of the body—'Out of Space, out of Time'—by every conceivable device of science fiction. Even the famous fold-in techniques were prefigured by Poe. It was Poe who wrote in *MS Found in a Bottle*:

> An incident has occurred which has given me new room for meditation. Are such things the operation of ungoverned Chance? I had ventured upon deck and thrown myself down, without attracting any notice, among a pile of ratlin-stuff and old sails, in the bottom of the yawl. While musing upon the singularity of my fate, I unwittingly daubed with a tar-brush the edges of a neatly-folded studding-sail which lay near me on a barrel. The studding-sail is now bent upon the ship, and the thoughtless touches of the brush are spread out into the word DISCOVERY.

Discovery is dependent on the chance observation, the chance methodology, in the cracks of an intellectual system. Imagination needs to be caught off guard by the chance word, the rhyme word, the juxtaposition of events, the hazards of reading. Scissors merely help along that revolutionary insight, like Marxists giving a push to the inevitable revolution.

But Burroughs outdoes Poe as a time traveller and space traveller, by taking 'coordinates', while walking the tight-rope of his 'association lines'. The aim is to expand consciousness, to tap the coded messages beyond literary earshot, to retrace the secret of Egyptian and Mayan hieroglyphs, to reach the silence beyond words in soundless, universal images and patterns 'at the extreme limit of readability'. Imagination is all. So the image is all. Is not 'all writing in fact cut-ups'? Is not the *Aeneid* a cut-up of the *Iliad* and the *Odyssey*? *Don Quixote* of chivalric romances? Burroughs's Junk City is ravaged by need, by the cancer of unconsummated desires: infantilism, apathy, and sexual helplessness, controlled by technological power groups (doctors, psychiatrists, judges and the police). Homosexuals are only the more conspicuous part of the 'soft machine', that 'terminal sewage', that universal cannibalism where mankind is at once predator, parasite, incubus and addict. Like junk, homosexuality in *The Naked Lunch* seemed only to offer 'arrested motion', a passive manipulation, symbolic of evil. But from his vision of homosexual abuse as controlled degradation, Burroughs moved to his vision of wild boys, rising armed to destroy the police machine. Sexual astronauts, they escape 'from flesh through sex', leaving the limits of their bodies through repeated orgasms, breaking through their nerve-racked urban prison to pastoral space. 'To travel in space', Burroughs told Daniel Odier in 1969,

> you must learn to leave the old verbal garbage behind. God talk, priest talk, mother talk, family talk, love talk, party talk, country talk. You must learn to exist with no religion, no country, no allies. . . . You must learn to see what is in front of you with no preconceptions.

These 'technologically-equipped homosexual warrior packs' are freed from the influence of state, tribe, family and women: 'a whole generation arose that had never seen a woman's face nor heard a woman's voice'.

At last he can openly celebrate that 'fervid comradeship', that 'adhesive love', to which Walt Whitman looked forward in *Democratic Vistas*:

> for the counterbalance and offset of our materialistic and vulgar American Democracy, and for the spiritualization thereof. . . . I say Democracy infers such loving comradeship, as its most inevitable twin or counterpart, without which it will be incomplete, in vain, and incapable of perpetuating itself.

Yet Burroughs calls his *Wild Boys* a 'Book of the Dead'. For it is only after an apocalyptic catastrophe that this heir of

Whitman can imagine a conflict-free eternity, where the pleasure principle, the Freudian *libido*, may rule. 'Nothing is true', runs the refrain. 'Everything is permitted.' It is a Golden Age vision, where, in the words of Tasso's Aminta: *S'ei piace, ei lice.*

It was Henry Adams who set up the American terms of the debate—between dependency and attraction, between technological energy (of the political power complex) and sexual energy (of redeeming love). Adams spelled out the need for a multiple, open response. Burroughs claims that such an open, multiple response is only possible with an expanded consciousness of homosexual experience that smashes the woman-centred and woman-dominated heterosexual world to regain an inner freedom: 'Mary, the Virgin Whore, in the next stage is to be replaced by Christ, the male bastard of a male god with male disciples who self-generate.' Such (in Mottram's words) is Burroughs's reply to Adams's Virgin and Dynamo. Or as Burroughs himself once put it: 'Find yourself in a matriarchy walk don't run to the nearest frontier. If you run, some frustrate, latent queer cop will likely shoot you.'

Like a latter-day Whitman, Burroughs extends his democratic revolution from literature to politics. He even picks up where the Yippies, some ten years earlier, left off: political sabotage, by scrambled electronic cut-ups, swamping the mass media with total illusion. Grinning from ear to ear, he celebrates his own maverick brand of Nigger Minstrel Show:

> Everybody doing it, they all scramble in together and the population of the earth just settle down a nice even brown color. Scrambles is the democratic way, the way of full cellular representation. Scrambles is the American way.

Such freedom is paradoxically billed as freedom from social traumas of impotence and psychic sterility. But it is all too reminiscent of the opening of *Moby-Dick*—of Ishmael's escape from New Bedford with a potent Queequeg, only to be trapped, aboard the *Pequod*, by an impotent Ahab. Melville long ago had already explored this tension between sex and technology in all-male society. For it is not so much the matter that is new, but the manner: the virtuoso parody of pop art in all its forms from science fiction and blue movies to strip cartoons.

Burroughs is not so much a metaphysician, whatever his own claims to the priesthood, as a farceur; and his best work, mingling eroticism and violent death, should be read in the antic tradition of burlesque.

Bohemia was never so much a way of resolving the problems of the world, or of single societies in that world, as the intractable-seeming problems of single, isolated individuals. The inhabitants of old-style bohemian ghettoes, in San Francisco or New York, today are mainly homosexual. By the 1970s bohemias of another kind were dispersed from coast to coast, from New England to New Mexico. These neo-Bohemias, or Arcadias, tend to attract individuals who feel peripheral, subordinate, incapable of independent existence. Living in the cracks of the capitalist Cockaigne, they flaunt a paradox: internal émigrés contemptuously living off that culture (with women, some dope, and a record player, a pile of comics, a telephone, a Coke, a piece of chicken, good friends) who are at the same time its largest and most recent leisure class.

At the magnetic centre of such collectives or extended families again and again is to be found a patriarchal head, long-haired guru or shaman, dispensing power, advice, instruction—not necessarily as malignant or even as neurotic as Charles Manson but of whom Manson is now the recognizable type. That oriental vocabulary of masculine dominance comes readily to mind:

> She said, 'Byron was the first really real man I ever made it with. He was the first one who could make me feel like a real woman. . . . Not that it is a sex trip . . . it's more like a head trip. He just really smoothes your head out . . . like, he *knows*, he really *knows*.'

A harem closeness of feeling apparently develops between such women till they seem exactly like their suburbanite mums sharing the same doctor or psychoanalyst.

Some communes merely display defiance: the energy of children openly ungrateful to their parents. To smash is freedom; the tigers of wrath are wiser than the horses of ecology. Others are therapeutic, organic, ecological, where

211

sun-people stir their macrobiotic mush with pensive fore-fingers. Yoga, meditation, natural childbirth and *porphyra umbilicalis* (or purple laver) gently reprove the envious, lonely, competitive culture of Coca-Cola, drugs, missiles and Tastee Bakes. But here too sexual anarchy lurks behind the suburban proprieties. Others again are hardly communes at all, merely associations of convenience knit together by urban economics: houses for twelve being cheaper than a dozen separate apartments. But there are also political houses, true covens of communards dedicated to the destruction of U.S. imperialism, founded in response to the politicians and the corporations. These are seedbeds of revolutionaries *at war*, whose proto-communes, as often as not, turn out to be prisons (for blacks) and mental institutions (for whites).

At some such extended family communes, busy with babies and dogs, Zen Happiness may mingle with Passover Seder back on the land:

> Sixty people live in three rooms, and at night all available floor space is covered with matresses. Members of short standing usually sleep on these matresses, while the more permanent residents sleep on huge carpentered double-decker beds, some-times three to a bed. The beds belong to the women. If you want to sleep in a bed, or if you want to sleep with a woman, you are supposed to ask her at some time during the day if it is all right with her. . . . The ones that are pregnant look forward to bringing new children into the Family, though they may not know who the biological father is. The children are cared for by all the women of the Family, and they sleep together on two buses parked in the yard.

Here is a sanctuary for mystery and initiation, without money and with coy Gothick names: Lord Byron, Lady Samantha, Lady Lily, Sir William. But the final effect is more like a coed sorority-cum-fraternity, only now with even more bizarre graduation honours and even more self-conscious publicity: 'we want to pledge the whole *world*.'

Such new monastic centres were built to survive these Dark Ages and herald a coming apocalypse of love. Others again remain perpetually on the move like mendicant friars, or Johnny Appleseeds 'just spacin' around' selling their acid from California to Oregon to Alaska. Here or there they meet at some caravanserai, some community crash-pad on the Grand Tour, replete with teenage pilgrims from nowhere to nowhere weighed down with back-packs, paperbacks and guitars. Their cult is one of poverty—non-competitive, neighbourly, voluntary, neo-Franciscan poverty in the richest of rich countries this earth has ever known.

12

In the Dark

The scene is Los Angeles—Disneyland, fun city, Hollywood—itself a stage-set within a stage, a gimcrack paradise beyond parody. The Strip, Sunset Boulevard, Westwood Village, Scandia, Farmers Market casually indicate the topography for all habitués of this collective dream-world. Its epic days, like those of Greece, lie in the distant past. There Jean Harlow, Lana Turner, Ann Sheridan, James Stewart, Clark Gable, Johnny Weissmuller, *et al.*, *et al.*, brood like benign, tough, buxom, slender gods and goddesses. Each governs some eternal aspect of classical passion. Their presence is a constant reminder of the Homeric dogma that '*in the decade between 1935 and 1945 no irrelevant film was made in the United States*'.

Yet the moviegoer, adrift on fantasy—absorbed in his dark, imaginative quest from downtown Roxy to Tivoli, from Loews to suburban Bijou—was more pertinent than any product (in film or fiction) of the dream factory. For he was its passive consumer. His impotence, his rôle-playing, his self-destructive irony were all related to Hollywood. 'I am attracted to movie stars', the hero of Walker Percy's *The Moviegoer* (1963) admits, 'but not for the usual reasons. I have no desire to speak to Holden or get his autograph. It is their peculiar reality which astounds me.' The celluloid world, though visible, is inaccessible. That is its thrill and torment. Like photographers with a telescopic lens, we are all conscripted as spies, as peeping Toms. Again and again the camera closes in. Furtively we study the actor's person. Studiously the actor pretends the camera is not there; he never stares back. Scott Fitzgerald's Monroe Stahr, in *The Last Tycoon*, well understood this melodramatic art: this 'furtive, privileged inspection of people under stress'.

Peculiar to Hollywood was the packaging and marketing of such voyeuristic fantasies as self-realization. Hollywood's job was to tell stories and sell stories. Its aim was not so much life as art: a perfectly integrated system of signs (of cuts, close-ups, slow dissolves, flashbacks) to explore its own developing form. All experience was apparently subsumed under its various conventions: situation comedy, screwball comedy, horror, thriller, gangster, women's pic, film *noir*, epic, biblical, western, costume, adventure. As Irving Thalberg (Monroe Stahr's original) wrote of what in 1929 he still called 'photo-plays':

> Other arts generally appeal to a selected group, but the motion picture art, and it is an art, must have universal appeal. This is fundamental, for the motion picture industry, with its invest-ment of hundreds of millions of dollars, is based on the hope that it will appeal to the people of a nation and of a world.

If all actors were furtive artists, however, all artists (by the same Hollywood canon) were furtive actors. That is the essence of Cornel Wilde as Chopin, Paul Muni as Zola, or Kirk Douglas as Van Gogh. This is fundamental to Orson Welles's career, down to his punning take-over by radio of H. G. Wells's *The War of the Worlds* (1938). Hollywood could even upstage traditional art with its own ever more vociferous populist assertions. As Mervyn Le Roy put it in *Hard to Handle*:

> *The Blue Boy* is a beautiful picture, but comparatively few people have seen it. The *Mona Lisa* is one of the greatest pictures the world has ever known, but more people have seen Lana Turner. My answer to that is: People want entertainment. If the Blue Boy sang like Jolson, they'd go to see him. Or if Mona Lisa looked like Heddy Lamarr, more people would go to the Louvre.

But the viewer, as voyeur, remains basically an outsider— more than that, a victim. The 'cut' is not only syntactic, as a point of transition, but a metaphor of severance, of irrational wounding, of ruthless intrusion. The audience lies helplessly exposed. The projector moves in to attack like the hand (at the opening of Luis Buñuel's *Un Chien Andalou*) that draws back the eyelid, like the razor slicing through the eyeball. In darkness alone can such imagery pierce our defences. As Bette Davis remarked in *Hush, Hush ... Sweet Charlotte*: 'It only works in the dark.'

No wonder Jews were drawn in such numbers to Hollywood. For they instinctively grasped this new rôle—of outsiders, of dreamers in the dark, of cultural voyeurs alienated from the mainstream of W.A.S.P. tradition. More than voyeurs merely, victims exposed to irrational wounding, to ruthless intrusion. Their very fantasies—whether in life or art—were marked by insecurity and isolation. No wonder they displayed such zeal for acting in films, for making films, for promoting films. Take Nathan Weinstein (born 1904), Arthur Wolff (born 1907), Daniel Fuchs (born 1909). All belong to a single generation. All were born of recent immigrant stock. All grew up with the movies. All gravitated west to California.

Nathanael West's four novels were all comparative failures. In select literary circles he enjoyed a *succès d'estime*, film rights were even bought, but—unlike Hemingway, Fitzgerald, Sinclair Lewis, Steinbeck—he never once earned enough to concentrate full-time on his own writing. An exile in the sun-drenched Siberia of Los Angeles, he wrote his apocalypse, *The Day of the Locust*, and at the age of 37, in a car crash as horrific and absurd as any of his fictional exploits, he died. He was on his way back from a weekend's quail and duck shooting south of the Mexican border.

Since that tragic date, in December 1940, his stock has steadily risen. A few discerning friends and literary acquaintances must always have foreseen this. Fitzgerald for one, who died a day earlier, had a deep professional regard for West; and his unfinished *Last Tycoon* shows the unmistakable marks of West's Hollywood novel. Outstanding among his supporters from the earliest days were West's sister Laura and her husband, S. J. Perelman. It was they who safeguarded his correspondence, short stories, poems, jottings, clippings. Though West confused his acquaintances with an astonishingly fertile dream life (as big-game hunter, connoisseur, adventurer, First World War veteran), such tall tales were merely an extension of the novels; and both concealed, in ironic layer upon layer, the essentially shy, haunted, suffering aesthete who was born Nathan Weinstein. Born a decade earlier, he might have become a kind of Jewish Firbank creating his private fantasies from maps of literary London and artistic Paris. There remained a touch of Max Jacob about him:

> *Vous allez donc alors au Cinématographe,*
> *Me dit un confesseur, la mine confondue.*
> *—Eh! mon Père! Le Seigneur n'y est-il pas venu?*

Such mingling of divine folly with the mass media—such a vision of Christ on a cinema screen—was to become West's trademark. All his life he drew doodles of suffering saints, martyrs or Christ figures with enormous heads set on emaciated bodies, with thick noses, heavy lips and fiercely staring eyes. He sketched this figure into copies of *The Dream Life of Balso Snell* and left a trail of this suffering man—who was West, of course, as well as Miss Lonelyhearts and Tod Hackett—in the margins of his books, on scraps of paper, and on restaurant napkins.

What saved him was certainly not his three brief months in Paris. Born in New York of Jewish émigré parents from Lithuania, son of a highly successful building contractor, West already felt lost long before he joined the 'lost generation'. He became an expatriate, an internal émigré inside America and, whether he adopted aristocratic poses or aesthetic poses or Dadaist poses, he needed neither Paris manifestos nor economic crises to teach him that irrationality prevailed there and that he hated its commercial life. All aspects of that life, as he saw it, touched on the grotesque and the absurd. In a world of 'boosters', to use the slang of his day, he was a natural-born 'knocker'. Even as undergraduate, at Brown, West spoke of himself as a 'Jewish outsider', a 'Jew and a not-Jew at the same time'; and his legal change of name in 1926 froze him in that awkward transitional posture.

The archaic 'Nathanael' struck him as peculiarly distinguished, though a cousin on Wall Street had long been using the name 'West'. In one bizarre sense it proved prophetic. As he told William Carlos Williams: 'Horace

Geeley said, "Go West, young man". So I did.' So eventually he did, to that Golden West where Charlie Chaplin and more recently the Marx Brothers had made their names and fortunes. Years earlier he had met S. J. Perelman, their script-writer, when both were students at Brown. But it was more than zany, knockabout routines he was after. 'In America violence is daily', West was to complain:

> What is melodramatic in European writing is not necessarily so in American writing. For a European writer to make violence real, he has to do a great deal of careful psychology and sociology. He often needs three hundred pages to motivate one little murder. But not so the American writer. His audience has been prepared and is neither surprised nor shocked if he omits artistic excuses for familiar events.

Only holocausts and surrealist extravaganzas could compete. Such spectaculars he reserved for the final scene of his last completed novel.

In 1927 he returned from Paris to a real estate crash that undermined his family fortunes. West settled down to an assistant manager's job at the Kenmore Hall Hotel (a Weinstein sinecure), from which he was transferred as manager to the Sutton Club Hotel at 330 East 56th Street. The depression years there became his apprentice years: *The Dream Life of Balso Snell* was published; S. J. Perelman introduced him to 'Susan Chester', the pseudonymous sob columnist of the *Brooklyn Eagle*; and in 1931 he was appointed joint editor with William Carlos Williams of *Contact*. But there was to be no annus mirabilis; only the *anus* mirabilis, or back passage, of a Trojan horse. As in *Balso Snell* the hero had entered the Trojan horse of illusions, so in *The Day of the Locust* Tod Hackett was to find among the 'dream-dump' of old Hollywood sets 'the wooden horse of Troy'. Like Tod, West was to follow the path of Balso through a world littered with the rubble of hopes and dreams. Even *Contact* ran for only three issues, *Contact* whose first title-page had announced its intent 'to cut a trail through the American jungle without the use of a European compass'. So he was stalled, writing by day, on hotel duty at night, surrounded by lonely, shabby-genteel, desperate, often suicidal vagrants. His small world seemed more like a whole

'Winesburg, U.S.A.' of grotesques, comprising a mass culture of bankrupt fantasy lives. He steamed open mail addressed to guests in order to study their private lives. At his night desk he kept a diary of the ambitions and dreams of the whole hotel. In the dark he could play voyeur. Only West fully understood that his fiction, far from being burlesque, was factual.

'Miss Lonelyhearts' became West's Messiah of these secret dreams: 'Saviour to the pawnshop of the spirit'. William James, Dostoevsky, Freud, all served this parody, this comic-strip gospel whose impotent hero is committed to the greatest of all illusions, the personal redemption of urban masses. When Liveright, his publisher, failed, West's hopes for his own future too collapsed, thrusting him west to that mill-town of ready-to-wear fantasy—Hollywood of the gilded 1930s. Again he was to write on location, as it were, in the Pa-Va-Sed apartment hotel on N. Ivar Street, just above Hollywood Boulevard, this time surrounded by bit-players, stunt-men, midgets, blonde prostitutes, all those down-and-out extras of the American Dream. Their Horatio Alger fable of success he had already inverted in *A Cool Million*, whose dismantled hero was reduced to a martyr of fascist thuggery (based on *Mein Kampf*). His Californian folk fantasy was to end in a frenzy of proletarian violence outside a film première.

In Hollywood he remained as private and curiously innocent at heart as in New York. Out of that innocence sprang a satirical drive unique in American letters. 'He had some furious hunger', Philip Wylie remarked, 'for a different humanity that was hidden by his deep, empathetic, outraged yet somehow, at bottom, loving regard for people.' Outwardly his life became increasingly normal, fulfilled, successful. Somewhat diffidently he performed his hack-work on film scenarios; he went boar-shooting with Faulkner on Santa Cruz Island and duck-shooting in the Tulare Marshes; he wrote an anti-war play (based on Liddell Hart); and married Eileen McKenney (model for her sister Ruth's *New Yorker* sketches, published as *My Sister Eileen*). To the end he played with new fictional ideas: a Melvillean adventure on some border-line between Coney Island and the South Seas; an investigation of Golden Friendship Clubs; or, more enticing, Turgenev's *Sportsman's Sketches* revised Californian-style. But something mysterious—hurt—was kept concealed. Seldom did he show his claws. But then he pounced. There was 'very little to choose' between Hollywood and Hitler, he once wrote to a friend, 'since in Munich they murder your flesh, but here it is the soul which is put under the executioner's axe'.

Dutifully he scripted *The President's Mystery, It Could Happen to You, The Squealer, Ticket to Paradise, Follow your Heart* for Columbia Studios, R.K.O. and M.G.M. Fashionably he flirted with communist and other anti-fascist fronts. But his affinity lay less with Marx than with James Ensor's suffering *Ecce Homo, ou, Le Christ et les Critiques*. (Tod Hackett's 'The Burning of Los Angeles' is reminiscent of several of Ensor's paintings.) For aesthetic perception alone was not to be deceived; and West was an artist, a seer, a Jewish prophet in Hollywood (who failed to observe the boulevard 'stop' sign and met his doom).

West's officer's moustache and tightly pinned collar insisted on formality and constriction; freedom was reserved for fiction. Arthur Wolff affected the same composed and tight-laced British appearance. But his art was to turn life itself to masquerade, to convert his very origins to fiction. He was the paragon of rôle-playing and consumption. For years he remained adrift, pursuing his dark and devious fantasies. It was left to his son Geoffrey to perfect his father's fondness for extempore lies and aliases by writing fiction. Not that *The Duke of Deception* is fiction. Nor another *Life with Father*. It is a classic account of an American drifter as sponger and unscrupulous confidence-man.

For Duke Wolff was no more a duke than Brer Wolf, or that parasitic Duke on Huck's raft with his sidekick the Dauphin. Arthur Samuels Wolff, alias Arthur S. Wolff II, alias Arthur S. Wolff III, alias Arthur Saunders Wolff III, alias Saunders Ansell-Wolff III, sounded like Hemingway. Ex-Groton, ex-Yale, he had volunteered (he said) for the R.A.F. in 1940. His talk was all of courage and candour and reticence. Yet his English accent was a sham. He had neither been to Groton, nor to Yale. He had done no military service. Father was a phoney, a faker, a 'bullshit artist'. Father, it turned out, was a Jew.

'Am I a Jew?' young Geoffrey, in bed, asked his father. 'Of course not. You're a baptized, confirmed Episcopalian.' 'I don't mean that. That doesn't count. Are you a Jew?' 'I'm a confirmed Anglican.' 'Was your mother a Jew?' 'She was Dutch, Van Zandt, fine family, Lutherans, I think.' 'Your father?' 'Atheist.' 'I'm not asking about religion. I'm asking what I am.' 'For Christ's sake! You know I'm not an anti-Semite. I wouldn't be ashamed to be a Jew, if I was. I'm not, that's all. Why would I lie to you? Wolff is a German name, Prussian. Your grandfather and grandmother were English. That's all.'

All fathers are bound to seem to lead double lives. In their sexual and social concerns, by definition, they transcend their sons. So much is commonplace. But, if like Ackerley, Sr., or Wolff, Sr., the fathers actually lead double lives—if they foster a third and secret identity beyond their domestic and professional rôles—they are likely to become exposed as the very type of paternal ambiguity. For it is in them that the mind seizes the essential puzzle of paternal ambiguity. Geoffrey's father was a counterfeiter, in the sense that he hurt and cheated countless innocent people. He was an impostor, disguised as a yacht club commodore. Yet he was also an immoralist, in the Gidean sense, capable of creating himself out of himself in his own image.

Commonly judged, Arthur Wolff was a monument of self-deception, a pathological mess of self-mutilation and self-denial. The need to 'pass' into a new priesthood of the elect—a chosen people—had long become an obsession with secularized Jewry. Adrift in an alien world, the urge was to identify with privilege, with power, with exclusive values. Bernard Berenson, notoriously, elected the aesthetic values of the Renaissance; Arthur Wolff preferred the values of Mayfair, as embodied by Lobb, by Dunhill, by Jaguar, and Holland & Holland. Such lives were bound to be corroded by inner shame. Yet it was an existential choice, something Sartre might in principle have applauded. It was fulfilment of a kind: a denial of essence (the genetic Jew) through the play of desire. Its results might be viewed as a state of transfiguration, in religious terms, or, in literary terms, as a fiction.

The link between father and son was certainly fiction. The

social construction of the one became the literary reconstruction by the other. Yet their two fictions are not complementary. The son's quest is for truth, for the certainty of origins; it entails a sleuth-like endeavour to nail his father, to document him. The father's fiction was itself an evasion, a repudiation of social origins: of his Jewish milieu in Hartford, Connecticut, of his father's hospital and summer house at Crescent Beach. Irving Howe, in *World of our Fathers*, has pointed out that the 1930s were a time for fast breaks and self-creations, that 'upon its sons and daughters the immigrant Jew branded marks of separateness, while inciting dreams of universalism. They taught their children both to conquer the gentile world and to be conquered by it.' Young Arthur Wolff concentrated on his father's wealth: on the potential drama of the doctor's library and music room, on cooks and maids and the chauffeur with Pierce-Arrows and Rolls-Royces. Geoffrey Wolff is astute on the covert conspiracy of such families to exacerbate that evasion:

> From the beginning my father heard talk about the best of this, the best of that: the best neighbourhood, school, automobile, mind, family. And if Jews with educations and without accents were better than Jews with accents and without educations, couldn't it follow that best of all was to be no Jew at all?

Arthur's atheist father, who never entered Hartford's Temple Beth Israel, had him educated in a succession of exclusive Episcopal schools. Young 'Duke', as he was nicknamed for his proud airs, grew up into a stuttering spoilt brat. The brat developed into a natty dresser, a swell, whose native *chutzpah* was disguised as aristocratic hauteur—what his son was to call 'a Bartleby-like refusal to play ball'. But such fantasies of grandeur depended increasingly on bluff. Flunked again and again from more prestigious institutions, he ended up as a playboy and drop-out from the University of Miami: 'a gonif, a schnorrer. He was just a bum. That's all he ever was.'

So his official education was a failure. By the 1930s he was deep into the fragmented fiction of modernism (Joyce, Williams, Eliot, Stein, Hemingway). Fiction itself became his ultimate confidence trick—as a dispersal of social reality. He learnt to fly. He married into a naval family. The patriarch doctor died. But almost broke, it turned out. The young couple headed west to Hollywood, to the very edge of American illusion, for the new break, the new start. On that fantastic shore, by the 1940s, everyone could pretty well invent their own credentials. He became an aeronautical engineer on wholly fraudulent degrees, movinng from Northrop to Lockheed to North American in time for Lend Lease and the Battle of Britain. He eventually rose to Assistant Chief Designer for the R.A.F.'s new Mustang, quartered in Park Lane with the honorary rank of Air Corps major. Father was no fool. But he squandered his jobs, like his cash, hustling his family by moonlight flits about the States. His marriage cracked. He was pursued by the F.B.I. Again and again he was fired for amassing debts. By opting for his father, his son (as he later came to realize) had opted for a life built on lies—without security, without stability, without definition, except that of its own constant shifts and migrations.

The scale of the deception was immense:

> He was a chameleon. He gave his clients what he thought they wanted: companies got his constipated management jargon, headmasters got piety, car salesmen got bank references, car mechanics got engineering lore. He was a lie, through and through. There was nothing to him but lies, and love.

The Duke's one and only unquestioned mastery was that of the American charge account. The Duke charged. 'He charged and charged ahead. There was something about him, what he wanted he got. Salesmen loved him, he was the highest evolution of consumer.' But a crash was always imminent. The rake's progress had at some point, somehow, to end. And the end, when it came, was seedy enough: in a San Diego jail on a fraud charge. (Father read *The Wind in the Willows* in jail and especially liked Mr. Toad.) There were to be more bad cheques, more jail sentences, more paroles. After a final two-year stretch, father died alone, neglected, in a tacky apartment by the Pacific.

The chronic inertia and hurt indifference of that retreat was suicidal. Like the bartender of Daniel Fuchs's *The Apathetic*

Bookie Joint (1938), he might have groaned: 'It's better if a person has a disposition that lets him see the funny side of life. . . . The trouble is, the whole trouble is, it's not so easy to have a sunny disposition.' *Miss Lonelyhearts* was published only a year before Daniel Fuchs's first novel; and he was to make the move from east coast to west in 1937. Those youngsters of his Brooklyn period who discussed *Ulysses* on park benches with their girl friends, or spotted butterflies in the subway, or tootled flageolets, were all dreamers, lost to adult chores. Even his barber's assistant concocted barbershop scripts for Mickey Mouse. *The Apathetic Bookie Joint* is tell-tale of all those separate, inturned, lonely consciousnesses, from Owen D. Larkin Park to Flatbush Avenue, that once formed his beat. This Jewish comedy of humours is one of submerged soliloquies suddenly erupting, like the Manhattan subway, into the open:

> 'Take the average guy that's married. They go around secretly thinking how nice it would be if their wife suddenly dropped dead of heart failure with none of the blame attaching to themselves and if that's an exaggeration, I'll eat my hat!'

> 'When I had my butcher shop, I was worth eighteen hundred dollars, cold cash. Today I'm a ruined man through no fault of my own.'

> 'Nobody understands me. I'm all alone. I am in a desert.'

> 'After all, after all, I am only flesh and blood. What could a man do? We had lovely times together, and I am only human too.'

> 'We're really a very happily married couple—sixteen years now—but my wife, she wants to make sure my affections aren't straying. So she pulls these tantrums and I have to go chasing all over the country after her.'

> 'A squirrel cage. Look at them. They laugh and cry. They get happy, they feel bad. They're all excited. But what does it all mean? What does it all add up to?'

Shared intimacies multiply anywhere. A stranger blurts out his life story in the washroom at Cheyenne airport, while a porter croons a Bing Crosby number leaning against the wastepipes. The lingering note is one of sadness, of lost hope, lost opportunities, lost beauty, lost youth, lost illusions, lost love.

Behind all the bravado, the phoney accents, the wishful reveries of his people's lives lay the shadow of futility. Long before he himself had transferred to Hollywood's dream factory, Fuchs had charted those celluloid dreams of Walt Disney and girls who called themselves Ginger on Manhattan Beach. Most Walter Mittyish of them all is the despatch clerk who actually flies (alias James Joyce) via Chicago and Salt Lake City to Burbank and back to Newark in a couple of days. Such is the exuberant climax to all those early dreams in which a flight to Hollywood itself becomes only the illusion of an action, a performance to impress the girls in the collection department. Stasis is everywhere, even in the air. Or, fog-bound, passengers are grounded, with planes circling at different levels overhead. Intimacies are shared, without meaning or resolution, before each character continues on his or her separate journey.

These stories clearly display Fuchs's own frustration and eventual escape from the movie-houses of Williamsburg to Celluloid City. (The silent screen, as he points out, had been the great egalitarian educator of the immigrant masses.) But nothing could have been more futile. His *Hollywood Diary* (1938) only reveals yet another unpredictable and inconsequential world, where writers sit in comic isolation playing cards, while producers in the 'front office' trump them with Jokers. His decent characters, again and again, are trapped between insecurity at home and isolation at work, stalled in their good intentions. The shift from deprivation (in Brooklyn) to the good life (in Beverly Hills) produces more effervescence, but little fundamental change. Affluent parties there explode with the exhaust of emotions overheard. That have-it-all, do-it-all, have-done-with-it-all society of Los Angeles fairly sizzles with bickering and sexual antagonism and corroded dreams. Still dreams. But no longer dreams of a brighter future elsewhere, rather of an eternal beauty and eternal youth. The characters can remodel their homes now, but not their complexion, or waistline, or bust:

'The other night we're going out somewhere, and suddenly she starts hollering it's gone, it's gone, her figure is gone, and right then and there she leans up against the wall mirror and bursts out bawling, crying her eyes out, and everything is *my* fault!'

'And then there was that time in the dress shop—everybody talked about it for days—when she walked all over the place in her girdle. "My God, she talks like people will live a thousand years!" Mrs. Hergle screamed. "Don't you understand? There is no time, *there is no time!*" '

Daniel Fuchs is the Jewish laureate of that dream-bound future and this dream-locked past, shuttling between the Atlantic and the Pacific. But in moving to the Golden West, the final illusion of all is lost—that of wonder. In California there was no more wonder, only (by the 1950s) signs of film studios collapsing, rumours of Fantasy Production Inc. itself closing down. *The Golden West* (1954) is as doom-laden, in its way, as *The Cherry Orchard*. The East Side momma, who had followed her golden boy to the coast, alone preserves her faith, as she gazes down from Bel Air to the glittering field of lights stretching from Santa Monica to Malibu. ' "Isn't it gorgeous?" she said to me. "It's like a fairyland, David. It's like magic!" '

In his youth he had secretly prided himself that he could tell almost on sight what a man did for a living,

> what he aspired to, the kind of home he had, what his parents looked like, his uncles. They were limited, held down, moving in swarms over the pavements, on their way to and from their jobs, to and from the subways. [He] knew what they would give to be here, how they yearned for the spaciousness, the ease of the life.

Here, working in the studios, he was stimulated by the vitality of his colleagues, 'by their escapades and high spirits, their good looks, their shining good health, their open generosity and bravura style'. Yet slowly, inexorably, the X-ray vision that had seen through the Brownsville section of Brooklyn, where he had grown up, sees through the desperate, hysterical *failure* of Beverly Hills. The glamorous, lacquered, look-alike guests make a doom-laden chorus. The stars disintegrate. Things fall apart. As in those barbershops and hosiery shops long ago, futility stares the protagonists in the face. Fuchs's

Golden West is bleak, rank with matrimonial and professional failure. No one is quite what he was thought to be. No one has the answers. The celebrities are themselves riddled with uncertainty. The gap between a smash hit and smash-up runs closer every time. For now the stakes are even higher, outbidding monotony with the craziest bids. The ultimate terror is impotence—the cry of the errant wife pleading with her husband: 'Nothing happened. Nothing happened. He couldn't do anything.' In other words, flops.

In *Twilight in Southern California* (1953), a bankrupt novelty manufacturer—some central European Leopold Bloom—crosses from Coldwater Canyon to Benedict Canyon in a final desperate search of a loan. On Mulholland Drive the air is clean. The view extends for miles on every side. This is the Promised Land, yes, but he is in captivity nevertheless, 'back in the desert wilderness, in the time of the Pharaohs'. Lean years are succeeding the fat years. Up there on his mountain top, between the Valley and the Pacific, this cheating, bullying, bouncing *shlimazl*—from that remote and ultimate exile—cries out for forgiveness.

Such are the antics of despair.

We can all put down jokers. Aristotle, from the start, put them down as low, trivial, knavish fellows. Yet Charlie Chaplin and Nathanael West and the Marx Brothers remain as exuberant today as ever. More challenging than their straight, romantic rivals. For it is not protagonists (of order) for whom we long in the dark so much as antagonists (of disorder). It is not a divine chaos that now threatens us so much as the ever-encroaching restraint of social uniformity and control. It is not heroic champions that we seem to need so much as comic champions, or 'Lords of Misrule'. Such as Huckleberry Finn, such as Groucho Marx, such as Charlie Chaplin, or (in our own day) Randle Patrick McMurphy: artful dodgers all, man and boy, for ever festive, defiant, outwitting an alien world with their duplicity, inscrutability and guile.

'Comedy', as A. W. Schlegel said as long ago as 1808, 'is the democracy of poetry, and is more inclined even to the confusion of anarchy than to any circumscription of the general liberty of its mental powers and purposes'. Or as Felix Krull wrote, on deciding to reject Lord Strathbogie's offer to make him his heir (in return for services rendered):

> The main thing was that a confident instinct within me rebelled against a form of reality that was simply handed to me and was in addition sloppy—rebelled in favour of free play and dreams, self-created and self-sufficient, dependent, that is, only on imagination.

Yet Hollywood, from the start, was resigned to serving as society's censor; it consistently triumphed over dissenters. Its *virtus*, like that of ancient Rome, enforced a strict subordination to clan and country. Only a bureaucratic establishment was right-thinking; the Hays Office alone could sponsor the rules. So quixotic clowns, in the end, had to go. They had finally to be ousted. From that pantheon of Hollywood's golden age, celebrated by Gore Vidal, they remain conspicuously absent. There was no place for Miss Lonelyhearts or Charlie Chaplin on that Olympus.

Bibliography of Key Secondary Sources

ALDBRIDGE, JAMES, *One Last Glimpse* (London: Michael Joseph, 1977)

ARNOLD, LLOYD, *Hemingway: High on the Wild* (New York: Grosset & Dunlap, 1977)

BAKER, CARLOS (ed.), *Ernest Hemingway, Selected Letters 1917–1961* (London: Granada, 1981)

BALL, GORDON (ed.), *Allen Ginsberg, Journals: Early Fifties Early Sixties* (New York: Grove Press, 1978)

BASSETT, JOHN (ed.), *William Faulkner: The Critical Heritage* (London: Routledge & Kegan Paul, 1975)

BENSON, JACKSON J. (ed.), *The Short Stories of Ernest Hemingway: Critical Essays* (Durham: Duke University Press, 1975)

BERGHAHN, MARION, *Images of Africa in Black American Literature* (London: Macmillan, 1977)

BICKLEY, R. BRUCE, Jr., *The Method of Melville's Short Fiction* (Durham: Duke University Press, 1975)

BLOTNER, JOSEPH, *Faulkner, A Biography* (London: Chatto & Windus, 1974)

BLOTNER, JOSEPH (ed.), *Selected Letters of William Faulkner* (London: The Scolar Press, 1977)

BUSCH, FRIEDER, *Natur in Neuer Welt: Bericht und Dichtung der Amerikanischen Kolonialzeit 1493–1776* (Munchen: Wilhelm Fink, 1974)

COWLEY, MALCOLM, *The Faulkner-Cowley File: Letters and Memories, 1944–1962* (London: Chatto & Windus, 1966)

DOUGHTY, HOWARD, *Francis Parkman* (New York: Macmillan, 1962)

DURAND, RÉGIS, *Melville: Signes et Métaphores* (Lausanne: L'Age d'Homme, 1980)

FELTSKOG, E. N. (ed.), *The Oregon Trail* (Madison: Wisconsin University Press, 1969)

FITZGERALD, SALLY (ed.), *The Habit of Being: Letters of Flannery O'Connor* (New York: Farrar, Straus & Giroux, 1979)

GARDNER, RALPH D. (ed.), *Horatio Alger, A Fancy of Hers & The Disagreeable Woman* (New York: Van Nostrand Reinhold, 1981)

GAYLE, ADDISON, Jr., *The Way of the New World: The Black Novel in America* (New York: Doubleday, 1975)

GIFFORD, BARRY (ed.), *As Ever: The Collected Correspondence of Allen Ginsberg and Neal Cassady* (Berkeley: Creative Arts, 1977)

GRANT, DOUGLAS, *The Fortunate Slave: An Illustration of African Slavery in the Early Eighteenth Century* (London: Oxford University Press, 1968)

HEERMANCE, J. NOEL, *Charles W. Chesnutt: America's First Great Black Novelist* (Hamden, Conn: Archon Books, 1974)

HERBERT, T. WALTER, Jr., *Marquesan Encounters: Melville and the Meaning of Civilization* (Cambridge, Mass: Harvard University Press, 1980)

HOBSON, FRED C., Jr., *Serpent in Eden: H. L. Mencken and the South* (Chapel Hill: University of North Carolina Press, 1974)

HUMPHREY, ROBERT E., *Children of Fantasy: The First Rebels of Greenwich Village* (New York: John Wiley, 1978)

IRWIN, JOHN T., *American Hieroglyphs: The Symbol of the Egyptian Hieroglyphics in the American Renaissance* (New Haven: Yale University Press, 1980)

JACOBS, WILBUR R. (ed.), *Letters of Francis Parkman* (Norman: Oklahoma University Press, 1960)

KATZ, ELIA, *Armed Love: Communal Living—Good or Bad?* (London: Blond Briggs, 1972)

KAWIN, BRUCE F., *Faulkner and Film* (New York: Frederick Ungar, 1977)

KUEHL, JOHN and BRYER, JACKSON (eds.), *Dear Scott/Dear Max: The Fitzgerald-Perkins Correspondence* (London: Cassell, 1971)

LATHAM, AARON, *Crazy Sundays: F. Scott Fitzgerald in Hollywood* (London: Secker & Warburg, 1972)

MACLEOD, ANNE SCOTT, *A Moral Tale: Children's Fiction and American Culture, 1820–1860* (Hamden, Conn: Archon Books, 1975)

MARTIN, JAY, *Always Merry and Bright: The Life of Henry Miller* (Santa Barbara: Capra Press, 1978)

MARTIN, JAY, *Nathanael West: The Art of his Life* (London: Secker & Warburg, 1971)

MERIWETHER, JAMES B. (ed.), *William Faulkner: Essays, Speeches and Public Letters* (London: Chatto & Windus, 1966)

MILFORD, NANCY, *Zelda Fitzgerald* (London: Bodley Head, 1970)

MORRIS, WILLIE, *North Toward Home* (Boston: Houghton Mifflin, 1967)

Bibliography of Key Secondary Sources

MOTTRAM, ERIC, *William Burroughs: The Algebra of Need* (London: Marion Boyars, 1977)

PIZER, DONALD, *The Novels of Theodore Dreiser: A Critical Study* (Minneapolis: University of Minnesota Press, 1976)

PORTE, JOEL, *Representative Man: Ralph Waldo Emerson in his Time* (New York: Oxford University Press, 1979)

QUINN, PATRICK F., *The French Face of Edgar Poe* (Carbondale: Southern Illinois University Press, 1957)

RUBIN, LOUIS D., Jr., *William Elliott Shoots a Bear: Essays on the Southern Literary Imagination* (Baton Rouge: Louisiana State University Press, 1975)

RUBIN, LOUIS D., Jr., and HOLMAN, C. HUGH (eds.), *Southern Literary Study: Problems and Possibilities* (Chapel Hill: University of North Carolina Press, 1975)

SAYRE, ROBERT F., *Thoreau and the American Indians* (Princeton: Princeton University Press, 1977)

SCHEICK, WILLIAM J., *The Half-Blood: A Cultural Symbol in Nineteenth-Century American Fiction* (Lexington: The University Press of Kentucky, 1979)

SEELYE, JOHN, *Melville: The Ironic Diagram* (Evanston: Northwestern University Press, 1970)

SINCLAIR, ANDREW, *Jack: A Biography of Jack London* (London: Weidenfeld & Nicolson, 1978)

STERN, MILTON R., *The Golden Moment: The Novels of F. Scott Fitzgerald* (Urbana: University of Illinois Press, 1970)

STOEHR, TAYLOR, *Hawthorne's Mad Scientists: Pseudoscience and Social Science in Nineteenth-Century Life and Letters* (Hamden, Conn: Archon Books, 1978)

THOMSON, DAVID, *America in the Dark: Hollywood and the Gift of Unreality* (London: Hutchinson, 1978)

TOCQUEVILLE, ALEXIS DE, *Democracy in America*, translated by George Lawrence, edited by J. P. Mayer and Max Lerner (New York: Harper & Row, 1966)

TOMKINS, CALVIN, *Living Well is the Best Revenge: Two Americans in Paris 1921–1933* (London: André Deutsch, 1972)

TURNBULL, ANDREW, *Thomas Wolfe: A Biography* (New York: Charles Scribner's, 1968)

WADE, MASON, *Francis Parkman, Heroic Historian* (New York: The Viking Press, 1942)

WADE, MASON (ed.), *The Journals of Francis Parkman* (New York: Harper, 1947)

WADLINGTON, WARWICK, *The Confidence Game in American Literature* (Princeton: Princeton University Press, 1975)

231

WALKER, FRANKLIN, *Irreverent Pilgrims: Melville, Browne, and Mark Twain in the Holy Land* (Seattle: University of Washington Press, 1974)

WOLFF, GEOFFREY, *The Duke of Deception: Memories of My Father* (London: Hodder & Stoughton, 1980)

Index

Index

Index

Index

Index

237

Index

238